Democracy and Democra
in Comparative Perspective

MW00710491

This book provides an introduction to democratic theory and empirical research on democracy and democratization. It first examines conceptions of democracy from the origins in ancient Greece to the present day, and then tracks when and where modern democracy has developed. On this basis, the book reviews the major debates and schools of thought dealing with domestic and international causes and consequences of democratization. Based on a systematic distinction between minimalist and maximalist definitions of democracy, it provides a comprehensive and critical assessment of existing theories. Furthermore, using a comparative, historical perspective, it not only sketches the development in the conceptions of democracy and the corresponding empirical reality, but also discusses whether causal relationships differ across periods. Finally, the book documents the way in which all of this has been reflected by the development within the literature. In doing so, it offers a coherent framework that students and scholars can use to grasp the literature on democracy and democratization as a whole.

Democracy and Democratization in Comparative Perspective will be of interest to students of political science, democracy and democratization, comparative politics, political theory, and international relations.

Jørgen Møller and **Svend-Erik Skaaning** are Associate Professors in the Department of Political Science at Aarhus University, Denmark.

Democratization Studies
(Formerly Democratization Studies, Frank Cass)

Democratization Studies combines theoretical and comparative studies with detailed analyses of issues central to democratic progress and its performance, all over the world.

The books in this series aim to encourage debate on the many aspects of democratization that are of interest to policy-makers, administrators and journalists, aid and development personnel, as well as to all those involved in education.

Democracy and Democratization in Comparative Perspective

Conceptions, conjunctures,
causes, and consequences

**Jørgen Møller and
Svend-Erik Skaaning**

LONDON AND NEW YORK

First published 2013
by Routledge
2 Park Square, Milton Park, Abingdon, Oxon OX14 4RN

Simultaneously published in the USA and Canada
by Routledge
711 Third Avenue, New York, NY 10017

Routledge is an imprint of the Taylor & Francis Group, an informa business

British Library Cataloguing in Publication Data
A catalogue record for this book is available from the British Library

Library of Congress Cataloging-in-Publication Data
Democracy and democratization in comparative perspective : conceptions, conjunctures, causes, and consequences / Jørgen Møller and Svend-Erik Skaaning.
       p. cm. — (Democratization studies ; 22)
    Includes bibliographical references and index.
    1. Democracy. 2. Democratization. I. Skaaning, Svend-Erik. II. Title.
    JC423.M652 2012
    321.8—dc23   2012016747

ISBN: 978–0–415–63350–5 (hbk)
ISBN: 978–0–415–63351–2 (pbk)
ISBN: 978–0–203–08399–4 (ebk)

Typeset in Times
by Keystroke, Station Road, Codsall, Wolverhampton

To Bjørn
(Jørgen Møller)

To my grandparents
(Svend-Erik Skaaning)

Contents

Illustrations

Figures

Tables

Preface

> The great problem of our time is the organisation and establishment of democracy.
>
> (Tocqueville 1988 [1835]: 311)

Tocqueville's sentence was written more than 175 years ago, but the message is arguably as relevant for our time as it was for his. In this book, we seek to elucidate Tocqueville's problem from a number of different angles. The title – *Democracy and Democratization in Comparative Perspective: Conceptions, Conjunctures, Causes, and Consequences* – conveys this nicely. The book is divided into the four parts listed in the subtitle: conceptions of democracy, empirical developments (conjunctures), causes of democracy, and consequences of democracy. As the main title reflects, each of these four parts is approached from an unapologetic comparative perspective, including comparisons across both space and time. Indeed, the most important difference between this book and existing textbooks is to be found in the historical take on the subject. What we set out to elucidate is not only contemporary aspects of democracy and democratization but also the historical evolution of the concept and the concomitant empirical developments in different periods.

The book is based on an equivalent which we published in Danish in 2010 under the title *Demokrati og demokratisering: en introduktion* (*Democracy and Democratization: An Introduction*). The book was well received and was awarded the 'Sven Henningsen Prize 2010' for best Danish popular book within the areas of contemporary history, political science, and international relations. Furthermore, we used the book in a graduate seminar in 2010 and in a lecture series on Comparative Politics in 2011, and both times received positive feedback on it from the students. All of this convinced us that it would be worthwhile making an English edition. We are grateful to our Danish publisher, Hans Reitzels Forlag, for granting us permission to do so. Our original intention was simply to publish an English translation, but, as it were, the process has taken on a life of its own. This is probably the place to reveal the working title of the book: *The Long Journey of Democracy*. Not only was this our tentative title virtually until we submitted the final manuscript, it also turned out to be an apt description of the process. Our long journey originally commenced in 2008 when we set out to write the Danish version, but it was very much prolonged when we began to rework the English translation. Not only have we completely rewritten, updated, and expanded most of the chapters of the translated version, we have also added an entirely new part on the consequences of democracy.

We received valuable comments from a number of colleagues when working on the original version of the book (these inputs are acknowledged in the Preface of the Danish version). This time around, we have received comments from additional scholars, including Gerardo L. Munck and three anonymous reviewers. But we have privileged receiving input from the target audience. We presented drafts of all chapters of the English version to a group of remarkably skilled graduate students in 2011 as an integrated part of a co-taught seminar on democracy and democratization. We are indebted for the comments we received from David Andersen, Kim Andersen, Jonas Axelgaard, Michael Sejlstrup Ellegaard, Jakob Gjørup, Jákup Emil Hansen, Jens Lyhne Højberg, Maria Juhler-Larsen, Allan Knudsen, Maj Kathrine Larsen, Nina Larsen, Rasmus John Franklin Lindholm, Casper Sakstrup, Christian Stenz, Rasmus Storgaard Suikkanen, Jens Damgaard Thaysen, and Anna Windfeldt Thorning. On this basis, we once more revised the manuscript in the spring of 2012. During this process, we received valuable help from Anne-Grethe Gammelgaard and Lasse Lykke Rørbæk.

The long journey has been rewarding for both of us. It is an instructive exercise to attempt to cover one's entire research field in a single book, and the process of doing so has forced us into corners of the theoretical and empirical literature on democracy and democratization which we had not visited before. As Lazslo Brust (former PhD supervisor of Jørgen Møller) has put it, "the very essence of any scientific learning process is to get cornered and see if you can get out – because if you get out, you will have learned something." We have certainly been cornered on a number of occasions during our work on this book. Most conspicuously, this was the case when writing the chapters on classical conceptions of democracy. However, here we have been so fortunate as to benefit from several readings by Mogens Herman Hansen. Mogens' lucid comments have made it possible to escape at least this corner relatively unscathed. Whether we have been equally adept at getting out of other corners is less certain. What is certain, however, is that we have both learned quite a lot along the way. Our hope is that the readers will benefit from our efforts.

Introduction

What is democracy? Where and when – and in what guises – have there been democracies? Why has democracy emerged and held its own in some countries but not in others? What are the consequences of democracy? In this book, we present a long-term, comparative perspective on democracy and democratization, including a critical discussion of prominent answers to these questions. Others have reviewed the extant literature on democracy and democratization (e.g., Grugel 2002; Sørensen 2008; Haerpfer et al. 2009). However, our take is novel in several ways. First, we use a general conceptual distinction between 'thinner' and 'thicker' definitions of democracy to show that many of the current disagreements – and some seemingly irreconcilable findings – can be bridged. This conceptual edifice enables us to appreciate a pivotal message of this book, namely that the distinction between different kinds of democracy has become very important in recent decades, both theoretically and empirically. Second, our proposed structure is arguably the first to integrate *Conceptions, Conjunctures, Causes, and Consequences* of democracy into a coherent framework, which students and scholars can use to grasp the literature on democracy and democratization as a whole. Third, we use a historical focus to not only lay bare the development in the conceptions of democracy and the corresponding empirical reality but also to discuss whether causal relationships differ in different periods and to assess the way this has been reflected by the development within the literature.

This is not as such a chronological take on democratization, but it is surely a logical one. We first need to understand conceptions before we can describe empirical trends, and only then does it make sense to discuss the causes of these trends, which, finally, paves the way for a discussion of the consequences of those very developments. This is a neat way of covering both democratic theory ('the what?'), the empirical dynamics of democratization ('the when and where?'), explanations of this development ('the how and why?'), and the consequences of democracy ('the so what?'). The book is structured in strict accordance with this series of issues. The first part discusses the competing definitions of democracy in the literature and presents our own position. The second part analyzes the development of democracy across time and space based on these conceptual distinctions. In the third part, we provide a critical overview of attempts to explain democratic development in the past as well as in the present. In the final part, we assess the potential consequences of democracy.

Before delving into these issues, however, a more comprehensive introduction to the theme of democracy and democratization is called for. First and foremost, we need to explain why the issues of democracy and democratization are attracting so much attention today – and, by implication, why it is worthwhile reading a book such as this. This can be broken down into two sub-questions. First, why is democracy a term of universal praise? Second, why does the study of democratization figure so prominently within political science?

Democracy: from pejorative to honorific concept

'Democracy' comes from the Greek *demokratia*. It is a synthesis of *demos*, meaning people, and *kratos*, meaning rule, and it thus signifies 'rule by the people'. Over its considerable life span, the term (and the concept) has been the object of continuous disagreement and conflict. In a book outlining the history of democracy, John Dunn (2005) retells its stormy history. It is widely held that democracy was conceived in ancient Greece – more precisely in the 6th century BC (Hansen 2010b: 14–17) – where it thrived for more than four centuries before falling to the sword of Rome in 146 BC. Indeed, the proportion of democracies among the Greek *poleis* grew during this period. In the first half of the 4th century BC, about two-fifths of all city-states were democracies but in the early Hellenistic Period – before the Roman conquest in 146 BC – the majority of the Greek *poleis* were democratically governed. From then on, however, oligarchy made a comeback, and in the late imperial period democracy had all but disappeared (Hansen 2010b: 16–17).

At the same time, the very word 'democracy' fell into disfavor. A major reason for this was that all the influential philosophical tracts, which survived from ancient Greece, were written by critics of democracy. Most vehement was Plato, who considered it to be the penultimate form of misrule, only just better than tyranny. But according to Dunn (2005), much of the blame must be attributed to the less hostile treatment of Aristotle. In his political writings, Aristotle referred to a well-functioning and stable democracy as *politeia*, while reserving *demokratia* for its pathological twin; what the Greek historian Polybius would later refer to as 'mob rule' (*ochlokratia*). Crucially, Aristotle sometimes construed *politeia* as an approximation of a mixed constitution, i.e., a blend between democracy and oligarchy (Hansen 2010a: 519–520).[1] This distinction was not quickly forgotten. Democracy retained some honorific meaning as a part of the so-called mixed constitution but only when tempered by monarchical and aristocratic institutions, and not on its own.

For almost 2000 years, democracy was not only extinct as a regime form, it was also – in its pure form – perceived as a regime that only had misery to offer. Democracy was used pejoratively throughout the Middle Ages. Thomas Aquinas, for one, described it as an unjust form of government (*iniquum regimen*) (Naess et al. 1956: 92).[2] Nor do we, with a few New Englanders as the sole possible exception, find self-professed democrats during the period from the Renaissance to the French Revolution (Naess et al. 1956: 95). Hobbes, for instance, subscribed to Aristotle's view of democracy as the tyranny of the poor, a position we also meet much later with Edmund Burke (Naess et al. 1956: 99–113).

Aristotle's distinction between unjust democracy and the preferable mixed constitution thus held all the way until the reintroduction of democracy in the 19th and 20th centuries. A large part of the reason was that democracy was constantly equated with direct democracy, rather than with representative democracy. As documented by Mogens Herman Hansen (2010b: 13), both Diderot's *Encoclopédie* (1754) and the contemporary *Encyclopædia Britannica* (1771) did so, and therefore construed democracy as a purely historical phenomenon associated with Antiquity.

Dunn (2005) traces democracy's return to the two major 'Promethean revolts' of the 18th century: the American (1776) and French (1789) revolutions. The American revolutionaries, however, did not describe themselves as democrats. James Madison, for one, did everything in his power to shore up against what he perceived to be the chaotic forces of democracy. In the *Federalist Papers*, he distinguished between a democracy (as in Athens) and a republic (as in America). While the former was subject to the whims of the masses, the latter was guided by elected representatives who were held accountable by an effective separation of powers.

As has often been pointed out, in his *Rights of Man* Thomas Paine (1996 [1791]: 136–137) precociously suggested a fusion of democracy and representation:

> By ingrafting representation upon democracy, we arrive at a system of Government capable of embracing and confederating all the various interests and every extent of territory and population. . . . It is on this system that the American Government is founded. It is representation ingrafted upon Democracy. . . . What Athens was in miniature America will be in magnitude.

However, in this respect Paine's was a lonely voice in the American debate. The course of events on the other side of the Atlantic played out differently. During the most rabid phase of the French Revolution, Maximilien Robespierre's so-called reign of terror, democracy returned as a rallying cry, at least for one particular group of actors. The revolutionary Jacobins in France were drawn to the word precisely due to its tantalizing message implying equal access to the exercise of power – that is, the very notion that Madison and his peers had warned against. Robespierre's grand project was scuttled by its own excesses, but the term democracy and the ideal of equality that was associated with it were to be denied no longer. This was also the case with Madison's corrective, however. And the democratic ideal of equality and the republican notion of freedom were forged together over time, which serves to emphasize how popular sovereignty has been combined with barriers establishing limits on the power of the people (Manin 1997; Dunn 2005).

Hansen (2010a: 513) points to the year 1828, in which Jefferson's and Madison's Democratic-Republican Party changed its name to The Democratic Party, as "the epoch-making year for modern representative democracy." "It was the first really important mass movement launched under the banner of democracy," thereby marking a fusion of the democratic principle and the principle of representation and the separation of powers. As already argued, the European development was more lethargic, but from the revolutions in 1848 we increasingly encounter a liberal adherence to democracy (Naess et al. 1956: 124). Arne Naess et al. (1956: 125–126) document this historical shift by demonstrating how Alexis de Tocqueville's use of the term changed from referring to social equality to describing a political method (in his speeches in 1848). Tocqueville was not alone in changing his views at this point in time. Piggybacking the great liberal revolutions of the 19th century, democracy once again became an honorific term in some circles, only now associated with representatives, not the direct rule of the people.

Even during the second half of the 19th century, this was more the exception than the rule, however. It took a First World War – proclaimed by American President Woodrow Wilson as a war to "make the world safe for democracy" – to render democracy broadly popular. In his *Modern Democracies*, James Bryce (1921: 4) could thus note the "significant change" which had produced "the universal acceptance of democracy as the normal and natural form of government" (see also Kelsen 1920). Over time the bourgeoisie accepted democracy for the very reason that it had been purged of its mob rule connotations. More precisely, the notion of popular became fused with the notion of representation, civil liberties, and the rule of law (Manin 1997; Dunn 2005). This happened exactly because liberals – and in time most conservatives along with them – came to the conclusion that even a relatively broad (male) suffrage did not necessarily imperil property rights.

In this *Gestalt*, democracy has managed to strangle all of its challengers. To be sure, democracy was again placed on the defensive in the years leading up to World War II, but only briefly. And this challenge was not so much reflected in a renewed pejorative use of the word; most undemocratic forces actually framed themselves as democratic forces (see, e.g., Kelsen 1955: 1). As the genuinely democratic countries emerged victoriously from the epic confrontations of the 20th century – first with fascism and later with communism – the road was paved for the current status of the word as the label for the 'best' form of political rule.[3] In fact, democracy has assumed an entirely unique position in the vocabulary of contemporary mankind. It has come to shine so brightly that it is hardly necessary to defend its merits. Anyone renouncing democracy is excluded from good company, more or less regardless of their reasons for doing so.

We will return to this issue. However, the consensus in recent decades regarding the virtues of democracy does not mean that there is – or ever has been – common ground when it comes to defining democracy. Most telling is the fact that many of the decidedly non-democratic states of the 20th century were – by the governing elites – referred to as democracies. This is the case with the Eastern European 'people's democracies' during the communist period and with a number of military regimes, such as Nasser's 'presidential democracy' in Egypt, Sukarno's 'guided democracy' in Indonesia, Franco's 'organic democracy' in Spain, and Trujillo's 'neo-democracy' in the Dominican Republic (Finer 1962: 242). In all of these cases, the dictator or party has claimed to serve as the guarantor for putting the actual interest of the people into practice. The corresponding assertion has been that the regime was therefore more democratic than the states in which the members of an ignorant population made a more or less informed decision at the ballot-box.

Showing that these cases involve an implausible 'conceptual stretching' of the word democracy is relatively straightforward (cf. Sartori 1970). However, this is hardly the final word in this matter. On the most general level, it is necessary to distinguish between *substantive* definitions (defining democracy in terms of its content), which, for example, emphasize the need for economic equality, or the existence of 'public deliberation', as opposed to *procedural* definitions, which focus narrowly on the presence or absence of an institutional framework consisting of characteristics such as competitive elections, civil liberties, and the rule of law. We account for the various conceptions of democracy throughout the ages – from ancient Greece to the present day – in Chapters 1 and 2, and against this background we provide a systematic ordering of procedural definitions in the form of a typology of democratic regimes in Chapter 3.

The democratization literature

The disagreements concerning the definitions have not prevented politicians, political scientists, historians, philosophers, and others from attempting – as long as democracy has existed – to take a step backwards and reveal its source. In other words, there is a veritable cornucopia of explanations as to what promotes democratization; that is, movements in the direction of (more) democracy. One of the first offerings was handed down by the aforementioned Aristotle. According to Aristotle (2008 [350 BC]): 170 [1296a]), there are two possible explanations as to why autocratic rule in a city-state, a *polis*, collapses and democracy emerges in its place. First, the masses can revolt on the grounds that they have been treated unjustly. Second, internal conflicts can arise between the governing oligarchies, after which one faction allies itself with the masses.

Aristotle's explanation may appear somewhat superficial; a popular takeover is, after all, pretty much the definition of a transition to democracy. But for the first 2000 years after the birth of democracy in ancient Greece, it was more or less always such rather obvious explanations being pursued in the field. A telling example may be found as late as in the Renaissance, where Niccolò Machiavelli (1970 [1517]: 160, 247 [I.17, i.55]) postulated that a democracy – what he referred to as a republic – emerges when the citizens are equal and virtuous, while an aristocracy or monarchy results when the citizens are unequal and corrupted.

This shallowness is probably due to a feature of both Antique and Renaissance political thinking, which Bertrand Russell (2004 [1946]: 471) has observed with specific reference to Machiavelli, namely the preoccupation with concrete lawgivers or great founders and the concomitant absence of an understanding of other (less actor-centered) causal drivers of political change. On this basis, Russell (2004 [1946]: 471) notes that:

The conception of a community as an organic growth, which the statesmen can only affect to a limited extent, is in the main modern, and has been greatly strengthened by the theory of evolution. This conception is not to be found in Machiavelli any more than in Plato.

Looking for 'deeper' explanations accounting for democratization, we must therefore fast-forward to the first half of the 19th century. In his portrayal of the American democracy of his day, *Democracy in America* (*De la démocratie en Amérique*), Tocqueville (1998 [1835/1840]) attributes its vitality to finely branched voluntary organizations; what we today would call a strong civil society. According to this perspective, democracy is interlinked with the capacity of the citizenry to keep the state authority on a short leash.

Another example is found half a century later. In the first pages of *The Protestant Ethic and the Spirit of Capitalism* (*Die protestantische Ethik und der 'Geist' des Kapitalismus*), Max Weber (2005 [1904/1905]) formulated the thesis that the democratic development in Great Britain should be traced back to the Protestant Reformation. Here, it is the individualism produced by Protestantism which accounts for the emergence of democracy. Finally, proceeding another 50 years forward in history, Seymour Martin Lipset (1959) wrote an article entitled 'Some Social Requisites of Democracy: Economic Development and Political Legitimacy' in which he pointed to a general connection between affluence and democracy. Lipset's admirably simple observation was that affluent countries are typically democratic, whereas this is rarely the case with impoverished countries.

Beginning with Lipset, the modern democratization literature has gradually established itself as a distinct discipline within political science. But though Lipset and a few other great names from the field, including Robert A. Dahl and Barrington Moore, provided a number of important contributions in the decades to follow, the democratization literature first gathered sustained momentum in the mid-1980s. The turning point was the publication of the four-volume work entitled *Transitions from Authoritarian Rule* in 1986. The fourth volume, which is a brief concluding essay, was written by Guillermo O'Donnell and Philippe Schmitter (1986). They took odds with the previous focus in the literature on structural conditions. Instead, they directed their attention to the societal elites and emphasized how the introduction of democracy is primarily the result of the contingent choices made by the significant actors and that democratization can therefore appear in the most unexpected places.

O'Donnell and Schmitter's essay has since established itself among the most frequently cited works in the democratization literature. It is also said to have had a direct influence on activists in non-democratic countries such as South Africa during Apartheid. O'Donnell and Schmitter thus set a course that has been followed ever since. In recent decades the field has developed into a veritable industry. Explaining the emergence of democracy still takes up the most space, but it goes hand-in-hand with practical recommendations for the promotion of democracy and democratic quality. In other words, it is now possible to talk about democracy assistance in much the same vein as we have previously referred to development assistance/aid. In many cases the two have actually merged. The field is therefore populated by innumerable researchers, experts, and consultants who – based in university milieus, think-tanks, aid organizations, and civil service apparatuses – contribute to the theoretical literature as well as providing advice to politicians, aid workers, and activists.

In this book, we make a general distinction between four kinds of explanatory perspectives within the democratization literature (modernization theory, the social forces tradition, transitology, and international factors). We discuss each of these perspectives in detail in Chapters 7 to 10 and we discuss the possibility of combining some or all of them in Chapter 11. Here, we are preoccupied with a distinct question: Why did a discipline that enjoyed a relatively modest status within political science in the first decades following World War II suddenly ascend to the prominent position it presently occupies?

The third wave of democratization

The increased attention has certainly been fed by the veritable explosion in recent decades in the number of democratic countries. Samuel P. Huntington (1991) introduced his renowned book about democratization, *The Third Wave: Democratization in the Late Twentieth Century*, with a thrilling description of the Portuguese 'Carnation Revolution' in 1974. Huntington's point was that the bloodless revolution was the first indication of what he refers to as the 'third wave of democratization'. In the years to come, this wave flooded Southern Europe, where first Greece (later the same year) and subsequently Spain (1978) turned their backs on their autocratic regimes. But that was not all. The tide continued, soon reaching Latin America and Southeast Asia before finally arriving in Sub-Saharan Africa and the former communist countries, where the fall of the Berlin Wall (1989) and disintegration of the Soviet Union (1991) symbolized the crumbling of some major barriers.

We analyze this third wave and the two previous waves in Chapters 5 and 6, while the historical roots of representative democracy are dealt with in Chapter 4. But a couple of figures quickly establish that the development has led to an unprecedented high water mark of democracy. According to our calculations, 26 percent of the world's countries were what we in this book term 'minimalist democracies' (see Chapter 3) in 1972. Twenty years later, this percentage had increased to roughly 53, and at the time of writing it is close to 60. Other counts indicate the same tendency, even though the absolute numbers vary. In short, and regardless of the measures used, the world has never been as democratic as in recent decades.

However, one could also argue that the category of democratic countries has never been as heterogeneous (cf. Mair 2008). Going back a single generation, most democracies were situated in Western Europe, North America, and Oceania. Today, we must look to the most remote corners of the world if we are to report every last democracy. This is where diversity enters the stage. Contemporary democracies all carry out competitive elections. Otherwise, they would be non-democratic by definition. But there is considerable diversity with respect to the other relevant characteristics, such as respect for political liberties and the rule of law.

This is best understood using the classic Latin *per genus et differentiam* principle, which explicitly or implicitly serves as the basis for most definitions. *Genus* is that which all members of a given category have in common. In the case of democracy, this is competitive elections. *Differentiam* is that which distinguishes the members of the category from one another. Here, the list is virtually endless in today's world. Of greatest relevance, obviously, are the elements referred to above: political liberties and the rule of law. As we shall see, this is because they are often directly tied to the definition of democracy. But the differences also outweigh the similarities in terms of accompanying properties – or possible consequences – such as international and domestic peace, economic growth, famines, and social equality, issues we return to in Chapters 12 and 13.

For our purposes, the important aspect is that the combination of the spread of democracy and the pronounced differences between distinct forms of democracy has stimulated interest in questions of democratization in at least two ways. First, the positions sway back and forth on the front lines of democracy; some countries democratize, while others relapse into autocratic rule. To many observers, this remarkable upheaval is more interesting than the general stability of Western democracies, where the great political battles are a thing of the past.[4] Second, the diversity within the democratic category is interesting in itself. For how can we explain that the rule of law in some democracies exists only on paper while in others it is woven into the social tapestry? And is it possible to tie the different forms of democracy together with the heterogeneous political, economic, and social development of the respective countries?

From autocracy to democracy

We will attempt to answer these questions – and many others – in this book. But suffice here to further elaborate on a particular reason behind the new interest in the subject of democracy, which we have already alluded to, namely that the variation within the democratic category has increased substantially in recent decades, and since the breakdown of communism in particular.

This is reflected in the focus of researchers dealing with political regimes. It is striking how the literature displayed far greater interest in autocracies up until the 1980s. From the 1950s until the early 1980s, very many researchers were interested in the variation in the non-democratic categories – conceptually as well as empirically (Mair 2008). Worth mentioning are the studies carried out by Hannah Arendt (1951) and Carl Friedrich and Zbigniew Brezinski (1968) of the Nazi and communist totalitarian regimes; O'Donnell's (1973) analysis of 'bureaucratic-authoritarian' regimes; Huntington's (1968) work addressing political instability in developing countries; and Juan J. Linz's (1975) renowned distinction between authoritarian and totalitarian regimes.

At present, it is instead the democratic category that is captivating scholars. David Collier and Steven Levitsky (1996) set about describing this new tendency in the mid-1990s, and they began by tallying the number of definitions of democracy found in the literature. They stopped counting after hitting 550! There is no evidence indicating that this development has since stalled. The literature teems with more or less systematic typologies of various forms of democracy, such as liberal democracy, electoral democracy, and defective democracy (Møller & Skaaning 2010). At the same time, it is striking how the autocratic category has, at least until very recently, been neglected. It is rarely included directly in typologies, and there are only a few systematic attempts at spelling out the variations between the various forms of regimes within the autocratic residual category, attempts which we briefly address in Chapter 3.

The democratic *Zeitgeist*

Another reason why democratization now occupies an independent and very central position in political science is the following: In the latest generation, democracy has won the battle for ideas to the extent that Francis Fukuyama (1992) proclaimed the end of history in the aftermath of the communist breakdown and the dissolution of the Soviet Union between 1989 and 1991. The non-democratic challengers – and particularly the totalitarian alternative – enjoy hardly any popular support in the new and old democracies alike. Whereas democracy was on the defensive for most of the interwar period and had a considerable opponent during the Cold War, it is now the 'last man standing' on the battlefield of political ideas.

While many of the new democracies are marked by corruption, judicial arbitrariness, and poor economic performance – and the respective populations therefore have a considerable lack of confidence in their elected politicians, the judiciary, and the police – a large majority nevertheless support democracy as the preferable form of political rule (Klingemann 1999; Chu et al. 2008; Norris 2011). In short, the notion of democracy stands stronger than it has in decades, perhaps stronger than ever before. The only partial exception to this pattern is political Islam (or Islamism), which has formulated an ideological alternative to liberal democracy. For the time being, however, this exception has yet to lead to actual democratic breakdowns.

More than a century ago, the English liberal politician Sir William Vernon Harcourt famously declared: "We are all socialists now." Today, keeping the above considerations in mind, it would hardly be an exaggeration to declare that we are all democrats now. The statement would at least appear to have greater validity than was the case with Harcourt's statement. This *Zeitgeist* has increased the interest in research in democratization in two ways.

First, the monopoly of democracy on legitimacy is one of the factors contributing to the third wave of democratization. More specifically, this is part of the reason why so many countries continue to carry out democratic elections, even though they are unable to maintain the rule of law ideal characteristic of Western democracies. In addition, as already pointed out, these illiberal combinations of democratic characteristics motivate many of the current studies addressing the subject. Second, researchers are humans too, and they are therefore influenced by their political convictions. Just think of the great interest in Marxism that followed in the wake of the 'youth rebellions' of the 1960s and thrived in university milieus in the Western world in the 1970s and 1980s. Today, democratic theory and the study of democratization processes are among the big draws.

In other words, there is good reason for writing a book such as this. In the course of this introductory chapter, we have directed the reader's attention towards some impulses that have contributed to stimulating interest in democracy and democratization. There is the explosion in the number of democracies that has simultaneously led to unprecedented democratic diversity, and there is the democratic *Zeitgeist*, which has rendered devoting one's scientific and political activities to democracy and democratization fashionable and interesting. This book represents an attempt at traversing this literature.

Part I

Conceptions

Democracy – what is it?

1 Conceptions of democracy in ancient Greece

> Yet a term that means anything means nothing. And so it has become with 'democracy', which nowadays is not so much a term of restricted and specific meaning as a vague endorsement of a popular idea.
>
> (Dahl 1989: 2)

These are the words of the most prominent scholar working on democracy after World War II. His message is indicative of the debate surrounding the concept of democracy. Democracy offers an apt example of what Walter Bryce Gallie has referred to as 'essentially contested concepts': concepts that are characterized by disagreement regarding the fundamental meaning. In fact, Gallie (1956: 184) suggested that democracy is the essentially contested concept *par excellence*, i.e., democracy is a construction about which there will never be agreement because it is multidimensional, abstract, qualitative, internally complex, and evaluative (see also Held 2006: 2).

There is definitely something in this; but social science requires clearly defined concepts (Sartori 1970). To determine if a given country is a democracy or the extent to which it is democratic, we must know what democracy is (and is not). This is also the case if we are interested in studying causes and consequences of democracy. The minimum requirement is therefore the ability to present one or more definitions of democracy. We return to this in Chapter 3, where we discuss some of the definitions frequently employed in empirical democratization research and order them in a typology.

Our purpose here and in Chapter 2 is somewhat different. In these two chapters, we outline the contours of some of the most significant conceptions of democracy through the ages. The structure and content of our discussion of conceptions of democracy is inspired by three central bodies of works dealing with this issue. The first is the influential overview provided by David Held (2006) in *Models of Democracy*. The second is the work of Robert A. Dahl, who has done more than anyone else to create clarity about what characterizes and justifies democratic rule. The third is the works of Mogens Herman Hansen on democracy in classical Athens and beyond.

Dahl, Held, and Hansen all situate the origins of democracy as both idea and practice in ancient Greece. Indeed, the most important theorists trace democracy back to the ancient Greeks.[1] This, therefore, is where we begin. More particularly, it seems pertinent to start with an excerpt from one of the most famous speeches of all times, the great Athenian statesman Pericles' Funeral Oration – or, more precisely, Thucydides' report of it:

> It has the name democracy because government is in the hands not of the few but of the majority. In private disputes all are equal before the law; and when it comes to esteem in public affairs, a man is preferred according to his own reputation for something, not, on the whole, just turn and turn about, but for excellence, and even in poverty no man is debarred by obscurity of reputation so long as he has it in him to do some good service to the state.
>
> (Hansen 1999: 73)

This passage is often used to summarize the Athenian understanding of democracy. In a historical perspective, the regime and ideology that Pericles is describing is nothing less than revolutionary. Throughout most of recorded history, human societies have been characterized by political hierarchy. This has generally assumed either the form of rule by a single person (monarchy/tyranny) or rule by the few (aristocracy/oligarchy). Some 2600 years ago, however, a number of Greek city-states began breaking down the monopoly on power held by the narrow elite. In *Democracy and Its Critics*, Dahl (1989) accordingly describes how the very idea of the 'rule of the many' emerged in ancient Greece, more specifically in Athens. Dahl refers to this as the *first democratic transformation*.

The understanding of liberty in the ancient *polis*

But what were the ancient ideas about democracy? It is often asserted that the classical understanding of democracy differs fundamentally from the modern, liberal view (see Sartori 1987: 158).[2] This claim is first and foremost founded in the understanding of liberty. Benjamin Constant (1988 [1819]), in his renowned lecture entitled *The Liberty of the Ancients Compared with that of the Moderns* (*De la liberté des Anciens comparée à celle des Modernes*), underlined that the citizens in the Greek city-states were only free in the sense that they participated in the political decision-making process. In other words, citizens were liberated by their political participation, regardless of which chains the decisions of the majority placed upon them (see also Berlin 2002 [1995]: 283–284; Fried 2007).

According to this view, one could also say that the citizens of the *polis* had no experience with civil liberties or the rule of law. The critics of Athenian democracy often refer to Socrates' trial in order to illustrate this point. Not only is this one of the most renowned trials in human history due to Plato's 'Socratic dialogues'; Socrates was actually sentenced to death for having led the youth astray, that is, for expressing his opinions. As such, the case arguably demonstrates the distance to the modern ideal regarding freedom of speech.

Inspired by Constant, Isaiah Berlin (2002 [1958]) drew a distinction between the 'positive' understanding of liberty in Antiquity and the 'negative' understanding of liberty among classical liberals. Whereas Berlin very much maintains Constant's modern liberty (the negative conception), without noticing it he alters Constant's ancient liberty (the positive conceptions). To Berlin, the positive conception of liberty demands not so much that people participate in politics but rather that they are able to control themselves, restrain their passions, and realize themselves via their reason (Hansen 2010d: 315–318). This is in contrast to negative liberty, which Berlin identified in the English liberal tradition, where liberty is defined as the absence of physical coercion, in particular from officialdom. According to Berlin, the negative sense of liberty (i.e., negative liberty as an ideal) was entirely absent in the Greek city-states, even if the citizens did occasionally enjoy genuine personal liberty.

The famous critique forwarded by Constant and Berlin against the antique understanding of liberty has not gone unchallenged, however. Others have emphasized how the Greek city-states produced a political idea closely resembling the modern understanding of democracy. Hansen (1989) thus points out that the Greek democracies celebrated two ideals: liberty (*eleutheria*) and equality (*isonomia*), and that liberty was paramount to equality. Among other sources, he draws upon Aristotle's famous description of the principles of democracy. This deserves to be quoted at length, as it is such a central factor in the disagreement over the respective understandings of democracy in ancient Greece:

> The basis of a democratic state is liberty; which, according to the common opinion of men, can only be enjoyed in such a state – this they affirm to be the great end of every democracy. One principle of liberty is for all to rule and be ruled in turn, and indeed democratic justice is the application of numerical not proportionate equality; whence it follows that the majority must be supreme, and that whatever the majority approve must be the end and the just. Every citizen, it is said, must have equality, and therefore in a democracy the poor have more power than the rich, because there are more of them, and the will of the majority is supreme. This, then, is one note of liberty which all democrats affirm to be the principle of their state. Another is that a man should live as he likes. This, they say, is the privilege of a freeman; and, on the other hand, not to live as a man likes is the mark of a slave. This is the second characteristic of democracy, whence has arisen the claim of men to be ruled by none, if possible, or, if this is impossible, to rule and be ruled in turns; and so it coincides with the freedom based upon equality.
>
> (Aristotle 2008 [350 BC]: 280)

Naturally, however, the crux of the matter is what liberty meant in the Athenian context. The problem is that the Greek *eleutheria* would appear to have been a rather vague term without a particularly well-specified meaning[3] (see also Held 2006: 16). On one level it denoted being free as opposed to being a slave, that is, a question of status. Within the democratic sphere, however, the word had other meanings. Hansen (1989: 10–11) notes that, in the quote, Aristotle presents *eleutheria* as two rather different things: the right to participate politically and the right to freedom from political repression, including the right to arrange one's life according to one's own choices. The latter meaning is very close to Berlin's negative sense of liberty.

Pericles' Funeral Oration likewise indicates that democracy was associated with the tripod of equality, liberty, and tolerance; three values that operated in the private and public sphere alike. As regards the notion of personal liberty, it was first and foremost freedom of speech and legal protection that distinguished the democracies from the oligarchies of the day. The Athenian statesman Demosthenes provides a telling example of the opposing perspectives on the freedom of speech when pointing out that while the Athenians had the right to criticize democracy and praise the Spartan constitution, the Spartans were unable to praise any constitution other than their own. And when Demosthenes was accused of non-democratic behavior by his opponent Aischines, because he had arrested an Athenian without basis in any decree adopted by the people, the emphasis was on the rule of law (Hansen 1999: 77).

In arguing the case for a negative conception of freedom in democratic *poleis*, Hansen also makes reference to Socrates' trial. While this was clearly an attack upon free speech, he sees the furore surrounding the trial as illustrating how the protection of personal liberties *was* an actual ideal. It was just that it was not always respected, which has also been the case in many modern democracies. What is more, the trial occurred in a period of upheaval for Athens, shortly after a brutal civil war, which makes the transgression part of a more general anomaly. Finally, we can observe that Aristotle's and Plato's famous criticisms of democracy owed much to their criticism of what amounts to a negative conception of liberty. In fact, Plato's outright dismissal of democracy seems to be a consequence of his understanding of the democratic freedom as the freedom of each citizen to do as he pleases (i.e., as negative liberty). Why would particularly Plato but also Aristotle spend so much effort denouncing the negative conception of freedom in the democracies of the day, had this not been something that existed on the ground?[4]

Note in this connection that Constant actually recognized that one antique exception to his scheme existed, namely classical Athens, where the liberty of the moderns – the right to live one's life as one pleased – was indeed recognized (Hansen 2010b: 6, 13). But Constant took Sparta, where no such negative liberty was recognized, as the symptomatic model of the classical *polis*, regarding Athens as an aberration. Ignoring Constant's distinction between Athens and Sparta, Berlin, on the other hand, claimed that even the Athenians did not appreciate negative liberty.

Direct democracy

One area where contemporary democracy undoubtedly distinguishes itself from the democracy of Antiquity is regarding our use of elected representatives, who appoint a government and pass legislation. The modern representative model would have seemed foreign to a citizen in ancient Greek democracies.[5] The democracy of the city-states was a direct democracy. All of the citizens had the right to participate in the popular assembly and debate political decisions. The basic ideal was for all (male) citizens to participate in the exercise of government and the legislative process, meaning that democracy was deliberately carried out by amateurs. None of the officeholders could be professional, since, if professionals are involved, they will always manage to take over and transform democracy into an oligarchy (Hansen 1999: 236, 308). The Greeks knew nothing about the 'career politician' – the politician making his living from politics – although statesmen such as Themistocles, Pericles, and Demosthenes dominated the Athenian *polis* in different periods.

In practice, maintaining direct democracy without an administrative apparatus was impossible. Nevertheless, in order to be able to respect the amateur principle as much as possible, the Greeks applied an approximation in the form of a rotation principle based on drawing lots. In every part of the civil service, the citizens took turns attending to the public offices. These offices were usually held for a relatively brief period of time, and the appointment was normally decided by lots drawn among the candidates who volunteered. Athenian democracy was thus a 'democracy by sortition', where the citizens took turns ruling one another. Indeed, the core characteristic of Greek popular rule is to be found in the use of lot, which was seen as the only genuinely democratic principle. Tellingly, Aristotle categorizes the elections of magistrates as oligarchic (Manin 1997: 41–42; Russell 2004 [1946]: 183–184).

The amateur principle did of course have its limits. The appointment of generals (*strategoi*), for example, was not subject to the rotation principle. Here, skill was the ultimate requirement, particularly in times of war. But the pivot of the democratic *polis* was the absolute political equality of the citizens as guaranteed by direct participation in legislative and court proceedings (Held 2006: 27). The modern distinction between state and society in general and civil servants and citizens in particular was therefore not especially crisp in the Greek city-states. Some scholars have even argued that there was no general distinction drawn between citizens, politicians, and civil servants (e.g., Holmes 1979). As Held (2006: 14–15) writes:

> The principle of government was the principle of a form of life: direct participation. And the process of government itself was based on . . . free and unrestricted discourse, guaranteed by isegoria, an equal right to speak in the sovereign assembly . . . Accordingly, the ancient democratic polis can be thought of as an attempt to enable men of different backgrounds and attributes to express and transform the understanding of the good through political interaction . . . Decisions and laws rested, it was claimed, on conviction – the force of the better argument – and not mere custom, habit or brute force.

Other scholars have argued that – in practice – the *polis* of Athens operated with distinction between public and private eerily similar to modern practice (e.g., Hansen 1998: 86–95). However, this distinction was not founded in the existence of individual human rights as it is in the modern liberal conception (see Holmes 1979: fn. 118). In that sense, the ancient Greek understanding of democracy differed significantly from the modern liberal understanding, which allows private persons to remain private persons as political participation is voluntary (Holmes 1995: 31). Modern representative democracy, so to speak, makes no demands on the political vigilance of citizens.[6] Indeed, the negative conception of liberty expressly includes the freedom *not* to get involved in politics (Holmes 1979, 1982). Instead, modern democracy rests on a much more indirect control principle, namely that the citizenry have the right to elect and dismiss the government should they wish to do so.

In this context, it is telling that the Greek word for private person, *idiōtēs*,[7] would attain the meaning 'uneducated or ignorant' (hence the English 'idiot') in late vulgar Latin. For the Greeks, political participation defined democracy. Democracy had no meaning without participation, and this is probably where the observations made by Constant and Berlin about the distinction between ancient liberty or positive liberty as opposed to the modern negative liberty have most purchase (cf. Posner 2003: 144). Notice in this connection that Constant's distinction was anchored in the argument that modern liberty only became possible as a consequence of the disjunction between state and society following the Reformation. In Antiquity, where no such dividing line existed, individual rights against the encroachment of the state on society made little or no sense (Holmes 1982: 54–56).

A controversial ideal

Instead of distinguishing between state and society, the Greeks distinguished between public and private. What was public concerned the *polis* – a community of citizens (*politai*) only. Thus a basic distinction was citizen versus non-citizen. Of all of the residents of the *polis* of Athens, probably about half held full citizenship. However, women were excluded beforehand from any form of participation, as were the *metoik* – free non-citizens, who usually hailed from other parts of Greece – and of course the slaves. Although the economic importance and proportion of slaves to citizens has often been exaggerated (e.g., Held 2006: 19), to some extent it was the labor of the slaves that enabled the citizenry to attend to the requirements of political participation on amateur terms. According to Douglass North (1981: 104),

> Greek democracy was inseparable from Greek slavery (or helotry in Sparta) since the structure of political-economic organization which permitted direct democracy of citizens required a labor force of slaves or helots to perform the basic functions of the economy in order that citizens could be released for political, judicial and military activity.

Though this exaggerates the economic and political importance of slaves, it is certainly the case that it was the down-sizing of the *demos* that made direct democracy possible. In this sense this was obviously a society based on privileges. This is where later democrats have stood in line to point fingers at the democracy of the Greek city-states. As Dahl (1989: 22) puts it, we are dealing with an ideal that is by definition exclusive, both externally and internally. It could never be extended beyond the *polis*, and never further than to the citizens in the *polis*. Against that background, the whole modern notion of human rights or merely abstract principles about equality in relation to the law made little sense to the Greeks. Liberty was exclusive, since it was inextricably connected to the status as citizen of the city-state community (Held 2006: 19). Modern democrats have therefore asserted that Greek democracy was in fact an oligarchy, where a select few attended to the interests of the many.

Somewhat paradoxically, the notion of direct democracy – without vigorous liberal counters – has at the same time been criticized for inevitably leading to the tyranny of the majority.[8] The whims of the people become the compass for politics. Ostracism and arbitrary violations of the lives and property of private persons became the order of the day, together with adventurous foreign policy. This was James Madison's (1987 [1788]: 126) point in *The Federalist Papers* when he thundered against the ancient democracies. Until the mid-1800s, the great thinkers and statesmen practically stood in line in order to denounce the ancient direct democracy. Indeed, we already meet these points of criticism in the heydays of Athenian democracy. There are hardly any surviving philosophical tracts defending democracy (Held 2006: 13). Most of the elaborate descriptions of the understanding of democracy that we do have were written by those who criticized democracy – although there are isolated fragments from its supporters, such as Pericles' Funeral Oration. The great Greek philosophers were either skeptical, such as Aristotle, or outright hostile, such as Plato, towards the democratic ideal. In this context, it is worth noting what Aristotle called for to replace democracy. As mentioned in the Introduction, Aristotle, in his classical regime typology – depicted in Figure 1.1 – distinguished between well-functioning and stable popular rule, *politeia*, and a perverse variant thereof, *demokratia*.[9]

The basic difference between *politeia* and *demokratia* is that, in the former case, the citizens have the means to equip themselves as Hoplites (foot soldiers) to serve the city-state militarily, meaning that this form of popular rule rests on the armed citizen.[10] The *politeia* is consequently based on the existence of a large middle

	One ruler	Few rulers	Many rulers
Good constitution	Monarchy *(basileia)*	Aristocracy *(aristokratia)*	Citizenship constitution *(politeia)*
Perverse constitution	Tyranny *(tyrannis)*	Oligarchy *(oligarchia)*	Democracy *(demokratia)*

Figure 1.1 Aristotle's classical regime typology

class of peasant-soldiers rather than an impoverished mass of citizens: on middle-class rule rather than on the rule of the poor (which characterizes *demokratia*).

In the more empirical parts of his *Politics*, Aristotle largely ignores monarchy, since virtually no specimens were in existence in the Greece of his day (Sparta, with its two kings, being a partial exception). Instead he contrasts the rule of the few and the rule of the many and teases out the different degrees of purity with which each type can be encountered (Hansen 2010a: 519–520). The purer the form (denoted by *oligarchia* and *demokratia*, respectively), the more perverse is the type. Contrariwise, the golden mean between the two (rendered by either *aristokratia* or *politeia*) was perceived by Aristotle as the best constitution in practice. *Aristokratia* and *politeia* are thus seen as closer to being a 'mixed constitution', which in Aristotle's version fuses the rule of the few with the rule of the many. According to Aristotle, the social classes or the political institutions or both must be mixed to produce such a regime form. The typical examples from Antiquity are those of Sparta and Rome. The felicitous consequence of such a combination is that the democratic power of the majority is tempered, which puts a damper on arbitrariness.

We even meet the ideal of the mixed constitution in some of Plato's later writings (Held 2006: 27), and it is important to note that it was this very ideal about the favorable, mixed constitution that served as the basis for much of the democratic theory in the 18th and 19th centuries. Oftentimes, it has not been Aristotle's classical scheme but the slightly different version of Polybios which has been most influential. Polybios differs from Aristotle in two important ways. First, he renders the good version of popular rule as *demokratia* whereas he terms the bad version mob rule (*ochlokratia*). Second – and this is where his imprint upon later thinking has been the biggest – he maintains that the mixed constitution actually fuses all of the three types of monarchy, aristocracy, and democracy (Hansen 2010a: 519–521).

Understanding the notion of the mixed constitution in this way, we may say that democracy shed its skin after ancient Greece while significant elements in Western political thinking have been quite constant. It is telling that Thomas Aquinas, who railed against democracy as a pure type, celebrated the mixed constitution. Indeed, the doctrine about the golden mean, including its democratic element, was celebrated throughout the period in which democracy, on its own, carried derogatory connotations.

Conclusions

We further pursue the importance of the mixed constitution in the next chapter. Here, two points are important. On the one hand, Athenian democracy undoubtedly deserves the title. This is, after all, where the notion of popular sovereignty had its origins; it was here that the autocratic chains were systematically broken for the first time. Similarly, we have seen how supplementary values such as freedom of speech and the rule of law were already valued and enforced (albeit with significant exceptions) in ancient Greece. On the other hand, the liberal doctrine that the individual unto himself possesses a set of inviolable rights was not prevalent (Holmes 1979; Held 2006: 13–14, 26). To quote Sartori (1987: 285):

> The ancients did not, and could not, recognize the individual as a person and, concurrently, as a 'private self' entitled to respect, for the obvious reason that this conception came with Christianity and was subsequently developed by the Renaissance, by Protestantism, and by the modern school of natural law. What the Greek individualistic spirit lacked, then, was the notion of a *legitimate* private space conceived as the moral as well as the juridical protection of the single human person.

We can return one last time to Socrates' trial here. As Dahl (1989: 219) underlines, Socrates in any case did not have a 'constitutional right' to preach dissenting views as have citizens in modern, liberal democracies. In that sense, it would appear as though the modern negative sense of liberty – in the form of basic human rights that exist prior to and stand above the political process – had yet to make its mark.

In our discussion, we have concentrated on the conception and practice of democracy in the classical era. This entire discussion begs the question in one particular regard, however: Just how much has the Athenian precedent mattered for modern democracy empirically? It is interesting to note that Hansen (2010c), being so adamant about the basic similarity between Athenian and modern democracy – in particular as an ideology – categorically asserts that we neither find an unbroken tradition, nor a broken tradition nor even just inspiration linking modern democratic institutions to those of Athens. In fact, according to Hansen (2010c: xxxii):

> Not one single Athenian institution seems to have left its mark on posterity neither in the Middle Ages nor in the Early Modern period – when democracy was still conceived as direct rule by the people – nor in the 19th century – when democracy became conceived as representative government based on elections.

To the extent that Antiquity inspired the modern crafters of first republicanism and later democracy, the Roman precedent was the important one. This is exactly where the doctrine of the mixed constitution comes to the fore. Before examining how the modern, liberal sense of freedom fused with democracy, we must therefore outline the role of republicanism. This also means that we are now seeking to elucidate the road which leads to Dahl's (1989: ch. 2) *second democratic transformation*, i.e., the coming together of republicanism, representation, and the logic of equality. This is the objective of Chapter 2.

2   Conceptions of democracy
from ancient Rome to our time

Elements of the ancient Greek understanding of democracy could be found in Rome and later yet in the northern Italian republicanism of the late Middle Ages. However, over the course of the past 200 years, modern – or liberal – democracy has replaced the classical understanding of democracy (Dahl 1989).

In this chapter we set out to capture the shift in the conceptions of democracy that brought about the dominant (although not undisputed) conception of the present era, namely that of liberal, representative democracy. We do not rigidly follow a timeline, as we to some extent divide the conceptions of democracy thematically (cf. Held 2006). In this connection it is important to understand that there has not merely been a shift in the ideas about democracy but also a shift in the level of the political unit. Whereas the Greek understanding of democracy and the republicanism of the late Middle Ages revolved around the city-state, the *polis* or *civitas/città* (a micro state), modern democracy is tied to the national or territorial state (a macro state). The main thrust of Robert A. Dahl's *second democratic transformation* is exactly that the conception of democracy became adapted to the national state and that representation replaced direct democracy. According to Dahl, this shift only occurred in the 18th and 19th centuries; but, as we shall see, its roots should be traced further back in time.

Republicanism – from ancient Rome to the Renaissance

Horace, the great Roman poet, coined the famous line about how "Conquered Greece conquered her brute victor and brought her arts into rustic Latium." One may further argue that ancient Rome also carried the torch after Hellas in the political sphere, even though Roman republicanism had different roots than ancient Greek democracy. The Roman republic kept the notion of popular sovereignty alive, but only to a limited degree, since the republic was an oligarchy rather than a democracy, even when only considering the group of people possessing Roman citizenship (Held 2006: 28). Henrik Mouritsen (2001: 1) argues that "On the one hand, the Roman people wielded tremendous, almost unlimited powers . . . On the other hand, Rome was also an aristocratic society, where the elite controlled vast economic resources and monopolized public office." Republican Rome was characterized by a limited number of families largely controlling public affairs.

Unequal voting rules, political privileges, and patron–client structures (*clientele*) meant that these *nobiles* – a jumble of powerful patrician and plebeian families – took turns electing members as consuls, which was the highest office in the republic. Moreover, they dominated the Senate and provided most of the tribunes of the plebs.

In addition to incorporating certain elements of the notion of popular sovereignty, Roman republicanism also included innovations that are important from a democratic perspective. First, the republic was characterized by separate organs, such as the consuls, the Senate, and the tribunes, which balanced each other. As Machiavelli was later to note, the republic constituted a clear instance of a mixed constitution with elements of monarchy (the consuls), aristocracy (the Senate), and a popular element (the assembly and the tribunes). Second, the Roman legal practice was far more developed than anything we know from ancient Greece (Gress 1998: 99). Cicero, the greatest Roman thinker, emphasized that a true *res publica* must secure equality in liberty, *aequa libertas*. Crucially, the core of *libertas* was equality before the law (Hansen 2007: 59). Following the rediscovery of Roman law in the 11th century, these innovations exercised considerable influence over the political theory of the Middle Ages. This was especially reflected in the importance attributed to the precept of "that which affects all people must be approved by all people" (Tierney 1982: 21; Manin 1997: 88).

Above all, the Roman heritage became the pivot for the republicanism emerging in northern Italy almost a millennium after the fall of the (Western) Roman Empire. The early humanists and the later thinkers of the Enlightenment were inspired far more by ancient Rome than by ancient Greece (Held 2006: 28, 34). Niccolò Machiavelli (1970 [1517]) represents a telling example. His republican masterpiece was *The Discourses on Livy*; the Livy who produced a famous history of Rome, from the mythical times until Augustus. We concentrate on this 'return of the republic'; that is, the republicanism of the Renaissance, as it arguably has the greatest significance for the modern understanding of democracy. Indeed, with its pantheon of prominent thinkers, such as Plato, Aristotle, Cicero, Machiavelli, Montesquieu, Jefferson, and Madison, it was extremely politically influential as recently as the 19th century, only to be eclipsed by liberalism (Hansen 2007).

The premise of this republican body of theory was that a city-state, as in the age of the early Roman republic, ought to be autonomous as opposed to being directly or indirectly ruled by monarchs or pope. This applied in theory as well as in practice. The city-states in northern Italy achieved *de facto* independence in the Middle Ages after a number of trials of strength with the Holy Roman emperors (Russell 2004 [1946]: 400–402). At the same time, arguments for popular sovereignty and independent city-states were refined and advanced for the first time since the fall of the Roman Republic (Held 2006: 34), most prominently in Florence in the 14th and 15th centuries.

Just as in the Greek democracies – but without any direct connection with the Greeks – public offices in the medieval republics were normally filled via sortition (Manin 1997: 41–42). The big difference compared to, for instance, democratic Athens was that only upper- and middle-class citizens were allowed to partake.

The enfranchised did not number all citizens but first and foremost the members of the gilds, or oftentimes only the most powerful gilds. The poor urban population and the inhabitants in the *contado* (i.e., rural areas of the city-state beyond the city walls) were precluded from political participation. As the Roman Republic 1500 years earlier, neither Florence of the High Middle Ages nor any of the other northern Italian city-states could thus be considered democracies as an elite (the *optimati* corresponding to the Roman *boni*) by and large monopolized government. Yet alongside the emerging European territorial states, the Florentine republicanism had some obvious affinities with the liberal democratic regimes of the 19th century (see Brucker 1984: 138).

The umbilical cord of republicanism of the Renaissance was the political autonomy of the city-state (*libertas*), meaning that the citizens were accountable to no one but their own community. Their autonomy was synonymous with the autonomy of the city-state, and political power was firmly placed in the hands of the citizens (Held 2006: 34). However, this autonomy depended on a generous measure of civic duty (*virtù*), understood as the willingness to emphasize public interests at the expense of private interests (Hansen 2007: 29–30). This, in turn, required a comprehensive public sphere characterized by vigilance. As in Antiquity, civic participation thus was the alpha and omega for republicanism. By implication, republican liberty has more in common with Constant's ancient liberty than with the modern/negative liberty of classical liberalism (cf. Chapter 1, this volume). At the same time, however, Roman law was also revitalized, and the notion of private property was exalted as being close to inviolable.

Developmental republicanism and protective republicanism

More generally, it is useful to distinguish between two forms of republicanism: protective republicanism and developmental republicanism (Held 2006: 35).[1] The latter, which was later taken up by Jean-Jacques Rousseau, is tied to Constant's ancient and Berlin's positive understanding of liberty. Developmental republicanism thus considers political participation a value unto itself. Citizens are only able to realize themselves through an active public life. For Rousseau (1993 [1762]), who provided the most celebrated articulation of this perspective in *The Social Contract* (*Du contrat social*), all citizens must be legislators and exercisers of power in a community. Therefore, the political unit must preferably be the smallest possible in order to bridge or even annul the gap between subjects and rulers (Held 2006: 45).

Rousseau was, accordingly, bitterly opposed to any distinction between state and civil society. In his opinion, a representative democracy has never been and cannot be a real democracy. Most famous, perhaps, is his remark that the British are only free when they cast their vote. As soon as the election is completed, they are again enslaved, as they are at the mercy of the dictates of their elected representatives (Rousseau 1993 [1762]: 266). The other side of the coin is that in a direct democracy the people must be completely sovereign. This touches upon a paradox in Rousseau's writings (see Berlin (2002 [1958]: 208). Personal liberty is an absolute value for Rousseau, but at the same time he is convinced about the existence of universal laws for how society is to be structured. These two ideas can obviously be at odds with one another. Rousseau solves this problem by pointing out that rational people can recognize the true laws. Because they are universal, they apply to everyone, and the general will therefore have the right to force people to be free.

Conversely, protective republicanism emphasizes that the community (city-state) should guarantee personal liberty. According to republican self-government, the judicial practice should be rule-based, not arbitrary, which enables individual citizens to predict the consequences of their actions. In terms of lineages, protective republicanism is closely tied to Machiavelli's (1970 [1517]) thoughts as expressed in *The Discourses*, and the legacy from Rome is therefore clearly evident.

For Machiavelli, republican liberty should be understood as the absence of arbitrary domination (Hansen 2007: 68), a notion that has obvious affinities with negative liberty. However, protective republicanism also calls for a high degree of political participation. Without such vigilance, civic virtue is all too easily corrupted, and the way is paved for individuals or factions monopolizing power (Held 2006: 35–36). The republican concept of corruption is thus much broader than that of our day, which is normally defined as the abuse of public office for private gains (World Bank 2011). To Machiavelli and his contemporaries, corruption comprised any attempt to put private interests above those of public welfare (Hansen 2007: 30). The patriotic citizen – another crucial concept in republicanism – is one who sacrifices his private interest on the altar of the *res publica*.

The basis of Machiavelli's political thought is that humans are driven by self-interest and that we have always had the same needs. But while human nature does not change, political institutions are able to dampen the harmful inclinations of humankind to the benefit of the common good (Held 2006: 41). Machiavelli here draws attention to that beacon of *virtù* (civic virtue) found in (or channeled by) the political institutions of ancient Rome. The Roman Republic distinguished itself in terms of its effective checks and balances. As noted previously, the constitution divided political control between the respective offices of the 'monarchic' consuls, the 'aristocratic' Senate, and the 'popular' tribunes. These three bodies balanced one another, thereby to some extent shielding the citizenry from the whims of the rulers.

This is the tripartite distinction of Polybius, which Machiavelli starts by invoking. But in his further analysis, he simply distinguishes between *grandi* (the patricians in the Senate) and *populo* (the tribunes of the plebs and the people's assembly) – the monarchical element he ignores (Hansen 2007: 67–68). For Machiavelli, it was – and this shocked his contemporaries – this constitutionally controlled discord between the upper class and the people that secured the preservation of power, with Rome serving as the pre-eminent example (Held 2006: 41–42).

As already mentioned, the advantages of a mixed constitution can be traced back to Aristotle. But one of the most important voices of protective republicanism,

Charles-Louis de Secondat Montesquieu, ventured further down this path by distinguishing between the executive, the legislature, and the judiciary, a distinction taken over, though modified, by James Madison, who called for an institutional balance of power in the form of checks and balances. Montesquieu's and Madison's notion of the separation of power differs in important ways from that of the mixed constitution. Basically,

> The separation of power is a theory about the division between three different functions: the legislative, the executive and the judicial. The mixed constitution is a theory about cooperation between different types of institution of which some are monarchical, some oligarchic and some democratic, and often the cooperation between the institutions cuts across functions.
>
> (Hansen 2010a: 523)

Hence, whereas the crucial republican concept of checks and balances is inherent in the idea of the mixed constitution, it is – at the logical extreme – incompatible with the notion of a separation of powers. Nonetheless, checks and balances are essential for the credibility of the separation of power theory, as some cooperation between the different branches of government is needed if the political system is to work in practice (Hansen 2010a: 523). What is important for our purposes, however, is that the doctrine of the separation of powers, including an emphasis upon checks and balances, was to become intimately linked with representative democracy for three, interconnected reasons. First, because Montesquieu in his *Spirit of the Laws* (*De l'esprit des lois*) interpreted the British government of his day in these terms. Second, because the American founders were heavily inspired by Montesquieu's treatise. Third, because the very idea of representative democracy first gained popular acclaim in the United States with the advent of Andrew Jackson's Democratic Party in 1828. After this crucial juncture, the separation of powers doctrine – which was heeded most closely in the American political system – simply fused with the notion of representative democracy (Hansen 2010a: 513).

In this way, representative democracy has become instilled with Machiavelli's protective republicanism. J.G.A. Pocock (1975) has convincingly argued that Machiavelli's thoughts on republicanism were picked up on the other side of the Atlantic 250 years after his death, though ultimately – due to Montesquieu and Madison – the doctrine of the separation of powers eclipsed the original doctrine of the mixed constitution.

To sum up, we encounter two strikingly different strands of republicanism. Somewhat paradoxically, developmental republicanism, which has popular sovereignty as its pivot, has provided ammunition to several of the non-democratic currents in the 20th century via Rousseau's writings (Talmon 1952; Holmes 1979; Held 2006: 44, 49). And, just as paradoxically, one can argue that protective republicanism, which explicitly targets the establishment of a kind of constitutional rule of the few, has contributed to developing the principles of liberal democracy via its emphasis on freedom from arbitrary domination, civil liberties, and checks and balances (Held 2006: 43). This observation neatly leads us to the next stop in our journey through the different understandings of democracy.

From liberalism to liberal democracy

As mentioned above, liberalism draws upon various aspects of republicanism. As an actual political ideology, however, it can only be traced back 400 years. Liberalism thus has its origins in Western Europe in the 17th century, and it was further elaborated in the 18th and 19th centuries. During this period, a string of great thinkers – some of whom were also mentioned in the context of republicanism, such as John Locke, David Hume, Jeremy Bentham, and John Stuart Mill in England; Montesquieu, Benjamin Constant, and Alexis de Tocqueville in France; Alexander von Humboldt in Germany; and Thomas Jefferson, Alexander Hamilton, and James Madison in the USA – formulated what we now refer to as classical liberalism.

The roots of liberalism are ordinarily traced back to Thomas Hobbes' (1985 [1651]) *Leviathan* and John Locke's (1993 [1690]) *Two Treatises of Government*. Hobbes was, at most, a 'proto-liberal'. While his thoughts were based on individualism, he believed that only an absolute state (the Leviathan) could protect the individual from the rapines of anarchy (Held 2006: 61–62). Locke, on the other hand, is a clear representative of constitutionalism. He, too, emphasizes the need to create strong state power capable of protecting order. But his addition was that the social contract depends upon the state protecting the individual, and that it therefore entails a right of rebellion if the contract is breached (Locke 1993 [1690]: 375–378; cf. Held 2006: 59, 64).

In many ways, the classical liberalism of the 18th and 19th centuries may be understood as a reaction against the prevailing conservative ideology of the day, which celebrated absolute monarchy. The liberals agreed that people needed to be ruled, as they are all too often controlled by their passions. Inspired by Hobbes, the first generations of liberals emphasized that liberty does not exist in the absence of the state. Mankind is not born free. Mankind wins his liberty by virtue of the intervention of the state. While the authorities might limit the freedom to act, it is genuine within these limits (Holmes 1995: 270). However, the liberals may be said to have drawn the logical consequence of this understanding. As pointed out by Locke, since those in authority are people like everybody else, they must also be kept on a short leash (Held 2006: 62). The liberal solution to the possible transgressions of the rulers was – besides the right to rebellion invoked by Locke – the separation of powers and constitutionally sanctioned rights. By dividing power between the legislative, executive, and judiciary branches as well as assigning inviolable political rights and civil liberties, it would be possible to prevent – or at least put limits on – abuses of power. As Stephen Holmes (1995: 271) argues, "Liberal government is a remarkable innovation for this reason, because it is meant to solve the problem of anarchy *and* the problem of tyranny within a single and coherent system of rules."

Classical liberalism may therefore be presented as the struggle for the rule of law and fundamental (negative) civil liberties; an endeavor to introduce legal barriers against arbitrary state powers with a view to safeguarding individual liberties. Liberalism thus necessarily entails constitutionalism; that is, that the exercise of power can only proceed on the basis of the law (Sartori 1987: 374; Holmes 1995: 5). More particularly, liberalism champions values such as the freedom to make one's own choices, reason, and tolerance. From the outset this was conceived as a protest against the violation of liberty under absolutism and the religious intolerance of the Roman Catholic Church (Held 2006: 59). In other words, the liberals wanted to separate state and (civil) society (Holmes 1979). Freedom of choice also entailed economic liberty, including private property rights and freedom of trade. For the liberals, all of this was anchored in reason. In a nutshell, the liberties are understood as human rights, which are not subject to earnest political debate.

However, it is important to avoid over-emphasizing this abstract understanding of liberty. The first generations of liberal thinkers surely based their work on the natural liberties of the individual, but their thoughts were also deeply rooted in historical imagination. For example, the English liberals in the 17th and 18th centuries were fighting for what they perceived as their ancient or time-honored rights (see Pocock 1957) as opposed to a non-historical, abstract liberty.

Like republicanism, liberalism is not a homogeneous category. Inspired by Held (2006), we once again distinguish between two distinct currents: 'protective liberalism' and 'developmental liberalism'. These perspectives parted in the 19th century, and this branching may also be argued to mark the end of classical liberalism. This is where modern democracy makes its direct entry. Protective liberalism emphasizes that only efficient political institutions, including an institutional separation of powers, can curb human whims, thereby ensuring the common good. This explains the need for that which Dahl (1956) referred to as 'Madisonian democracy'; constitutionalism is exactly where liberalism and modern democracy become intertwined (Sartori 1987: 388; Holmes 1995: 6). Developmental liberalism, on the other hand, places emphasis on political participation, which encourages vigilant and democratic citizens (Held 2006: 60).

Protective liberalism

Protective liberalism first and foremost refers to the writings of Locke, Montesquieu, Madison, Constant, Bentham, and James Mill. Locke struck the chord, as he presented the state power as a framework intended to ensure the free choice of the individual in society; that is, an aegis of personal liberty. The government ought to keep its nose out of all of the areas where civil society in itself is able to regulate the behavior between people. Similarly, many of the members of this tradition, such as John Milton (1927 [1644]) in *Areopagitica*, regarded free speech as an important value in itself and a shield against the ever-lurking 'lust for power' of the rulers.

Locke's thinking also justified important elements of representative democracy. Combined with Montesquieu's idea about separating powers in order to hold the authorities accountable, the ideational foundations for modern, representative democracy were thus laid (Held 2006: 64–65). If we compare Montesquieu's lessons with the republicanism existing before his intervention, he breaks new ground when pointing out that the defense against a corrupt political system is not so much to be found in the vigilance and participation of the citizenry. Instead, it lies in an institutional arrangement that prevents the abuse of power (Held 2006: 67–69). Madison (1987 [1788]: 356) expressly embraced this point. In the renowned *Federalist Paper No. 51*, he conveyed this in his famous remark that "if men were angels, no government would be necessary" but that, as men are not angels, "experience has taught mankind the necessity of auxiliary precautions"; that is, about the need for tempering checks and balances.

More generally, it is difficult to exaggerate the extent to which Montesquieu's ideas concerning the tripartite separation of powers influenced the liberal democratic constitutions which spread through 19th-century Europe and the Americas. This brings us to an important point. For protective liberalists such as Locke, Montesquieu, and Madison, representative government is deliberately justified in the name of liberty. Montesquieu (1989 [1757]: 159) argues that:

> As, in a free state, every man considered to have a free soul, should be governed by himself, the people as a body should have the legislative power; but, as this is impossible in large states and is subject to many drawbacks in small ones, the people must have their representatives do all that they themselves cannot do.

Bentham and James Mill further developed these points in the early 19th century. They directed attention towards a number of institutional mechanisms that can help keep the authorities in check. As with Locke and Montesquieu, the point was that by doing so it became possible to arrive at an auspicious balance between power and rights (Held 2006: 70). This is where we find the intellectual origins of the modern, liberal democracy. Indeed, excepting Thomas Paine (see the Introduction), the English utilitarians, and particularly Bentham, were arguably the first important modern thinkers to connect democracy with representative, not direct, democracy, and thereby to render democracy an honorific term (Naess et al. 1956: 103–104). The right to vote was simply added to the set of check and balance mechanisms already established by prior liberals.

Developmental liberalism

Before moving further along this line of thought, it is pertinent to touch upon the alternative liberal democratic understanding of the 19th century. The key figure here is James Mill's son and intellectual heir, John Stuart Mill. The protective liberals described above were by and large skeptical when it came to democracy. They merely regarded it as a safeguard for ensuring liberty rather than a good in itself. It is also telling that most of the liberal thinkers and statesmen were rather lukewarm towards equal and universal suffrage, regarding it as a possible threat to liberty.[2]

The younger Mill did not have the same reservations regarding democracy as his liberal forebears. Over time, he even began emphasizing the personal development that we have earlier outlined as part of developmental republicanism. For Stuart Mill, this personal development was possible even under representative democracy, a point transmitted in the very title of his influential *Considerations on Representative Government* (1993 [1861]). Another way of saying this is by noting that Stuart Mill accepted most of the practical recommendations about the regime that the past generations of liberals, especially Bentham, had arrived at. But one of his cardinal points was that democratic participation – not just at the ballot-box, but also in the local communities and the judiciary – could furthermore contribute to more well-rounded individuals (Held 2006: 79). In his own words, "The most important point of excellence which any form of government can possess is to promote the virtue and intelligence of the people themselves" (Mill 1993 [1861]: 207).

Inspired by Plato, John Stuart Mill (1984 [1869]) went so far as to argue for women's suffrage, which was rather unheard of in the mid-1800s. In a sense, he distanced himself from the somewhat cynical approach to human nature expressed by Montesquieu and Madison and dusted off the old participatory ideal from the classical understanding of democracy and parts of republicanism.

Towards a formula

By the end of the 19th century, all of the basic elements in the liberal democratic understanding of democracy had thus been formulated and shaped in a debate that in certain ways goes all the way back to ancient Rome. But it was not until the decades following World War I that democracy was defined systematically. This happened gradually in renowned works such as those of Hans Kelsen (1920) and James Bryce (1921). But here, we focus on the two most influential such endeavors, that of Joseph A. Schumpeter's (1974 [1942]) *Capitalism, Socialism and Democracy* and that of Dahl's (1989) *Democracy and Its Critics*. Both are explicitly written against the background of the notions about democracy as an ideal and practice expressed in the preceding two-and-a-half millennia.

Realistic competitive democracy

Schumpeter violently rejects the notion that democracy constitutes an arena where men of a Socratic stature reason together and arrive at 'true' solutions to the problems affecting society. Gods and archangels might be able to do so, but not mankind, Schumpeter asserts. Instead of focusing on the political issues, it pays to emphasize the election process itself.

> [T]he primary function of the electorate is to produce a government. . . . The principle of democracy merely means that the reins of government should be handed to those who command more support than do any of the competing individuals or teams.
>
> (Schumpeter 1974 [1942]: 272–273)

Schumpeter thus presents democracy as what he himself terms a *modus pro-cedendi*; that is, a political method solely characterized by political competition in the form of free elections.[3] To stay in the vocabulary, this is to be understood in contrast to what may be termed the democracy as a *modus vivendi* (a way of living). In that sense, democracy is not about getting people to agree with one another, representing different social classes, or educating the population in democratic values. It is about electing leaders: politics is essentially a competition between alternatives. These considerations lead Schumpeter (1974 [1942]: 269) to the following definition of democracy:

> the democratic method is that institutional arrangement for arriving at political decisions in which individuals acquire the power to decide by means of a competitive struggle for the people's vote.

Hence, Schumpeter is narrowly focusing on popular sovereignty as opposed to popular participation (other than at the actual elections) or political liberties. He categorically rejects civil liberties, such as the freedom of assembly, as defining characteristics of democracy. Not even equal and universal suffrage is a require-ment in this perspective, as Schumpeter (1974 [1942]: 243–245) underlines that every *demos* delimits itself, for example, by keeping women or the impoverished outside of the circle of eligible voters.

Schumpeter's formula has since become known as the 'minimalist' or 'realistic' approach to defining democracy. This reflects that Schumpeter's objective was to arrive at a "reasonably efficient criterion by which to distinguish democratic governments from others" (1974 [1942]: 269). His phrasing indicates that part and parcel of these endeavors was to disown the currents in the 19th century which turned democracy into a device for ennobling mankind through personal devel-opment. Indeed, Schumpeter's (1974 [1942]: 250) definition is an objection against that which he refers to as the 'classical doctrine', namely that democracy is the institutional arrangement which realizes 'the common good' for the people. Here, it should be added that Schumpeter's description of the classical understanding of democracy is coarse in the sense that it would appear to combine Rousseau's theory about the general will with the considerations regarding utility drawn from utilitarianism (cf. Svensson 1979). More generally, as we have already demon-strated, there exists no single classical model, no matter the period in which it is sought (Held 2006: 146). But here the point first and foremost underscores how Schumpeter turns against developmental republicanism as well as developmental liberalism.

Democratic process criteria and polyarchy

Like Schumpeter, Dahl has become a standard reference in discussions about what democracy actually is (Collier & Levitsky 1997: 431). By virtue of an impressive capacity to develop concepts and theories, his writings have become natural pivots for many of the contemporary discussions about the concept of democracy and, by implication, for empirical studies of democratization.

On the one hand, Dahl agrees with Schumpeter that democracy is not about self-development or reaching true solutions. On the other hand, he presents more comprehensive demands regarding the democratic process. First, all interests must be weighted equally. Second, all adults are generally sufficiently qualified to participate in the making of binding, collective decisions that impact upon their interests (Dahl 1989: 105). Dahl is of the opinion that there are weighty reasons to accept these assertions. On this basis, he proceeds to establish five criteria for a democratic process (Dahl 1989: 108–131):

1   *Effective participation.* Throughout the process of making binding decisions, citizens ought to have an adequate opportunity, and an equal opportunity, for expressing their preferences as to the final outcome. They must have adequate and equal opportunities for placing questions on the agenda and for expressing reasons for endorsing one outcome rather than another.
2   *Voting equality at the decisive stage.* At the decisive stage of collective decisions, each citizen must be ensured an equal opportunity to express a choice that will be counted as equal in weight to the choice expressed by any other citizen. In determining outcomes at the decisive stage, these choices, and only these choices, must be taken into account.
3   *Enlightened understanding.* Each citizen ought to have adequate and equal opportunities for discovering and validating (within the time permitted by the need for a decision) the choice on the matter to be decided that would best serve the citizen's interests.
4   *Control of the agenda.* The demos must have the exclusive opportunity to decide how matters are to be placed on the agenda of matters that are to be decided by means of the democratic process.
5   *Inclusiveness.* The demos must include all adult members of the association except transients and persons proved to be mentally defective.

Dahl acknowledges that a democratic government living up to these require-ments will probably never be achieved in full.[4] However, that does not alter the fact that – as a package – they represent an ideal measure for assessing reality; an ideal which we should constantly strive to approach (see Munck 2011). Dahl also points out that specific procedures cannot readily be derived from these criteria. Instead, he goes on to outline a number of institutions, which several countries have managed to achieve, that are necessary for obtaining the status as a modern representative democracy (Dahl 1989: 222). As Dahl reserves the concept of democracy – an ideal form of government – for regimes that live up to the five-process criteria, he instead uses the term 'polyarchy' to refer to countries fulfilling the following seven procedural criteria (1989: 218–222):

1   *Elected officials.* Control over government decisions about policy is consti-tutionally vested in elected officials.

2   *Free and fair elections.* Elected officials are chosen in the frequent and fairly conducted elections in which coercion is comparatively uncommon.
3   *Inclusive suffrage.* Practically all adults have the right to vote in the election of officials.
4   *Right to run for office.* Practically all adults have the right to run for elective offices in the government, though age limits may be higher for holding office than for the suffrage.
5   *Freedom of expression.* Citizens have a right to express themselves without the danger of severe punishment on political matters broadly defined, including criticism of officials, the government, the regime, the socio-economic order, and the prevailing ideology.
6   *Alternative information.* Citizens have a right to seek out alternative sources of information. Moreover, alternative sources of information exist and are protected by laws.
7   *Associational autonomy.* To achieve their various rights, including those listed above, citizens also have a right to form relatively independent associations or organizations, including independent political parties and interest groups.

These criteria serve as a second standard for Dahl. More precisely, they may be used to assess the extent to which existing political regimes are polyarchies. Note here that even though Dahl's polyarchy criteria are considerably less demanding than his requirements for (ideal) democracy, they are nevertheless much more comprehensive than Schumpeter's definition of democracy. Dahl essentially expands Schumpeter's formula by including requirements about, first, inclusive suffrage and the right to run for office (as opposed to the point about how every demos delineates itself), and, second, political (civil) liberties in the form of free speech and associational autonomy. This distinction is central for a number of the discussions in the remainder of this book.

Critiques of liberal democracy

The constitutive parts of liberal democracy are today cherished by most citizens and political theorists, and popular will and fundamental rights are more often considered to be mutually constitutive than mutually exclusive (cf. Habermas 1996; Merkel 2004). Nevertheless, though only few are willing to reject the value of free and inclusive elections, civil liberties, and the rule of law, the ideal of liberal democracy is far from undisputed as the terminus of democratic development. We therefore briefly describe some of the most influential criticisms of liberal democracy, which have one thing in common: they opt for more demanding conceptions of democracy.

Egalitarian democracy

For more than 150 years, the main challenger to liberal democracy has been the idea – or ideal – of 'egalitarian democracy'. Basically, the point made here is that a real democracy is not merely a question about the right to vote, political liberties, and government responsibility to the parliament (if the head of the executive is not directly appointed by the voters); it also requires an equal distribution of society's resources. This critique may be traced back to, among others, Karl Marx. Marx was, for a short time in 1848, quite positive towards bourgeois (liberal) democracy. Over time, however, he distanced himself from this understanding of democracy, as he believed that it reproduced the power of the propertied classes. Such is the case because democracy functions within the framework of a capitalist system, and the working classes – first and foremost the workers – would never be able to break the dominance of the economically privileged classes via the ballot-box (Svensson 1995: 120; Sørensen 1979). To use a famous quote from Marx and Engels' (1998 [1848]: 161) *The Communist Manifesto (Manifest der Kommunistischen Partei):* "The executive of the modern state is but a committee for managing the common affairs of the whole bourgeoisie." According to Lenin (2004 [1917]: 73–77), genuine democracy can therefore only be realized through the 'dictatorship of the proletariat' and the classless society that follows, in which the resources are to be distributed equally and class conflict is therefore a thing of the past (see Svensson 1995: 121).

Attempts to realize Marx's radical solutions to the problem of the political consequences of economic disparity were made under the communist regimes in the 20th century. But a milder version of the idea about egalitarian democracy, which should be achieved by means of a nationalization of the means of production, simultaneously attained a major influence in 20th-century debates about democracy. A number of political theorists have emphasized that a high degree of economic inequality undermines the political equality of liberal democracy. Here, there is no requirement about a *complete* equalization – the classless society – but rather about some measure of leveling of economic gaps. One of the most important authors espousing this view is Charles E. Lindblom (1977: 167–168), who underscored that even where one man has one vote, the business community enjoys disproportionate influence over political decisions.

Influenced by Lindblom, Dahl (1985: 54–55) eventually reached the conclusion that democracy demands a distribution of resources that is not too skewed. Unequal opportunities for income lead to disparity in education, in access to information, and regarding opportunities to participate in the political system, all of which undermine the formal political equality of democracy (see Svensson 1995: 286). Dahl thus provides arguments for extending the democratic process from the political to the economic sphere. More specifically, he hones in on the way in which private corporations can be democratized. As a minimum, he calls for the introduction of employee influence, but in some of his writings (e.g., Dahl 1982) he also debates questions of ownership, though without calling for an outright nationalization of the means of production.

As an alternative or supplement to this solution, the modern welfare state may be regarded as an institution for ensuring some measure of economic equality, thus avoiding the postulated erosion of political equality (Svensson 1995: 296). This perspective fits well with (the elder) Dahl's perspective, but in addition to the purely political procedures, it demands the introduction of measures that promote socio-economic parity. In other words, this involves a slide beyond the purely procedural approach, which Schumpeter launched and (the younger) Dahl elaborated in the form of polyarchy (Collier & Levitsky 1997: 445–446; Møller & Skaaning 2011: ch. 3).

Deliberative democracy

The other major modern challenger to the notion of liberal democracy is to be found in the current known as deliberative democracy. The deliberative model entails a clear break with Schumpeter's definition of democracy. In Schumpeter's rendering, political democracy is not really that attractive. Above all, it does not lead to good political craftsmanship. Infamous is Schumpeter's (1974 [1942]: 287) description of the woes of the democratically elected government leaders:

> Thus the prime minister in a democracy might be likened to a horseman who is so fully engrossed in trying to keep in the saddle that he cannot plan his ride, or to a general so fully occupied with making sure that his army will accept his orders that he must leave strategy to take care of itself.

The advocates of deliberative democracy cannot accept such a prosaic (even cynical) attitude towards democracy. Indeed, these thinkers to some degree build on the very currents of thought that Schumpeter distanced himself from, namely the ancient participatory ideal, developmental republicanism, and developmental liberalism (Held 2006: 253; Hansen 2007). The supporters of deliberative democracy level a massive critique of modern democracy, which is regarded as something akin to an empty shell, as the decisions rarely reflect the long-term interests in the political community. Seen from this perspective, the objective of democracy must be to replace raw power politics with reasoning and deliberation. Instead of emphasizing the preferences of the electorate and the logic of demo-cratic institutions, emphasis is primarily placed on the good arguments made by the citizens (Loftager 2004: 29–30). Accordingly, thorough public debate – actual deliberation – is required in order to avoid short-sighted decisions marked by narrow selfish interests. In Held's words (2006: 237):

> Deliberative democracy, broadly defined, is any one of a family of views according to which the public deliberation of free and equal citizens is the core of legitimate political decision-making and self-governance. Political legitimacy does not turn on the ballot box or on majority rule *per se* but, rather, on the giving of defensible reasons, explanations and accounts for public decisions.[5]

This is equal to saying that the democratic process and the outcome of this process, rather than the democratic procedures, is of the essence. Here, a public debate leading to rational political decisions is paramount (Loftager 2004: 41). Obviously, this entails a requirement concerning free speech; but compared with Dahl's definition of polyarchy, where freedom of speech is also a defining characteristic, there is much more at stake. The political procedures alone are not decisive; a flourishing 'public sphere' (cf. Habermas 1989 [1962]) is also required. In that sense, we are not merely dealing with an expansion of the definition of democracy as a political regime. Indeed, the outcome of the political process is decisive for the assessment of democracy. As with the economic expansions described above, these additions also fall under the category that we refer to as substantive definitions in the next chapter.

Democratic quality as a new research agenda

The literature has recently developed an emphasis on the 'quality of democracy', which includes elements of the more expansive definitions of democracy described above. The study of democratic quality emerged as a new field of research in the mid-2000s. This occurred in connection with two different projects with the participation of a string of leading scholars. First was Guillermo O'Donnell, who together with two co-authors published *The Quality of Democracy: Theory and Applications* (O'Donnell et al. 2004). In the first chapter, O'Donnell (2004) called for the expansion of the definition of democracy that may be said to touch upon some of the aspects pertaining to equality we have mentioned above.

That same year, the *Journal of Democracy* issued a special issue entitled 'Quality of Democracy'. The team involved a number of the grand old men from the field, including O'Donnell, who gave their consent to the study of the quality of democracy. This provided an occasion for the drafting of an actual manifesto. The whole point with the special issue was to convince students of democracy to go out into the field and 'take the temperature on democracy', so to speak. It is telling how the very title, 'Quality of Democracy', was modeled on the past distinction in transition theory between 'Liberalization of Authoritarianism' (LoA), 'Transition to Democracy' (ToD), and 'Consolidation of Democracy' (CoD). It was now time to move on to the fourth phase, namely QoD.

The editors of the special issue, Larry Diamond and Leonardo Morlino (2004: 20), set the tone by providing three normative reasons for why we ought to be interested in the question about democratic quality. First, democracy is a moral good, second, democracy risks collapse if it is not consolidated, and third, even established democracies must renew themselves in order to avoid the emergence of cynicism among the people. Bearing these premises in mind, Diamond and Morlino (2004: 22) divided democratic quality into eight dimensions. The first five are procedural, which hardly distinguishes them from the Schumpeterian and Dahlian definitions of democracy reported above. Here, it is rule of law, participation, competition, and vertical and horizontal accountability that are the objects of scrutiny. Vertical accountability may be compared with the usual control via democratic elections; it is the mechanism that makes the authorities accountable to the voters, as the citizens have the opportunity to 'throw out the rascals', but it also covers continuous control by the civil society. The horizontal addition concerns the balance of power (checks and balances) within the state. The point is that the citizens' rights are best guaranteed by different state institutions – particularly the executive, legislature, and judiciary powers – tempering and controlling one another.

But Diamond and Morlino add three more substantial dimensions. The first consists of the civil and political liberties being fully respected. Second, the regime is to emphasize genuine political equality. And third, and finally – and here we are dealing with a purely result-oriented dimension – the outcome of the process in the form of decisions and results is to correspond to the wishes of the people to the greatest extent possible. The last criterion is especially demanding, and also well-established, 'old' democracies can face significant problems in this regard. In fact, there is now an entire genre pointing out that the people are losing their involvement in the existing democracies (Moravscik 2002; Crouch 2004; Schmitter 2010). This cynicism and indifference is observed in phenomena such as low voter turnout, declines in active and passive party membership, as well as support for populist parties and a focus on political personalities rather than policy. This is a very interesting debate, which speaks volumes about the way in which the more narrow, procedural definitions of democracy are still being challenged in the literature; but it is not one which we will further pursue in this book.

Conclusions

Chapters 1 and 2 have provided a general review of how democracy has been understood in Western political thought.[6] We have shown how these thoughts have been formulated as part of a dialogue about democracy going all the way back to ancient Greece. The notion of popular sovereignty had already been born in Antiquity. This also applies to the participatory ideal, which pervades, for example, the current notion of deliberative democracy. Moreover, the modern ideas about liberal democracy draw upon the defense of the rule of law which is integral to protective republicanism. Nonetheless, it was with modern liberalism that these thoughts were first systematized into an intellectual defense of the modern, representative democracy as characterized by equal and universal suffrage, civil liberties, and the rule of law.

To some extent at least, the basis for this formula may be traced all the way back to Aristotle's ideas about the mixed form of government, which republicanism adopted as an ideal and which may also be found in liberalism. The mixed government may thus be said to constitute the red thread of Western political thought (Hansen 2010a). It is rather paradoxical that for over 2000 years it was used as an argument *against* pure democracy, only to be rediscovered in the 19th century in democratic guise as that which we now refer to as liberal democracy (Manin 1997). As we have already touched upon in the Introduction, the word has simply attained new meanings over time. Where it was previously tied to ideas about direct rule – often in the derogatory understanding of mob rule – it now refers to popular rule conditioned by representation, fundamental civil liberties, and the rule of law.

Together with Schumpeter's minimalist definition and Dahl's notion of polyarchy, this liberal definition of democracy is the most influential conception nowadays. However, these procedural definitions are not bereft of competitors. Both before and after, more substantive definitions – with a focus on social equality, deliberation, or participation – have challenged these conceptions of democracy. In the next chapter, where we present some more formalized definitions of democracy, we argue that the approaches developed by Schumpeter and Dahl have the most to offer when it comes to analyzing and discussing democratic development across time and space.

3 Typologies of democratic and autocratic regimes

The words *democracy, socialism, freedom, patriotic, realistic, justice* have each of them several different meanings which cannot be reconciled with one another. In the case of a word like *democracy*, not only is there no agreed definition, but the attempt to make one is resisted from all sides. It is almost universally felt that when we call a country democratic we are praising it: consequently the defenders of every kind of regime claim that it is a democracy, and fear that they might have to stop using that word if it were tied down to any one meaning. Words of this kind are often used in a consciously dishonest way. That is, the person who uses them has his own private definition, but allows his hearer to think he means something quite different.

The words are those of George Orwell (1962 [1946]: 2237) in a famous essay about the political abuse of the English language. As in so many other instances, Orwell's observation was an apt one. Recall from the Introduction that a veritable cornucopia of dictators have referred to their states as democracies – although often qualified by adjectives such as popular, organic, or new. As mentioned at the end of the previous chapter, there is also a very broad range of views within the academic literature about the meaning of democracy. The historical overview of the different conceptions of democracy is therefore important. But when describing the ups and downs of democracy in the latest 200 years (Part II), when discussing the extant explanations of these cross-temporal and cross-spatial processes of democratic development (Part III), and when assessing the consequences of democracy (Part IV), we need to refer to one or more specific definitions of democracy. In the words of Giovanni Sartori (1970: 1038), the basis for any such exercise is that "*Concept formation stands prior to quantification.*" Thus, to avoid the pitfall Orwell laid bare in 1946, we provide a systematic overview of the various definitions of democracy that we employ throughout the rest of this book.

Definitions – an itinerary

Before offering such specific definitions, it is crucial to say something about the logical rules of defining. The systematic clarification of concepts requires the ability to navigate the waters between a term, its denotation (i.e., its empirical

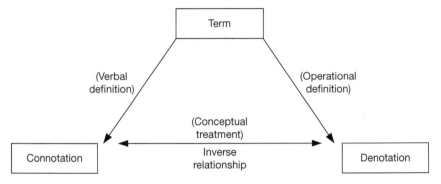

Figure 3.1 The Ogden-Richards Triangle

referents), and its connotation (i.e., its defining properties). These are the three elements binding a concept together. Ninety years ago, Charles Ogden and Ivor Richards summarized this structure in the so-called Ogden-Richards Triangle (Figure 3.1) (see Sartori 1984; Gerring 1999). This triangle serves as the basis of the present attempt to define democracy.

The first problem concerns the choice of the term itself. It must fit the concept, and it is important not to unsettle the semantic field (Sartori 1984: 51–54) by erratically introducing new terms. In the aforementioned essay, Orwell specifically recommends choosing the simplest and most easily recognizable words possible. With reference to Figure 3.1, the problem is one of avoiding ambiguity. Here, we are initially on safe ground with democracy, which after all has a celebrated history and upon which most people probably have a rather intuitive grasp. Yet later in this chapter, when distinguishing between various forms of democracy, the wording should be considered carefully and terminological innovations should, if at all possible, be avoided.

More important is the lower side of the triangle; that is, the relationship between connotation and denotation. The connotation involves the characteristics defining a concept. In the case of democracy, most scholars would at a minimum include the characteristic of competitive elections on the basis of which leadership is decided. The denotation is the cases which the concept covers; that is, specific instances of democracy. In order to denote these, it is necessary to operationalize the defining characteristics subsumed by the connotation. The aim here is to avoid vagueness. More generally, the golden rule of the triangle is that there is an inverse relationship between a concept's connotation and its denotation, meaning that the more demanding the definition, the fewer the cases it covers. This rule is decisive for the efforts to conceptualize and measure democracy. The best way of appreciating the rule is via what Sartori (1970) has labeled the 'ladder of abstraction'. Sartori's message is that we can place the different concepts on different rungs on one and the same ladder according to the level of abstraction at which they are operating. If defined by relatively few characteristics (the connotation), the concepts are relatively abstract in the sense that there can be relatively many empirical instances of them (the denotation). In other words, if democracy is to be defined by competitive elections alone, a large number of countries would be democratic. When we add more characteristics to the definition (e.g., by expanding the electoral criteria and/or adding political liberties and/or rule of law), the concept is displaced to a lower rung on the ladder of abstraction. The definition is now more demanding, and fewer countries can therefore be regarded as democratic.[1]

Substantive or realistic definitions?

A fundamental choice must be made before even thinking in terms of the logic of the ladder of abstraction. A general demarcation line in the literature runs between what are normally termed *substantive* and *procedural* definitions of democracy (Sartori 1987: 11; Collier & Levitsky 1996; Sørensen 2008: 10–16). The substantive definitions are the most demanding, as they emphasize the substance or content of democracy (sometimes even construing it as a *modus vivendi*, a way of living). Here, characteristics such as the economic distribution of resources or the opportunity to participate in a rational deliberation are often emphasized (see Held 2006: 1–2; see also Chapter 2, this volume). In other words, power is to be distributed in society in such a manner that everyone can participate on an equal footing, meaning that democracy is to some extent defined by its results.

The procedural tradition instead equates democracy with a political regime or a political method. This tradition can be traced back to Max Weber (see Held 2006: ch. 5) and Hans Kelsen (1920), and it was also prominent among Anglo-Saxon political scientists in the interwar period (Bryce 1921; Naess et al. 1956: 130–131).[2] These two strands came together in – and culminated with – Joseph Schumpeter's famous definition in 1942. As already reported, Schumpeter presented democracy as a *modus procedendi*, that is, a regime defined by the presence of a specific set of procedures. The perspective on democracy found in Weber, Kelsen, Bryce, and Schumpeter is also referred to as the 'realistic' approach (O'Donnell 2001), an adjective Schumpeter himself used about his formula.

Substantive and procedural definitions are so fundamentally different that it makes no sense to place them on the same ladder of abstraction. The former position thus entails that democracy is rendered as a 'What?', the latter position that it is construed as a 'How?' (Ross 1952 [1946]; Møller & Skaaning 2011: ch. 3). In a nutshell, if democracy is defined by its content (as a What?), it cannot be a political method (a How?). We therefore have a choice to make in determining which of the two has the most to offer. Here, it is appropriate to hammer home that the choice between competing definitions is not an abstract matter which can be conclusively determined via free-floating speculations, or simply logics. Instead, the choice depends upon the specific issue in question (the research question in academic parlance). Substantive definitions are surely preferable in some studies; for example, analyses of democratic participation or, perhaps, attempts at describing a democratic ideal.

In other cases, procedural definitions have more to offer. In this connection, several factors can be emphasized. First, there is considerable agreement as to which aspects are to be included and excluded when it comes to a realistic definition *à la* Schumpeter. Second, such definitions have the advantage of containing relatively few defining characteristics. This paves the way for testing whether characteristics couched in the substantive definitions, such as cultural, social, or economic traits, appear to be the causes or consequences of democracy. If, say, economic equality per definition is part of democracy, we are unable to study whether there is a positive relationship between economic equality and democracy (Karl 1990: 2; Alvarez et al. 1996: 18; Diamond 1999: 8; Linz 2000: 57–58). Finally, a more pragmatic argument is important. As the procedural definitions are realistic, it is relatively simple to assess whether a given country is democratic. Indeed, according to Guillermo O'Donnell (2001:11), this adjective simply means that we are dealing with "attributes whose absence or existence we can assess empirically."[3] In short, realistic definitions make it possible to operationalize and measure democracy in multiple cases without excessive problems of vagueness (Adcock & Collier 2001).

It is a different matter with the substantive definitions, where we often fumble in the dark as soon as we move from the theoretical reflections into the real world. For if democracy is, say, a form of deliberation which realizes the common good, who can determine with any certainty how democratic a given country is? Likewise, if all relevant resources have to be equally distributed, then exactly where do we draw the line between democracy and non-democracy, and how do we measure this cross-nationally?

Tellingly, most of the attempts at explaining democracy and democratization via comparative analyses opt for an extended version of the Schumpeterian formula (e.g., Lipset 1959; Huntington 1991; Przeworski et al. 2000). If these analyses mention the substantive definitions at all, it is only by way of the introductory conceptual discussion. As soon as the empirical material is brought into play, it is primarily the procedural formula that is applied in the field (e.g., Sørensen 2008). We follow this practice. But the choice of a procedural definition is merely the first step. For, even under the heading *modus procedendi*, it is possible to place several different properties, thereby operating on multiple levels of abstraction.

A typology of various forms of democracy

The next step is therefore to situate a number of relevant procedural definitions on the respective rungs of the ladder of abstraction by constructing a typology[4] of different kinds of democracy. We apply the *per genus et differentiam* logic, which is the basis for the ladder, moving down the rungs by adding characteristics. Doing this, we distinguish between three properties which have been emphasized as central in the democratization literature in recent decades:

1   Electoral rights
2   Political/civil liberties
3   Rule of law

We derive the electoral attribute from Schumpeter's (1974 [1942]) classic definition. Political liberties are anchored in Dahl's (1971, 1989) elaboration of polyarchy. The rule of law we embed with reference to O'Donnell's (2001) call for augmenting Dahl's definition (for a more general treatment of these issues, see Møller & Skaaning 2010, 2011: chs 1–3).

We have already justified the relevance of these procedural characteristics. However, it is necessary to underline one thing. Our typology systematically reduces the conceptual complexity via functional reduction (Lazarsfeld & Barton 1951); that is, by deleting empirically empty combinations of the serial operations on the three properties. The premise for doing so is that the real world is marked by a hierarchical relationship in the way countries score on the three characteristics. More particularly, countries should not do worse with regard to elections than with regard to political liberties, and they should not do worse with regard to political liberties than the rule of law. The exercise becomes much more complicated in the absence of such an empirical hierarchy, as the typology must then include all of the conceivable combinations of the three characteristics. This would include regimes where political liberties and the rule of law are upheld despite the absence of competitive elections. Such 'liberal autocracies' were actually in existence as recently as the period leading up to World War I, as many Western European countries had introduced the rule of law but did not hold free (inclusive) elections. Today, however, this is an extinct species (Diamond 1999: 4),[5] as elections now precede the rule of law. More particularly, in prior work we have demonstrated the empirical presence of a very clear hierarchy across the three characteristics (Møller & Skaaning 2010, 2011). In a nutshell, the countries of the world are most democratic as far as elections are concerned and least democratic with respect to the rule of law – political liberties are situated somewhere in between. Bearing this in mind, the diffferent types of democracies can be fleshed out and placed on the various rungs of the ladder (Table 3.1).

A couple of clarifications are pertinent. The first type, *minimalist democracy*, is based solely on Schumpeter's (1974 [1942]: 269) definition: "the democratic method is that institutional arrangement for arriving at political decisions in which individuals acquire the power to decide by means of a competitive struggle for people's vote." Along the same lines, Adam Przeworski (1991: 14) argues that democracy is a matter of institutionalized uncertainty, where all interests are

Table 3.1 A typology of democratic political regimes

	Competitive elections	Free, inclusive elections	Political liberties	Rule of law
Minimalist democracy	+			
Electoral democracy	+	+		
Polyarchy	+	+	+	
Liberal democracy	+	+	+	+

Note: The presence of an attribute is indicated by '+'.

subjected to competition. More particularly, (minimalist) democracy is defined by frequent elections characterized by '*ex ante* uncertainty', '*ex post* irreversibility', and repeatability (Alvarez et al. 1996: 50–51). What often goes unnoticed – or is at least downplayed – is that Schumpeter (1974 [1942]: 244–245, 270–271) explicitly gives leeway for grouping a country as a case of (minimalist) democracy even if the right to vote in the competitive elections is restricted to certain parts of the adult population or in the face of the political analogy to what economists refer to as 'unfair' competition (though at some unspecified point such fraudulent competition of course disqualifies a country from the set of democracies). The only hard-and-fast requirement is that the designation of the government follows from the voters' choice. This can be done either directly as in presidential systems or indirectly as with government responsibility to the legislature in parliamentary systems. In general, if genuine political competition exists, the result is thus democracy in the Schumpeterian sense, regardless of whether there are restrictions on the right to vote, moderate irregularities in the elections, or domains where tutelary powers can veto policies (but not governments). Conversely, if there is an absence of such competition, we are dealing with autocracy.

Electoral democracy is the next rung on the ladder of abstraction. Regarding this type, the elections are not merely characterized by competition; they are also free and inclusive. This means that suffrage is equal and universal, that there are no substantial irregularities associated with elections, and that there are no reserved domains where non-elected groups (e.g., the armed forces) have a veto on significant areas of politics (cf. Valenzuela 1992; Merkel 2004; O'Donnell 2004: 14). Electoral democracy is thus distinguished from minimalist democracy solely on the attribute of electoral rights.

Descending yet another rung, we encounter Dahl's notion of *polyarchy* (1971, 1989). In polyarchies, free and inclusive elections are supplemented by political/ civil liberties such as free speech and freedom of assembly and association. Finally, *liberal democracy* is situated at the bottom of the ladder and is thus the most demanding type. In this instance, free elections and political liberties are supplemented by rule of law, rule of law being understood as the regular and impartial administration of public rules (cf. Rawls 1971: 235).[6] The rule of law addition to the concept of democracy – hence *liberal* democracy – has been proposed by scholars such as O'Donnell (2001, 2004; see also Diamond 1999; Merkel 2004).

Notice that the typology to some extent treats the three characteristics differently as the electoral attribute has been divided into three: 'free, inclusive elections', 'competitive elections', and 'no competitive elections'. The other two charac- teristics have only been dichotomized. This conceptual difference reflects the hierarchical premise of the typology. In relation to democracy, the property of elections is simply in a league of its own. Political competition at the ballot-box is the *condicio sine qua non* of democracy; that is, a necessary condition for even the thinnest definition of democracy (cf. Collier & Adcock 1999: 559; Merkel 2004: 36–38; Føllesdal & Hix 2006: 534). With reference to Schumpeter, the existence of this kind of political competition therefore represents our minimal definition of democracy – and the core of all the other definitions situated at lower rungs. In other words, competitive elections are a basic condition for the typology of democracy, i.e., the main dividing line between democracy and autocracy. The other characteristics work to determine whether a country can live up to the more demanding definitions of democracy.

The logic of the ladder means that the lower rungs subsume the higher rungs by definition. Any empirical instance of polyarchy also fulfills the conditions for electoral democracy and minimalist democracy, but not for liberal democracy. However, when referring to actual empirical observations (countries), we use the most demanding definition of democracy they live up to. A country such as Norway is thus labeled a liberal democracy, even though it is also, in diminishing order, a polyarchy, an electoral democracy, and a minimalist democracy. Logically, then, ever fewer countries live up to the definitions of democracy as we move down the ladder. Relatively many countries will be minimalist democracies, while relatively few countries will be liberal democracies.[7] This is a result of the inverse relationship between connotation and denotation.

Autocracy and its sub-types

So far, we have squarely focused on the democratic side of the spectrum of political regimes. This will not do, as the autocratic side also merits attention. We have previously made it clear that we call all instances of undemocratic regimes autocracies. However, here we discuss to what extent this overarching category should also be disaggregated. The point of departure for this discussion is the simple observation that the focus on autocracy has recently made a comeback. Three influential strands may be identified here. First, and most generally, scholars such as Larry Diamond (2002), Andreas Schedler (2002, 2006), and Steven Levitsky and Lucan Way (2002, 2010) have drawn attention to 'electoral/ competitive authoritarian' regimes characterized by frequent and sometimes even intensively fought elections but which nevertheless belong to the set of autocracies. Second, and in terms of more elaborate classifications, scholars such as Juan Linz and Alfred Stepan (1996), Barbara Geddes (1999), Axel Hadenius and Jan Teorell (2007), and José Cheibub et al. (2010) have attempted to distinguish between different kinds of autocracies. Third, and regarding the consequences of this variation, scholars such as Jennifer Gandhi (2008), Jason Brownlee (2007, 2009), and Milan Svolik (2008) have argued that these distinctions matter with respect to the prospect of autocratic stability, democratic transitions, and democratic consolidation, respectively.

A seminal disaggregation of the overarching category of modern autocracies[8] was carried out by Linz (2000 [1975]) in *Totalitarian and Authoritarian Regimes*. His attempt to describe and understand various kinds of autocracies was later elaborated in an influential book with Stepan (Linz & Stepan 1996). Based on four dimensions – leadership, mobilization, ideology, and pluralism – Linz and Stepan distinguish between totalitarian, post-totalitarian, sultanistic, and authoritarian regimes.[9] The defining characteristics are summarized in Table 3.2.

Table 3.2 Linz and Stepan's typology of autocratic regimes

	Authoritarian regime	Totalitarian regime	Post-totalitarian regime	Sultanistic regime
Pluralism	Limited political pluralism. Often some space for semi-opposition and extensive social and economic pluralism	No significant social, economic, or political pluralism. Official party has de facto monopoly of power	Limited social, economic, and institutional pluralism but almost no political pluralism	Economic, social, and political pluralism subject to unpredictable and despotic intervention. High fusion of private and public
Ideology	No elaborate and guiding ideology but distinctive 'mentalities'	Elaborate, holistic, and guiding ideology with high level of commitment	Guiding ideology but only moderate level of commitment	Arbitrary symbol manipulation and extreme glorification of leader but neither elaborate ideology nor commitment
Mobilization	Normally no extensive or intensive political mobilization	Extensive mobilization into obligatory organizations with emphasis on activism and enthusiasm	Moderate mobilization within state-sponsored organizations but disinterest among leaders and ordinary citizens	Low but occasional manipulative, ceremonial mobilization without permanent organizations
Leadership	A leader or a small group exercises power within formally ill-defined but actually quite predictable norms	Leadership – often charismatic – rules with undefined limits and great unpredictability for all	Checks on (uncharismatic) leadership via party structures, procedures, and 'internal democracy'	Highly personalistic and arbitrary with strong dynastic tendencies and extreme patrimonialism

Sources: Based on Linz (2000 [1975]: 58, 151, 159), Chehabi and Linz (1998: 7), and Linz and Stepan (1996: 44–45).

Linz and Stepan highlight a number of diagnostic specimens of these categories: Nazi Germany and the Soviet Union under Stalin are cases of totalitarian rule, Hungary in the 1980s a case of post-totalitarian rule, Spain under Franco a case of authoritarian rule, and Haiti under 'Papa Doc' Duvalier and later 'Baby Doc' Duvalier a case of sultanistic rule.

More recent efforts to conceptualize the autocratic side of the regime spectrum differ from Linz and Stepan's framework in significant ways but have much in common with each other. Geddes (1999) has based her distinctions on the rulers' power bases and ends up with three prototypes: military rule, single-party rule, and personalist rule, plus a number of hybrid versions. To this list, Hadenius and Teorell (2007) add monarchies, remove personalist rule – because personalism characterizes all autocracies to some degree – and consider one-party rule to be a sub-type of a category of non-democratic which they term 'electoral regimes'.[10] Cheibub et al. (2010) agree with the first two adjustments but not with the latter. Moreover, they motivate the resulting distinction between monarchical autocracies, civilian (usually party) autocracies, and military autocracies in the following way:

> Monarchs rely on family and kin networks along with consultative councils; military rulers confine key potential rivals from the armed forces within juntas; and, civilian dictators usually create a smaller body within a regime party – a political bureau – to coopt potential rivals. Because real decision-making power lies within these small institutions, they generally indicate how power is organized within the regime, to which forces dictators are responsible, and who may be likely to remove them. They produce different incentives and constraints on dictators which, in turn, should have an impact on their decisions and performance.
>
> (Cheibub et al. 2010: 84)

The last part of the quote, hinting that the different forms of autocracy are systematically related to different outcomes, is particularly important for our purposes and we return to this point in our discussion of the causes of democratic transitions and stability. Though we do not embed the distinctions discussed in this section in our general typology of regime types, we draw on them where relevant.

A cursory glance at the world anno 2011

The actual description of the empirical development of democracy is found in Part II of this book. However, in order to put some flesh on the conceptual edifice, we briefly touch upon the empirical reality anno 2011. To do so, we draw upon the *Freedom in the World Survey*, an annual report issued by US-based Freedom House. This report provides two different scores for all countries. The first reflects the respect for 'Political Rights' and the second 'Civil Liberties'. For each dimension, countries are assigned a score between 1 and 7, with 1 indicating the highest level of freedom. In order to measure our types, we have used a procedure which requires both some elucidation and some explicit justification. In a nutshell, we argue that it is possible to use the Freedom House data to distinguish between autocracy and the four different types of democracy.

First, we use the scores on political rights, which primarily concern the extent to which elections are free, in order to distinguish between democracies with free elections (1–2), minimalist democracies (3–4), and autocracies (5–7). Since 1989 Freedom House has released a yearly list of 'electoral democracies'. The criteria for inclusion in this group very much overlap with our definition of minimalist democracies. Therefore, for the years 1989 and onwards, we use this list rather than the maximum score of 4 on political rights to assess if countries are included in the set of democracies. Next, we use the scores for civil liberties in order to further divide the democracies with free elections into three groups: liberal democracies (1 on civil liberties), polyarchies (2 on civil liberties), and electoral democracies (>2 on civil liberties).

This is of course a rather imperfect way to measure the three attributes but unfortunately we are unable to score political liberties and the rule of law independently of each other. The reason that this cannot be done is that Freedom House has only published its subcategory scores for the year 2005 onwards.[11] Using these sub-component scores will not suffice, as we venture much further back in time in this book. However, elsewhere we have established the hierarchy empirically for the years 2005 to 2010, as based on Freedom House's subcategory scores (Møller & Skaaning 2010, 2011). Insofar as this hierarchy is robust across the scrutinized period, our procedure should not be overly problematic.[12]

When applying this formula to the most recent Freedom House report from 2012, which covers the year 2011, we arrive at the distribution presented in Table 3.3. Freedom House includes 195 countries in its most recent survey. Of these, 49 fulfill the criteria linked to the definition of liberal democracy. Twenty-eight democracies do not perform quite on this level and therefore only meet the criteria for a polyarchy. A mere seven countries do not qualify as polyarchies but still live up to the definition of electoral democracy, whereas 33 countries just fulfill the criteria to be included in the set of minimalist democracies. Finally, there are no less than 78 autocracies. This is the lay of the land in 2011 according to our definitions, measured with the help of the Freedom House data. Orwell may not care much for the distinctions we have drawn between different kinds of democracy, but each type has a specific meaning, so there is hardly talk of any severe conceptual confusion. In the next part of the book we show when, where, and how democratic developments have unfolded over time.

Table 3.3 Distribution of countries in the typology, 2011

Liberal democracy (49)	*Polyarchy (28)*	*Electoral democracy (7)*	*Minimalist democracy (33)*	*Autocracy (78)*	
Andorra	Argentina	El Salvador	Albania	Afghanistan	Mozambique
Australia	Belize	Guyana	Antigua &	Algeria	Nepal
Austria	Benin	India	Barbuda	Angola	Nicaragua
Bahamas	Brazil	Indonesia	Bangladesh	Armenia	Nigeria
Barbados	Bulgaria	Jamaica	Bolivia	Azerbaijan	North Korea
Belgium	Croatia	Mali	Bosnia-	Bahrain	Oman
Canada	Dominican	Peru	Herzegovina	Belarus	Pakistan
Cape Verde	Rep.		Botswana	Bhutan	Qatar
Chile	Ghana		Colombia	Brunei	Russia
Costa Rica	Greece		Comoros	Burkina Faso	Rwanda
Cyprus	Grenada		Ecuador	Burma	Saudi Arabia
Czech Rep	Hungary		East Timor	Burundi	Singapore
Denmark	Israel		Guatemala	Cambodia	Solomon
Dominica	Japan		Lesotho	Cameroun	Islands
Estonia	Latvia		Liberia	Central	Somalia
Finland	Mauritius		Macedonia	African Rep.	South Sudan
France	Mongolia		Malawi	Chad	Sri Lanka
Germany	Namibia		Maldives	China	Sudan
Iceland	Panama		Mexico	Congo, Rep.	Swaziland
Ireland	Romania		Moldova	Congo,	Syria
Italy	Samoa		Montenegro	Demo. Rep.	Tajikistan
Kiribati	São Tóme		Niger	Côte d'Ivoire	Togo
Liechtenstein	& Prín.		Papua New	Cuba	Turkmenistan
Lithuania	Serbia		Guinea	Djibouti	Uganda
Luxembourg	South Africa		Paraguay	Egypt	United Arab
Malta	South Korea		Philippines	Equatorial	Emirates
Marshall	Suriname		Senegal	Guinea	Uzbekistan
Islands	Taiwan		Seychelles	Eritrea	Venezuela
Micronesia	Trinidad &		Sierra Leone	Ethiopia	Vietnam
Monaco	Tobago		Tanzania	Fiji	Yemen
Nauru	Vanuatu		Thailand	Gabon	Zimbabwe
Netherlands			Tonga	Gambia	
New Zealand			Tunisia	Georgia	
Norway			Turkey	Guinea	
Palau			Ukraine	Guinea-Bissau	
Poland			Zambia	Haiti	
Portugal				Honduras	
St. Kitts &				Iran	
Nevis				Iraq	
St. Lucia				Jordan	
St. Vincent				Kazakhstan	
& Gr.				Kenya	
San Marino				Kosovo	
Slovakia				Kuwait	
Slovenia				Kyrgyzstan	
Spain				Laos	
Sweden				Lebanon	
Switzerland				Libya	
Tuvalu				Madagascar	
United				Malaysia	
Kingdom				Mauritania	
United States				Morocco	
Uruguay					

Part II

Conjunctures

Democracy – when and where?

4 Medieval foundations of the second coming of democracy[1]

June 15, 1215, is an important day in the history of modern democracy. On this day, a number of England's most powerful barons rallied against King John (aka Lackland) at Runnymede, a short distance to the west of London. Under the threat of rebellion, the barons forced the English king to sign the *Magna Carta Liberatum*, the Great Charter of Liberties. As the name indicates, the Magna Carta codified a considerable number of liberties together with *habeas corpus*, the right to have one's case tried in the court system.[2] The Magna Carta thus served as a set of legal barriers against the arbitrary exercise of power by the king. Above all, it meant that the law placed limits on the power of the ruler. The charter also declared that the free subjects in the Kingdom (above all, the aforementioned barons) had the right of rebellion should the king fail to respect the legal concessions he had made. In return, the barons renewed their oath of loyalty to King John.

The Magna Carta was actually in no way unique. Similar charters of liberties were forced upon monarchs in even the remotest corners of Western Christendom over the course of the Middle Ages.[3] The right to resistance has been dated all the way back to the Oaths of Strasbourg in AD 842 (Bloch 1971b [1939]: 451–452), an occasion at which Charles the Bald and Louis the German pledged their allegiance to one another in an alliance against their brother, Emperor Lothar I. The Oaths of Strasbourg are remarkable for including the following point: If one of the kings broke the mutual oath, their soldiers – who had also taken the oath – were bound by duty *not* to assist their king. This was arguably one of the earliest reflections of the modern conception of popular sovereignty[4] which was to prove hugely influential in most of Western Europe in the High Middle Ages.

The importance of the precedent in Strasbourg should not be overstated, however. It was not until the 13th and 14th centuries that actual 'charters of rights' began spreading throughout Western Europe. In addition to the Magna Carta (1215), a number of so-called 'golden bulls' (*aurea bullae*) were issued in the 13th century. The most important of these was that of the Hungarian King Andreas II in 1222, which granted privileges to the Hungarian nobility relatively similar to those mentioned in the Magna Carta. The Aragonese Privilege of the Union (*Privilegio de la unión*) of 1287 and the the statute of Dauphiné of 1341 could also be mentioned as instances (Bloch 1971b [1939]: 451–452). The distinct historical status of the Magna Carta owes to the subsequent significance of the charter for English constitutionalism. On the European continent, the various charters of liberties were annulled or at the very least diluted following the advent of absolutism after the onset of the 16th-century military revolution (Downing 1992; Finer 1997b: 1298–1307). Conversely, the catalog of rights in the Magna Carta proved durable. In fact, the charter remains valid in England and Wales to this day. For example, it provides specific rights to the City of London and the Anglican Church. The Magna Carta thus assumes a prominent position in the traditional English notion of having an 'ancient constitution' that guarantees the time-honored Anglo-Saxon liberties (Pocock 1957).

The historical roots of representative democracy

Why this excursion to a southern English meadow in a distant past? This chapter outlines the second coming of democracy in the 19th century. At the time, more than one-and-a-half millennia had lapsed since ancient Greek democracy disappeared (Hansen 2010c: 16–17). But it is important to note that the modern European version of democracy did not represent the direct continuation of ancient Greek democracy. As already mentioned, though important similarities exist, ancient democracy was in significant ways – most notably with regard to representation, the scope of citizenship, and fundamental (liberal) rights – different in theory and practice from modern liberal democracy (Sartori 1987: 279; Manin 1997).

A number of features of liberal democracy should instead be traced back to the conceptions and institutional practices of the Middle Ages regarding popular sovereignty, legal rights, and representative institutions. It is on this basis that Mogens Herman Hansen (2010c: 30) – who identifies no unbroken tradition from Antiquity to modern democracy – grants that, with regard to representative democracy, "there is an unbroken tradition which connects modern legislatures with the medieval parliaments of the 13th century onwards, and modern governments with the king's council as known from the high Middle Ages onwards" (see also Acton 1972: 91). Robert A. Dahl makes a similar point in the following way:

> The first successful efforts to democratize the national state typically occurred in countries with existing legislative bodies that were intended to represent certain fairly distinctive social interests: aristocrats, commoners, the landed interest, the commercial interest, and the like. As movements toward greater democratization gained force, therefore, the design for a 'representative' legislature did not have to be spun from gossamer fibers of abstract democratic ideas; concrete legislatures and representatives, undemocratic though they were, already existed.
>
> (Dahl 1989: 215)

The estates of the realm (*États, Stände, Cortes*), first convened towards the end of the 12th century, in subsequent centuries popping up in even the remotest corners of Western Christendom (Myers 1975), were thus the forerunners of the contemporary parliaments. This is where the idea of political representation arose. The notion of being able to delegate one's decision-making competence to elected or appointed representatives is simply drawn from the estate-based society of the Middle Ages, including its corporative approach to rights (Finer 1997a: 1025). Furthermore, a charter – such as the Magna Carta – serves as a legal restriction on the power of the king, and in combination with the privileges of corporate groups we here find the seeds of the constitutionally guaranteed liberties of our time. To understand the advent of modern democracy, we thus need to capture the content of this prior medieval constitutionalism and to explain its origins. This is the twofold aim of the present chapter, which closes with a panoramic view of the second coming of democracy in the 19th century.

Medieval constitutionalism

The institutional manifestations of medieval constitutionalism were those of corporative rights, charter of liberties, and estates of the realm. Ideologically, constitutionalism was reflected in ecclesiastical and secular writings about the relations between rulers and community and about corporations (Tierney 1982). Most important was probably the doctrine of the right to resistance (Bloch 1971b [1939]: 451–452); that is, the notion that the loyalty of the people first and foremost follows from the king respecting the privileges that have been granted, for example, in connection with the charters, and that rebellion is justified insofar as the king transgresses these limits. One way of capturing constitutionalism would be by saying that the practical use of charters, the gathering of the estates of the realm, and the introduction of legal privileges for certain groups were the institutions which 'translated' the theoretical teachings about rulership into specific rights in the estate-based society of the day. The medieval milieu was simply pervaded with constitutionalist thoughts and practices (Tierney 1982: 40).

The importance of medieval constitutionalism has been stressed by Brian M. Downing (1992) in *The Military Revolution and Political Change*. Downing attempts to explain why certain parts of Western and Central Europe developed into what he unashamedly terms 'democracies'[5] after the Middle Ages, whereas absolute monarchy made inroads in other parts of this area. Downing draws attention to the 16th-century military revolution and the political impact of the subsequent geopolitical competition. But the actual premise of his explanation is that the constitutional basis for modern democracy existed throughout Western Christendom when the military revolution began in the 16th century. In the areas where the military revolution did not require absolutist state power because funds for warfare could be extracted without mobilizing the economy with force, such as the protected British Isles and the prosperous Netherlands, this heritage simply resulted in constitutional democracy. In the areas where the opposite was the case, for example, in vulnerable and exposed France and impoverished Prussia, constitutionalism was sacrificed for military efficiency. Instead of democracy, the absolutist state won the day.

Regarding the constitutional basis, Downing asserts that Western and Central Europe distinguishes itself from all other regions on this point. This is the one area where we find the constitutional infrastructure that led to modern, representative democracy (see also Hintze 1975 [1931]; Myers 1975; Poggi 1978; Finer 1997b). It is therefore, Downing argues, no coincidence that Western Europe, together with the European settler offshoots (in particular, the USA, Canada, Australia, and New Zealand, but to a lesser extent also Latin America), set the stage for the first representative democracies. In fact, Downing (1992: 10) goes so far as to suggest that it is difficult to imagine liberal democracy thriving outside of these areas. This last claim does not fit particularly well with the third wave of democratization (see Chapter 5), which really got going at the very point in time at which Downing sent his book to press. Nevertheless, Downing's failed prediction does not undermine his historical point. It is indeed striking that the modern resurrection – or second coming – of democracy was a purely Western phenomenon.

The origins of constitutionalism

It is one thing to conclude that the soil was prepared for representative democracy in Western Christendom. Entirely different is the question to what this favorable heritage owes. Downing shies away from opening up this Pandora's box. He more or less takes the historical background for granted – the medieval conception of popular sovereignty, representative institutions, and the rule of law (Downing 1992: 10) – and merely shows that similar institutions were not to be found in the countries of Eastern Europe and Asia (see also Myers 1975). Fortunately, we are able to find assistance elsewhere. Several of the great sociologists and historians of the 19th and 20th centuries addressed this issue extensively.

A majority of these scholars pointed to the European state system as a necessary precondition for constitutionalism. At least since the Hundred Years War (*circa* 1337–1453), this system has been characterized by what German historian Otto Hintze referred to as a systematic dynamic of *Schieben und Drängen* (push and pull). Since the fall of the (Western) Roman Empire, no one European power has been able to gain lasting temporal hegemony – as opposed to the great civilizations of Asia where empires, which by definition avoid competition between their constituent units, have been the norm (Jones 2008 [1981]: 104–108). However, what is peculiar about the European state system is not solely competition but also integration (Weber 1981 [1927]: 337; Hall 1989: 553). European competition was an effective facilitator of important developments, such as the spread of technologies, including bureaucratic and political technologies, exactly because the European space was close knit culturally (Jones 2008 [1981]: 45).

There is little doubt that the European multistate system was a precondition for the development of constitutionalism; but as a mono-causal explanation it is clearly insufficient. We can thus pinpoint at least two cases/sets of cases which contradict this. First, Warring States China (475–221 BC) was characterized by a strikingly similar state system, but one which did not produce constitutionalism (Finer 1997b: 1305 1306; Hui 2004, 2005). Second, Russia was gradually integrated into the European state system without developing constitutionalism (Finer 1997b: 1407–1411).

Tellingly, the classical sociologists and historians working on this subject eschewed mono-causal explanations. Instead, their work tends to show how a sometimes not even exhaustive configuration of factors combined to produce constitutionalism. Max Weber's sociological work is probably most influential (Smelser 1976: 123) but Otto Hintze (1962 [1929]; 1962 [1930]; 1975 [1931]) likewise finds the origins of medieval constitutionalism – what he refers to as the *Ständestaat* – in a unique combination of factors (Gerhard 1970: 35). Similarly, economic historians such as Eric L. Jones (2008 [1981]: xviii) have argued against the identification of one root cause in order to lay bare the configuration of factors explaining the rise of the West.

So, which factors must be included in the configuration that brought about medieval constitutionalism? Seen from the higher ground, the literature on state formation and regime change in Europe has tended to supplement the emphasis on the state system with two contextual (and possibly contingent) historical factors: first, religious–secular conflicts; second, European feudalism. Whereas the former factor both worked to sustain the competitiveness of the European state system and had a more direct effect upon constitutionalism, the latter factor first and foremost had an effect via the creation of a particular societal landscape characterized by a balance of power between rulers and privileged groups in society.

The religious–secular divide

Francis Fukuyama (2011) has recently proposed that the early European development of the rule of law was a contingent effect of the competition between secular rulers and the Catholic Church following the Gregorian Reforms in the 11th century and the subsequent Investiture Contest over the right to appoint ecclesiastical offices. Fukuyama here echoes a huge number of scholars who have pinpointed the religious–secular conflicts of Western Christendom as a precondition of the development of constitutionalism (e.g., de Ruggiero 1927: 19; Tierney 1982: 10; Zakaria 2003: 34). The claim is expressly not that Christian doctrines in themselves carried the seeds of such constitutionalism. As John A. Hall (1985: 119–120) pertinently points out, in the Orthodox Church similar Christian doctrines were used to defend *ceasaropapism*, that is, the notion that secular and religious rule should be fused into one, absolutist office. However, exactly the opposite occurred in Western or Latin Christendom. Conflict between the Church as an international organization and the secular rulers of Western and Central Europe has been ongoing since the 11th century. To quote Holmes:

> Throughout the Middle Ages people were confronted with two distinct and quite incommensurable realities: the towering stone castle and the towering stone cathedral; Caesar and Christ; sovereignty on the one hand and salvation on the other.
>
> (Holmes 1979: 125)

Moreover, in time, the Church itself was split into competing units due to the Reformation. The religious–secular divide meant that, at least since the Gregorian Reforms (roughly 1050–1080), no one authority has been able to gain omnipotence, neither ideologically nor politically. As such, the religious–secular divide has been an important impetus behind the extraordinary European state system, which has already been highlighted as a cause of constitutionalism. Furthermore, the Roman Catholic Church was the force that, via its institutional infrastructure and ecclesiastical doctrines, was the dominant factor in creating the cultural homogeneity which is the other key ingredient in the European state system.

The religious–secular divide may also be seen as the first important structural differentiation in the modernization process of the West. This divide paved the way for the development of quasi-independent social domains, i.e., spheres of society not beholden to the state (Holmes 1979: 124–125; see also Chapter 7, this volume). Here, we see dimly the roots of the civil society that has played such a pivotal role in the development of European constitutionalism (cf. Hall 1985). Harking back to Chapter 1, Benjamin Constant explicitly highlighted the disjunction of state and society as the precondition for the notion of modern liberty. In this view, individual rights developed as a response to the danger that the state would destroy the autonomy of society that has been brought into existence by the religious–secular divide in general and the Reformation in particular (Holmes 1982: 54–59).

Finally, the import of the religious–secular divide also works on the ideational or ideological level. Following the Gregorian Revolution, the Church was instrumental in spreading the doctrine that secular rulers were bound by Christian law. This doctrine, which had an important Old Testament precedent (Finer 1997a: 863–864), diffused across Latin Christendom via the activities of the Church (Hintze 1975 [1931]: 318). More generally, much theological work was done on the relationship between rulers and society, work that contributed to the development of theories about corporations, limited monarchy, and the mixed constitution, theories which later on migrated into political theory (Tierney 1982). These ecclesiastical teachings thereby provided the ideological backdrop of medieval constitutionalism.

The importance of the Catholic Church is manifested in the fact that constitutionalism eventually came to characterize all temporal units within Western Christendom. Yet, it never spread beyond the border of Western or Latin Christendom (Myers 1975; Poggi 1978). Most importantly, Russia never produced constitutionalism and neither did the remaining parts of Orthodox Europe (Myers 1975: 36–39).

Feudalism

But just as the state system did not in itself produce constitutionalism, so we must remain skeptical about whether the religious–secular divide in itself or in combination with the state system was sufficient to create constitutionalism. One additional factor needs to be highlighted, namely medieval feudalism. This, at least, is the claim we meet in the writings of a number of classical sociologists and historians (see, e.g., Hintze 1962 [1930]: 120, 139; Bloch 1971b [1939]: 451–452; Poggi 1991: 88–89), who consistently linked the rise of constitutionalism to feudalism.

The crystallization of feudalism was obviously facilitated by the religious–secular divide, especially via the creation of an independent and privileged clerical estate in society. But feudalism was also a contingent development partly offset by military requirements in a moneyless society (see Bloch 1971a [1939]). What interests us here is the political effects of feudalism. A number of famous examples of the nexus between feudalism and constitutionalism may be found. To mention only one, J.G.A. Pocock (1957: 109–111) recounts how Sir Henry Spelman used the concept of the *feudum* to show that the English Parliament "had [originally] been simply a feudal curia in which the barons met their king, as vassals their lord, to discuss the affairs of his lordship," something Pocock goes on to term "probably the most important single discovery that has ever been made in the historiography of the medieval constitution."

More generally, we can identify three characteristics of European feudalism as a form of government (cf. Stephenson 1942; Poggi 1978; Strayer 1987 [1965]), which set the stage for constitutionalism. First, sovereignty was divided into a vertical hierarchy between lords and vassals; there was thus no omnipotent power center as we later see in the absolute state. Second, the ties of dependence between lord and vassal were of a contractual character, which led to legal reciprocity. This asymmetrical contractual relationship paved the way for the notion of the right to resistance and for legal privileges for certain groups (estates). Third, the corporate immunities granted to these estate groups – initially the nobility and clergy, subsequently also the free towns – created a multiplicity of privileged groups which the rulers had to bargain with to obtain the wherewithal for warfare.

The representative institutions of the Middle Ages emerged out of this situation. In the words of Marc Bloch (1971b [1939]: 451–452):

> It was assuredly no accident that the representative system, in the very aristocratic form of the English Parliament, the French 'Estates', the *Stände* of Germany, and the Spanish *Cortes*, originated in states which were only just emerging from the feudal stage and still bore its imprint.

Various attempts have been made to identify a similar political feudalism, that is, feudalism as a form of government rather than a mode of production, outside of Western Christendom. Most notably, Japan from 1300 to 1600 and Zhōu China in the period 1046 to 256 BC have been emphasized as potential instances (see Coulborn 1956; Creel 1970: 319-320; Anderson 1974; Hui 2005: 196, fn. 143). However, if the three characteristics identified above are treated as necessary attributes, all non-European instances fall short. Discussing the case of Japan, Barrington Moore – while accepting Japan as an instance of feudalism – tellingly concedes that:

[t]he special character of the Japanese feudal bond, with its much greater emphasis on status and military loyalty than on a freely chosen contractual relationship, meant that one source of the impetus behind the Western variety of free institutions was absent.

(Moore 1991 [1966]: 253)

Towards liberal constitutionalism

The medieval landscape characterized by legal privileges of the various groups of the 'Polity of Estates' (Myers 1975) thus – somewhat paradoxically – represented primitive constitutional measures against arbitrary state power. The paradox consists of the fact that the pivotal point for liberal constitutionalism is that everyone is equal before the law. But the very judicial inequality before the law which marked the corporate privileges of estates paved the way for particular political and civil liberties which have since gradually become universalized (Ganshof 1952 [1944]: 154; Bloch 1971a [1939]: 228; Poggi 1991: 88–89). The causal mechanism of this broadening of the rights is to be found in the ongoing conflict between state power, personified by the monarch, and the privileged classes in society since the High Middle Ages (Schumpeter 1917/1918). The privileges proved to strengthen constitutionalism because they meant that the monarch was no longer able to treat his subjects arbitrarily. In the long run, however, the upper class was unable to prevent these rights from being extended to the lower classes in society, meaning that privileges in the form of liberties were universalized to the point where it no longer made sense to talk about privileges (de Ruggiero 1927: 4).

Taken together, the whole process, which leads to the development of European constitutionalism, is thus an obvious example of unintended consequences, rooted in the bargaining between rulers and ruled in the context of a competitive state system, religious–secular conflicts, and feudal institutions. The medieval heritage made Western Europe and the British settler colonies[6] uniquely prepared for the second coming of democracy, which fused checks and balances, representation, and political equality.

The great revolutions of the 18th century

Having outlined the medieval foundations of modern democracy, we fast-forward a couple of centuries. The history about the actual return of democracy begins towards the end of the 18th century. It had been fermenting for quite some time. The radical French and skeptical Scottish ages of enlightenment each represented their rebellion against privileged society. Yet, up until this point, it had merely been a rebellion in thought and speech, not action. Things did not begin happening in earnest until the American War of Independence (1775–1783) and the French Revolution (1789) (Dunn 2005: 71).

These two revolutions were markedly different as regards their respective perspectives on the democratic ideal. The fathers of the American constitution warned vehemently against the chaotic forces of democracy. In their self-understanding, the American revolutionaries were fighting to protect the time-honored (medieval) political liberties of the 13 colonies, including the right to political representation, a right that had developed even further in the 13 colonies than in England (Finer 1997b: 1400–1401). With the exception of a few radicals (e.g., Paine 1996 [1791]), the American revolutionaries were not occupied by the more democratic version. In that sense, the revolution represented a struggle to protect legal privileges rather than a fight to repeal them.

In France, the situation after the revolution of 1789 was strikingly different. From the very outset, a deliberate break with the privileged strata of society was the stated objective. This was expressed in several different ways: partly in the treatment of the royal family, the nobility, and the Church (i.e., the previously privileged groups), partly in the abstract principles laid down in the *Declaration of the Rights of Man and of the Citizens* (*Déclaration des droits de l'Homme et du Citoyen*) of August 1789. As mentioned in the Introduction, it was in connection with the French Revolution that democracy, which had previously been a derogatory word (Naess et al. 1956: 92), was suddenly used as a political slogan by a particular political grouping, namely the Jacobins under revolutionary leader Maximilien Robespierre.

The difference between the American and French revolutions is reflected in the reactions of the day. Most telling are those of Edmund Burke. Burke has come to be regarded as the father of conservatism, but his contemporaries saw him as a classic English Liberal, that is, a Whig, not a Tory. Like any Liberal would do, Burke defended the American revolutionaries. In his eyes, they were fighting to protect the ancient Anglo-Saxon liberties in the meeting with the arbitrary English central power in the guise of King George III and his representatives in the colonies. Conversely, Burke was antagonistic towards the French Revolution, as it represented a revolt against past rights (or privileges); that is, a radical break with the *status quo ante*. In his *Reflections on the Revolution in France* (1986 [1790]), he therefore warned vehemently against the radical program of the French Revolution.

In other words, the self-understanding of the American revolutionaries was that their rebellion was based on the constitutional basis of the Middle Ages, as was the case with the English Glorious Revolution of 1688. The French Revolution, contrariwise, was seen as an attempt to overthrow this very foundation. It is not for nothing that Karl Marx (1988 [1871]: 54) referred to the French Revolution as a gigantic broom that swept away all the medieval rubbish. Judging from these two cases, this proved to be a risky strategy. The French Revolution resulted in a bloody reign of terror under Maximilien Robespierre, which in turn paved the way for the Bonapartist reaction. Burke was not alone in coupling the pernicious consequences of the French Revolution to this radical break with the past. One of the central ideas in Alexis de Tocqueville's (1988 [1835/1840]) classic work, *Democracy in America*, was that a purely democratic state has an inherent tendency to centralize power, thereby threatening the liberty of the people. The absence of the privileged classes means that the state power is not being balanced by other social forces. In that sense, it may be argued that the English and

American gradualist paths to democracy were more stable than the radical French version.

The great revolutions of the 19th century

In the bigger picture, the most important thing about the 18th-century revolutions was that the genie was now out of the bottle. The medieval conceptions of popular sovereignty gradually merged with a rebellion against privileged society and thus a struggle for universal political rights. And for the first time since Antiquity, democracy was again a positive term, at least among revolutionary Jacobins. That said, democracy still had some way to go to attain the status it has today as a value that almost everyone swears by. The warnings issued by Plato, Aristotle, and restated by James Madison regarding the chaotic forces of democracy, continued to resonate throughout Western cultured society. Crucially, this was not just a position represented by conservative monarchists or supporters of the Catholic Church, who turned their backs on the Enlightenment and criticized the very notion of equality as well as the faith in human reason (see de Bonald 1796; de Maistre 1847 [1809]). Liberals were also uncomfortable with the democratic message about political equality (Przeworski 2009). Burke stated that democracy was "the most shameless thing in the world," François Guizot found that democracy is "the echo of an ancient call for social war" (our translation) of the impoverished majority against the propertied minority, and Guiseppe Mazzini similarly declared that democracy is "the cry of Spartacus, the expression and manifestation of a people in its first apprising" (Naess et al. 1956: 113, 115). Likewise, Benjamin Constant[7] and Tocqueville warned against the leveling consequences of universal suffrage. These messages echoed some of the great thinkers of the Enlightenment, who were not exactly beholden to democracy either.

As opposed to the conservatives, the liberal apprehensions did not concern the notion of equality, as such.[8] In contrast, they were occupied by the inviolability of private property. More generally, as already touched upon in Chapter 2, it is worth noting that the liberal political program – or at least the program of the classical liberals (Hayek 2006 [1960]: 343–356) – need not coincide with a democratic political program (Sartori 1987: 389). The liberal agenda aims at limiting the power of the state and ensuring the rule of law. It is a struggle for constitutionalism and political liberties rather than political equality. It was not until the great bourgeois revolutions in 1848 and 1849 that the liberals began to reconcile themselves with the term democracy.

It once again began in France. Already in 1830, a warning came in the form of the so-called July Revolution, where the bourgeoisie forced through a constitutional monarchy and replaced one king from the House of Bourbon with another. However, it was not until 1848 that things really got going. The Sicilians led off in January, when they ousted their own Bourbon king. In February it became the turn of the French Bourbons. This time around, the upheaval did not produce a new monarch, but rather a republic. Revolution subsequently spread throughout Western and Central Europe. In March, many of the German states underwent bourgeois revolutions, next came Austria-Hungary, and the revolutionary wave then reached countries such as Denmark, where absolutism suffered a sudden death. Even distant Brazil recorded a bourgeois revolution in 1848 (Weyland 2009, 2010).

The liberals marched under the banner of a free constitution, rallying against absolute monarchy. More generally, the bourgeois revolutions had a twofold objective: to establish constitutional rule, including civil liberties and the rule of law, and to introduce political representation. From this time on, the liberal program was therefore – at least partly – endowed with a democratic potential concerning political participation and competition. A number of liberal constitutions of 1848 to 1849 represent vestiges of this historical merger.

Equally telling is Marx's referral to democracy before and after the revolutions in 1848. Marx and Engels used the word as a synonym for 'the dictatorship of the proletariat' in *The Communist Manifesto* (Naess et al. 1956; Sørensen 1979). Democracy was thus equated with the masses taking over and the subsequent economic and political revolt against the propertied classes. But impressed by the liberal revolutions, Marx and Engels started using the concept in another sense, namely as the label for the broad movement against monarchy and feudal privileges (Sørensen 1979: 49). Here, democracy is equated with bourgeois democracy, which is a political regime rather than a social form of organization. However, Marx quickly turned against this ideal, increasingly regarding it as a mirage. As he saw it, genuine equality required economic equality, which could only be achieved via a radical break with the entire structure of society, as economic disparity would otherwise continue to be reproduced politically, regardless of whether or not there were free, inclusive elections.

The revolutions in the 19th century thus marked a fundamental shift in the view on democracy (Naess et al. 1956: 124). Indeed, increasingly it became a bourgeois rather than a radical ideal. Yet the liberals remained cautious as regards the extent of political equality because they regarded equal and universal suffrage to be dangerous. They were afraid that if suffrage was granted to people who were not property owners – or merely the smaller landowners – private property would be fundamentally threatened; for the impoverished masses would use their newfound political power to take from others what they did not have (and envied), first and foremost property (Przeworski 2009).

For the same reason, the 19th-century constitutions were almost without exception characterized by unequal and restricted suffrage and eligibility criteria. As recently as 1900, only 17 countries had placed all men on the same footing in this regard, and only a single country, New Zealand, could boast of genuine universal suffrage in the sense that women had also received the right to vote (Przeworski 2009). It was not until the first half of the 20th century that equal and universal suffrage finally made inroads in almost the entire Western world.

Conclusions

Modern, representative democracy is thus, at one and the same time, rooted in the estate-based society of the Middle Ages and represents a break with the privileges intrinsic to this society. Hence, representative democracy made its advent because, following the rabid phase during the French Revolution, it proved capable of combining political equality with political stability, fusing democracy with tempering aspects of republicanism and liberalism such as representation, constitutionalism, and checks and balances. Bernard Manin (1997: 238) goes so far as to proclaim modern democracy a mixture of aristocratic and democratic elements and, therefore, the "mixed constitution of modern times". John Dunn (2005: 130, 146), in a similar vein, describes this as a 19th-century balance between "the order of egoism" and "the order of equality". The advocates of inequality made political concessions, first and foremost continuously widening the suffrage, but at the same time, the absolute equality ideal was placed on hold.[9]

It is also possible to talk about a balance between personal and political liberty. Seen in this light, it is first and foremost the merging of liberalism and democracy – not egoism and equality, or aristocratic and democratic elements – that has paved the way for the triumph of modern democracy (Sartori 1987: 450; Holmes 1995: 6). The *quid pro quo* of this version of the narrative is civil liberties, including property rights, and checks and balances in exchange for equal and universal suffrage. This reading awards a prominent place in the narrative for Great Britain. For the classic English liberalism gradually reconciled itself with the ideal of political equality over the course of the 19th century; an ideal that, in itself, can be destructive but, combined with the liberal measures, strengthens a society (Holmes 1995: xi). It is precisely in this guise that democracy has triumphed over all of its challengers. In the next chapter, we look closer at how this has taken place and how democracy has spread to the rest of the world since its second coming in the 19th century.

5 Waves of democratization

A wave of democratization is a group of transitions from non-democratic regimes to democratic regimes that occur within a specified period of time and that significantly outnumber transitions in the opposite direction during that period of time.

Using this simple formula, Samuel P. Huntington (1991: 15) pinned down his famous wave metaphor about democratization. Huntington's general point is that democratic transitions and breakdowns wax and wane in wave movements. A first wave is followed by a reverse wave, which is followed by a second wave that in turn meets yet another reverse wave, and so on and so forth. However, this is not a symmetrical logic of ebb and flow. The decreases are less powerful than the increases. We should therefore understand it more in terms of a 'two steps forward, one step back' logic, implying that still more democracies come into existence, yet that this development is punctuated by considerable, albeit temporary, setbacks (Huntington 1991: 25).

This chapter deals with the wave metaphor and the reality it targets, and the objective is dual. First, we introduce Huntington's influential analysis. Second, we examine the empirical validity of his work more closely. The questions we address are these: What exactly does Huntington say about the democratizations of the latest 200 years? And can his claims be corroborated? This two-part exercise should provide a systematic historical overview of the democratic ups and downs since the return of democracy in the 19th century.

The three waves of democratization

Huntington wrote *The Third Wave* in the immediate wake of the collapse of communism, demarcated by the fall of the Berlin Wall in 1989 and the disintegration of the Soviet Union in 1991. He was undoubtedly impressed by the events of the day, as the book is considerably more optimistic than his work in general. It is probably no exaggeration to say that Huntington's authorship has been imbued with a general strain of pessimism. Some of his more celebrated claims include that in developing countries, modernization does not lead to democracy but to instability (Huntington 1968), that democratic institutions are generally overloaded by unrealistic demands (Corzier et al. 1975), and that cultural gaps prevent a peaceful world and the global ascendancy of democracy (Huntington 1996).

Not so the *The Third Wave*, which is based on the observation that democratization has tended to increase over time. Returning to Huntington's more particular claim about patterns of regime developments, he argues that over the course of the latest 200 years, democracy has swept over the world in three successive waves which have been separated from one another by two reverse waves. Huntington regards the Portuguese Carnation Revolution in 1974 as marking the beginning of the third wave of democratization. From Portugal, the wave spread to the rest of Southern Europe in subsequent years, on to Latin America and Southeast Asia in the 1980s, to Central and Eastern Europe in 1989, and thereafter to Sub-Saharan Africa. Huntington apparently took the collapse of communism as representing a democratic high water mark. Against that background, he suggested that a new reversal was probably imminent (Huntington 1991: 315). We address the validity of this contemporary prediction further in the following chapter. Here, we focus squarely on the historical patterns.

Huntington's definitions

As already mentioned, Huntington defines a 'wave' as a specific period in which the number of transitions to democracy clearly exceeds the number of democratic breakdowns. Analogously, a reverse wave is defined as a period in which the number of democratic collapses clearly exceeds the number of transitions to democracy (Huntington 1991: 15).

But what does Huntington mean by democracy? What kinds of regimes are born and die as a result of the lapping of the waves? Once again, Huntington is quite explicit. He refers to Joseph A. Schumpeter's (1974 [1942]) realistic tradition, which he sees as being superior to alternative approaches. As discussed in previous chapters, the basic thought here is that democracy is first and foremost a method in which competitive elections for the main political offices are especially important. More particularly, Huntington embraces Robert A. Dahl's elaboration of Schumpeter's definition. Democracy thus consists of free and fair elections combined with certain political liberties (i.e., polyarchy).

Huntington's analysis is not entirely consistent on this point. While Dahl includes equal and universal suffrage as part of his definition, this would in principle pose a problem for Huntington, as he lets the first wave begin with a limited expansion of suffrage in the USA in 1828. However, only 17 countries had implemented universal suffrage for men as late as 1900, and just a single country – New Zealand as of 1893 – had granted women the right to vote (Przeworski 2009). According to Dahl's definition, then, the 19th century was a non-democratic epoch (cf. Doorenspleet 2000), with the sole exception of New Zealand in the last decade of the century.

In this case, Huntington pragmatically argues that we must lower the bar when comparing past and present.[1] Democracy simply means something different in different periods.[2] In the 19th century, it meant competitive elections and that at least a large percentage of men had the right to vote and stand for election. Although the claim that there were no genuine democracies in the 19th century is correct based on Dahl's polyarchy criteria, it means that we are unable to appreciate some interesting developments and variations. We therefore follow Huntington's logic when testing his claims. But as opposed to Huntington, we do so in a consistent manner, as we apply our concept of minimalist democracy which merely requires competitive elections, not necessarily equal and universal suffrage.

Huntington's analysis revisited

First, Huntington's own results must be scrutinized. In Table 5.1, we have reproduced his overview of the three waves and two reverse waves. The first long – and somewhat sluggish – wave lasted from 1828 to 1926. During this period, the Anglo-Saxon countries and Northern Europe were democratized first, followed by parts of continental Europe and Latin America. A reverse wave started in 1922 and lasted until 1942, draining continental Europe as well as Latin America of democracies. A new wave of democratization surged forward in the period 1943 to 1962. This time, the wave led to the reintroduction of democracy in the parts of Europe that had been liberated by the Western Allies, while advances were also made in large parts of the Third World. From 1958 until 1975, a reverse wave almost evened out the advances of the second wave. Finally, the third wave of democratization began in 1974. It swept over Southern Europe and spread to Latin America and Southeast Asia before reaching the former Eastern Bloc and Sub-Saharan Africa after the end of the Cold War.

More than anything else, Huntington's book is renowned for having identified these waves. Nonetheless, he actually uses more energy on explaining the third wave. Instead of trying to provide a mono-causal explanation, he weaves a number

Table 5.1 Huntington's waves of democratization

Wave	Period	Countries
First (long) wave	1828–1926	Western Europe, North America, Australia, New Zealand, parts of Latin America, and Central and Eastern Europe
First reverse wave	1922–1942	Central and Eastern Europe, parts of Latin America
Second (short) wave	1943–1962	Countries liberated/occupied by the Western Allies, parts of the former European colonies, and Latin America
Second reverse wave	1958–1975	Former colonies and parts of Latin America
Third wave	1974–	Southern Europe, Latin America, Southeast Asia, Africa, and the former communist countries (the Middle East as the only major exception)

of partial explanations together (see Kitschelt 1992: 1033–1034; Mahoney & Snyder 1999: 22–24). According to Huntington, five factors are important.

1   *Legitimacy crisis*: The non-democratic regimes suffered a widespread legitimacy crisis beginning in the 1970s, which was partially caused by an economic crisis rooted in 'oil price spikes' or 'Marxist-Leninist constraints' (Huntington 1991: 59). In many cases, autocracies had lagged behind the democracies in terms of economic growth. And compared with democracies, authoritarian regimes have a hard time legitimizing themselves with reference to their political regime, which is obviously not free. In short, they must be able to deliver the goods in terms of results in order to muster widespread popular support.

2   *Economic development*: Focusing on the absolute level of wealth rather than short-term growth rates, Huntington (1991: 59) states that "by the early 1970s, many countries had achieved overall levels of economic development that provided an economic basis for democracy and that facilitated transition to democracy."

3   *International influences*: A significant shift in international relations took place in the form of the governments of North America and Western Europe increasingly encouraging democratization.

4   *New stance of the Catholic Church*: The Roman Catholic Church adopted a new position regarding democracy in the 1960s. Catholicism was for long argued to be detrimental to democracy. However, the Catholic Church had already shifted in a more democracy-friendly direction during the Second Vatican Council (1962–1965), and in the 1970s and 1980s the Catholic Church in South America actually began actively fighting against the local authoritarian regimes, as did the Catholic Church in the struggle against communism in Poland.

5   *The 'snowball effect'*: When a snowball first starts rolling, it keeps growing. Whereas the other factors explain the particular onset of the third wave, this factor explains the general dynamics of the waves. The democratization of neighboring countries simply increases the tendency to follow suit. This logic of contagion also applies to democratic breakdowns (once offset by more particular factors). During the third wave, this snowball (aka domino) effect has even hopped from continent to continent.

As is his wont, Huntington's (1991: ch. 2) analysis is easy to understand, and there is no reason to dwell on it further. Instead, we turn our attention to some of the criticism directed against the analysis, which also paves the way for scrutinizing Huntington's statements more closely.

Can the wave thesis be corroborated?

The literature includes two general points of criticism against Huntington's analysis. The first is technical in the sense that it concerns the actual definitions and how the numbers are tallied. The basic claim is that the wave movements are not nearly as salient as Huntington describes. The second point of criticism is analytical in that it challenges the uniformity of the wave movements – particularly the third wave. According to this claim, it is possible to identify a fourth wave as of 1989 and henceforth, which is both qualitatively and quantitatively distinct from the previous third wave. We first discuss the technical critique, which we use to investigate the existence of waves of democratization and reverse waves. At a later stage of the chapter, we return to the arguments for teasing a fourth wave out of the third wave.

Doorenspleet's critique

Nine years after the publication of *The Third Wave*, Renske Doorenspleet (2000) delivered a lucid criticism of Huntington's assessment. She first points out that Huntington ignores Dahl's criterion regarding equal and universal suffrage – which he otherwise claims to endorse – for the 19th century. As observed above, if we take this criterion as read, the first wave of democratization started in the 1890s rather than in the 1820s.

As opposed to Doorenspleet, however, we argue that is it more fruitful to apply Schumpeter's more minimalist perspective to the 19th century. More needs to be said here, however. Doorenspleet (2000: 386) also argues that Huntington's counting rules leave a lot to be desired:

> Huntington has estimated the incidence of transitions to democracy in terms of the *percentages* of world states involved. Since the denominator in this equation, that is, the number of states in the world, is far from constant, this measure can be misleading. As we shall see, for example, the number of (minimal) democracies in the world grew from thirty in 1957 to thirty-seven in 1972, thus appearing to reflect a small but noticeable 'wave' of democratization. Considered as a percentage, by contrast, this same period seems to have been characterized by a small *reverse* wave, in that the proportion of states that were democratic fell from 32 percent to 27 percent. The explanation for this apparent paradox is simple: largely as a result of decolonization in Africa, the number of independent states in the world – the denominator – grew from 93 to 137; hence, although there was an absolute increase in the number of democratic regimes, their proportion of world states actually fell.

Doorenspleet's critique of Huntington's method thus addresses the fact that he is examining the percentage of all of the countries in the world that are democracies. This calculation fails to account for shifts in the total number of countries. In our opinion, the crucial problem is that this procedure is not in accordance with Huntington's own definition of waves, which specifically emphasizes the number of transitions, not the percentage (Doorenspleet 2000: 394). In addition to the observation that the first wave begins very late (due to the absence of equal and universal suffrage in the 19th century), Doorenspleet's analysis demonstrates that there actually was a reverse wave in the interwar period. However, its magnitude was smaller than Huntington describes. In turn, it was countered by a second wave following World War II, but there was no subsequent (second) reverse wave. The second wave merely becomes weaker towards the late 1970s, after which it again begins to surge.

This criticism is rather convincing, and our replication is heavily inspired by Doorenspleet. Nevertheless, we do not reach the exact same results for a number of reasons. First, we use an updated dataset. Second, as mentioned above, we follow Huntington and accept countries with competitive elections as (minimalist) democracies in the 19th century. This gives a somewhat longer spread-out of the first wave. Third, Doorenspleet excludes interrupted regimes from her analysis; that is, instances where a country is characterized by the absence of a central authority, wartime occupation, or ongoing political upheaval. We choose to include all of these instances based on the reasoning that the only significant distinction must be whether a country has a democratic government or not.[3]

What do the figures show?

The measurement of global empirical tendencies places great demands on the data. We are in a slightly unfortunate situation here, as there is actually only a single dataset stretching far enough back in time to identify possible early wave movements – the so-called POLITY IV project, which applies a rather narrow definition of democracy.[4] Of the three characteristics that we have used to define different types of democracy – electoral rights, political liberties, and the rule of law – POLITY IV only covers the first. This means that here we solely distinguish between (minimalist) democracies and authoritarian regimes. Fortunately, that is exactly the distinction we are interested in here, meaning that the scarcity of data does not present too much of a measurement problem.

Regarding the more concrete operationalization, we follow Doorenspleet's procedure, as she also uses the POLITY IV data in her analysis.[5] It is worth mentioning that the analysis only includes countries with a minimum population of 500,000, as countries smaller than that are not included in the dataset. We start the analysis in 1800 in order to be able to identify the spring of the first wave earlier than Huntington did insofar as the data provide a basis for doing so. In Figure 5.1, we follow Huntington and report the share of democratic countries of all of the countries in the entire period.

We see that the three waves and two reverse waves are clearly delineated. According to the POLITY data, the first wave already begins in 1808, when the USA joins the set of democratic countries. After a sluggish start, the wave begins to surge in the mid-1800s and peaks in the early 1920s. Thereafter, the first reverse wave is identifiable, illustrating the rather disheartening political developments in the late 1920s, throughout the 1930s and in the early 1940s involving the reintroduction of different kinds of autocracies as well as Nazi Germany's occupation of established democracies. The second wave of democratization follows, although it

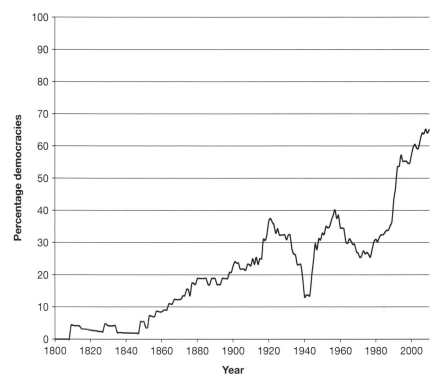

Figure 5.1 Percentage of democratic countries of all countries, 1800 to 2010

already dies out around 1960. A strong reverse wave is felt, especially in Latin America and Sub-Saharan Africa, before the third wave breaks through the autocratic dikes in the 1970s. At the end-point of the analysis (2010), a clear majority of the countries are democratic, while this figure was only a quarter as recently as the 1970s.

Figure 5.1 thus supports the general contours of Huntington's waves, but it also goes to show that Huntington's calculation methods are somewhat problematic. One slightly banal but telling example is that it is possible to identify a decreasing tendency immediately after the onset of the first wave of democratization begins in 1808 – a weak retreat lasting all the way until 1828 when Peru joined the democratic camp as the second country. This is because only a single country, the United States, was democratic during this period. But as the number of independent countries is slightly increasing, the number of democracies as a percentage of all countries falls. Referring to a reverse wave in such a situation is obviously nonsensical, which supports Doorenspleet's point about the percentage (instead of the number) being misleading. A corrective consisting of the absolute numbers is therefore appropriate. In Figure 5.2, we have illustrated the tally of democracies over the entire period.

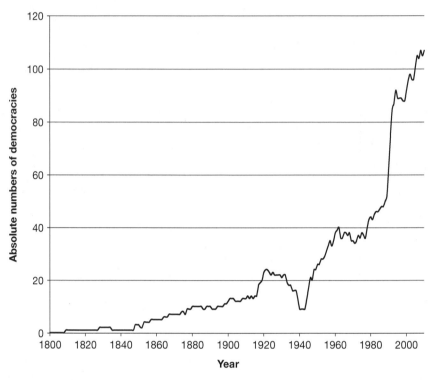

Figure 5.2 Absolute numbers of democracies, 1800 to 2010

When mapping the development in this manner, the picture changes somewhat. The first long wave – punctuated by an abrupt increase immediately after World War I – remains evident, as does the first reverse wave in the 1930s, which is more distinct in our analysis than in Doorenspleet's. As already mentioned, this is because Doorenspleet excludes the countries that were occupied during World War II, such as the Netherlands, Denmark, and Norway. We count these as democratic breakdowns, even though this was the result of foreign occupation rather than internal collapse. Next, a clear outline of the second wave emerges; yet the same cannot be said about the second reverse wave. At most, we find a period with a reasonably stable number of democracies in the 1960s and 1970s. This period, characterized by status quo, is followed by a very salient third wave, which begins towards the end of the 1970s, gains momentum in the 1990s, and remains forceful in the 2000s (see also Berg-Schlosser 2009).

Recall at this point that Huntington (1991: 15) perceives a wave as "a group of transitions from non-democratic regimes to democratic regimes that occur within a specified period of time and that significantly outnumber transitions in the opposite direction." As a final assessment of the existence of the waves we therefore compare the absolute number of democratic transitions with the absolute

Table 5.2 The number of democratic transitions and breakdowns in specified periods

Period	Democratic transitions	Democratic breakdowns	Difference
1808–1926 (first long wave)	37	15	22
1922–1942 (first reverse wave)	3	18	−15
1943–1962 (second short wave)	43	12	31
1958–1975 (second reverse wave)	33	30	3
1974–2010 (third wave)	120	46	74
1974–1988 (delineated third wave)	25	12	13
1989–2010 (fourth wave)	95	34	61

number of democratic breakdowns within each of the periods Huntington identifies (see Table 5.2).

At this point, we focus on the first five rows (we return to the last two below). During Huntington's first long wave – here understood as the period from 1808 to 1926 – the number of democratic transitions (37) clearly outnumbers the number of democratic breakdowns (15). The first reverse wave in the 20-year period 1922 to 1942 is equally obvious. Here, democracy broke down 18 times, whereas democratic transitions only took place three times. Finally, the existence of the second (short) wave is also corroborated, as we find 31 more democratic transitions than democratic collapses in the period from 1943 to 1962.

The picture then changes. The data do not support the existence of a second reverse wave in the period from 1958 to 1975 as the number of democratic transitions (33) is actually higher than the number of breakdowns (30). Huntington has apparently been led astray by the circumstance that many of the decolonized countries, especially in Africa, began their independent existence in the 1960s as autocracies. As these countries were not democracies from the outset, we argue that it is inaccurate to speak of any 'de-democratization' or reversals.

Finally, the analysis clearly confirms the existence of a remarkable third wave in the period 1974 to 2010, a period witnessing 120 democratic transitions against a mere 46 collapses. Bearing this in mind, we conclude that all of Huntington's three waves of democratization are identifiable, while the same can only be said about one of his two reverse waves. Logically speaking, it is therefore somewhat tempting to merge the second and third waves. Dirk Berg-Schlosser (2009) has actually done this in an analysis in which he talks about a second long wave. Analytically, however, different dynamics seem to be playing out, as the tendencies shift dramatically in the second half of the 1970s after a couple of decades marked by stagnation. This then leads to the other critique of Huntington in the literature, which suggests that – for analytical reasons and with reference to the frequency – two separate waves should be teased out of the period since 1974.

A fourth wave?

Using Huntington's framework, the third wave of democratization began way back in 1974 and has continued up until the time of writing. Vis-à-vis the long first wave, this is obviously not much of a time span. When considering Figures 5.1 and 5.2, however, it is equally obvious that the wave changes character over the period. Above all, there is a salient break around the collapse of communist regimes in 1989 to 1991, where a slow development is suddenly transformed into a steep increase in the share and number of democracies. As Table 5.2 illustrates, the 1974 to 1988 period is characterized by a modest difference of 13 more democratic transitions than breakdowns, while the 1989 to 2010 period produces a positive difference of no less than 61. Several researchers have accordingly argued that the third wave transforms into a qualitatively different fourth wave at some point (e.g., Bunce 2000; McFaul 2002; Doorenspleet 2005). While it may appear problematic that there is no reverse wave separating the two, the same is actually the case with the second and third waves, as we have just demonstrated.

That is not all. Theoretically, Huntington's wave metaphor builds on a domino effect. If there are two different rows of dominoes – one in Southern Europe and South America in the 1970s and 1980s and another in Eastern Europe and Sub-Saharan Africa in the 1990s and 2000s – that is in itself a strong argument for dividing the third wave into two. Michael McFaul (2002) makes this very point in his article entitled "The Fourth Wave of Democracy and Dictatorship". This title nicely conveys McFaul's two criticisms of Huntington. First, a fourth wave – of a different ilk than the third – is identifiable. Second, while it has led to democratization in some places, it has also led to the instant reintroduction of autocracy in other places.

First and foremost, McFaul emphasizes the development in the former Eastern Bloc. He begins with the observation that the latest (fourth) wave of democratization required the division of a number of multiethnic states into their constituent units, including most prominently the disintegration of the Soviet Union, Yugoslavia, and Czechoslovakia. This was only possible because the Soviet Union, under the leadership of Mikhail Gorbachev, abandoned the so-called Brezhnev Doctrine in the late 1980s. The doctrine dictated that an internal or external threat against the socialistic order in a socialist country was a shared problem for all socialist countries, which were therefore obligated to respond to this threat, including with military means. This means that the impulse behind this wave was exogenous, that is, it came from the outside, except, of course, as regards the center of the Soviet Empire (Russia).

That clearly distinguishes this wave from the previous third wave, where the dominant impulses came from within the individual countries, domino effect or not (cf. O'Donnell & Schmitter 1986). McFaul accordingly points out that the factors encouraging democratization in Southern Europe and South America did not have the same importance in Eastern Europe (and the rest of the world) after 1989. The causal relationships simply differ. It is possible to further extend McFaul's argument, as this development may also be observed outside of Eastern

Europe in the 1990s and 2000s. Here again, an exogenous impulse obviously exists. Intensive international pressure to democratize first became effective once the balancing act between the Cold War superpowers – the USA and the Soviet Union – was relegated to the ash heap of history.

Moreover, and here we are exclusively talking about the former Eastern Bloc, McFaul reminds us that there have been transitions to autocracy as well as to democracy. From their shared background, the post-communist countries have proceeded in different directions. This is why he refers to a fourth wave towards democracy *and* dictatorship, rhetorically asking: "Why, after all, should the emergence of *dictatorship* in Uzbekistan be subsumed under the third wave of *democratization?*" (McFaul 2002: 242). In our opinion, this second point of criticism is less convincing than the first. McFaul is obviously correct that not all regime changes run in a democratic direction. Yet, there have been both democratic transitions and democratic breakdowns in the entire period analyzed in this chapter. And as we have shown, the democratic transitions have clearly been in the majority in the 1990s and 2000s. There is thus more to McFaul's argument about how the democratizations in the 1990s and 2000s were qualitatively different from the 1970s and 1980s (see also Levitsky & Way 2010: 34–35).

Conclusions

Taking a step back, our assessment of democratic waves has shown that, as of the beginning of the 19th century, the number of democracies increased gradually up until the end of World War I, which triggered an abrupt increase. This trend was followed by a brief drop in the 1930s and early 1940s. The end of World War II was then marked by a strong increase followed by a gradual increase in the number of democracies until a period of stagnation set in from the beginning of the 1960s to the end of the 1970s, where the incremental increase begins again. Finally, there was a very abrupt increase following the collapse of communism in 1989 to 1991, which was then followed by a less remarkable but nevertheless positive development.

What can we conclude against this background? Huntington's analysis has been agenda-setting, its greatest merit being that it has directed attention to the international dynamics which have tended to mutually reinforce either democratization or de-democratization since the second coming of democracy. However, our replication and discussion indicate that the wave metaphor is problematic, as it draws no distinction between abrupt and gradual developments, including pivotal conjunctures such as those occurring in 1848 to 1849, 1919 to 1922, 1945 to 1948, and 1989 to 1991 (cf. Berg-Schlosser 2009). Moreover, it is unclear whether a stagnant period or an actual decrease separates two different waves. In order to follow up on these issues in general and McFaul's points in particular, we must examine the third wave more closely, in that connection focusing on the development in different regions. This is the objective of the next chapter.

6 The third wave of democratization in different regions

The third wave of democratization, which broke through the autocratic dikes from around the mid-1970s, has left a large number of new democracies in its wake. This has not been ignored in the literature. A particularly big impression was made when the wave broke through the Berlin Wall and reached a hitherto unseen momentum in the aftermath of the collapse of communist party rule in 1989 to 1991. In considerable parts of the academic community – as well as with politicians and in the media – the expectation was that democracy would now go from strength to strength.

But the mood can turn quickly, and so it did in the second half of the 1990s. A number of researchers began addressing the dark sides of some of the new democracies. The general point, made initially by scholars such as Guillermo O'Donnell (1992), Fareed Zakaria (1997), and Larry Diamond (1999), was that many of the newly democratized countries were situated in a 'gray zone' (Carothers 2002) between democracy and autocracy. Moreover, these hybrid regimes showed a certain measure of stability, since they did not appear in transition towards democracy proper. For example, both O'Donnell (1993) and Zakaria (1997) referred to particular versions of them, such as 'illiberal democracy', as new species that ought to be taken seriously for the very reason that they could be thought to establish themselves as durable political phenomena. Thus, the gray zone was not necessarily a temporary stopover on the road to liberal democracy. More particularly, Diamond and Zakaria pointed out that the major problem in the gray zone was that free and inclusive elections were far too often carried out in the absence of political liberties and the rule of law. As such, these were countries that fulfilled the democratic requirements regarding the electoral dimension but failed in relation to that which may, generally speaking, be understood as the liberal dimension. Hence, what Diamond (1999: 10) referred to as a "gap between electoral and liberal democracy." Or, as Zakaria (1997: 23) eloquently proclaimed: "Today the two strands of liberal democracy, interwoven in the Western political fabric, are coming apart in the rest of the world. Democracy is flourishing; constitutional liberalism is not."[1]

Thomas Carothers (2007) has characterized this development as a shift from democratic optimism to democratic pessimism (see also van de Walle 2002: 66; Merkel 2010). In this chapter, we grapple with the empirical tendencies that first led to the optimism and later on to the pessimism. Our general objective is to provide an overview of the third wave. However, we seize the occasion to investigate whether the pessimistic perspective can be corroborated. We retain Samuel P. Huntington's original division and do not distinguish between a third and a fourth wave in our analysis of the development since the beginning of the 1970s. This is not to belittle the analytical arguments made in favor of teasing out a fourth wave but, on the contrary, because we are interested in identifying and discussing such shifts over the latest two generations. In other words, rather than accepting the 1989 cut-off point in advance, we further scrutinize whether the general development is in fact punctuated at this point in time.

This is reflected in the fact that – compared with the previous chapter – we carry out a more detailed analysis of the tendencies in two ways. First, we apply our fine-grained typology; that is, the distinction between liberal democracies, polyarchies, electoral democracies, minimalist democracies, and autocracies, as presented in Chapter 3. Second, we do not merely refer to the global level, but also provide overviews for each of the world's major regions. To do so, we change the dataset used to measure democracy. Instead of POLITY IV, we again apply Freedom House's *Freedom in the World Survey* (see Chapter 3). Furthermore, we adopt Freedom House's regional division of the world. After an introductory global overview, we thus, in due order, zoom in on Western Europe, the Americas, South and East Asia, Eastern Europe, Sub-Saharan Africa, and the Middle East and North Africa.

A global overview

Beginning with the global overview of the development since 1972, Figure 6.1 shows that the third wave is also easily identifiable using our more fine-grained distinctions.

More than anything else, the figure brings out the way in which the ratio of democratic regimes has risen steadily since the end of the 1970s. As recently as the late 1980s, these categories contained less than 40 percent of all countries; today they contain around 60 percent. Three other tendencies leap to the eye. First, the most dramatic surge in democracy occurred shortly after 1989. Second, it was not until the turn of the millennium that there was a serious increase in the number of liberal democracies, that is, regimes characterized by both free and inclusive elections, political liberties, and the rule of law, and in 2011 they still only represented around a quarter of all countries.[2] Third, both the overall percentage of democracies and the percentage of liberal democracies seem to have declined modestly since 2006.

This brings us to another conspicuous tendency. The ratio of electoral democracies – characterized by free and inclusive elections but lacking the liberal barriers against state repression – actually did peak when the pessimistic concerns were first voiced in the latter half of the 1990s. Roughly 10 percent of all countries were at the time found in this category. What is more, the proportion of liberal democracies fell slightly during this period. It is thus tempting to conclude that the data

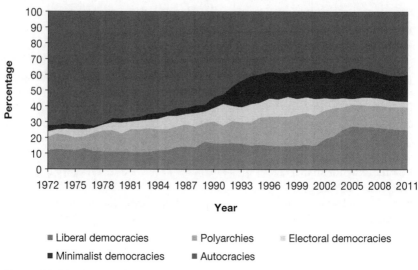

Figure 6.1 Distribution of political regimes on the global level, 1972 to 2011

support the gap between electoral and liberal democracy identified by Diamond and Zakaria. Yet looks may be deceiving for two reasons. First, even in the 1990s there were substantially more minimalist democracies than electoral democracies. Second, the percentage of electoral democracies has fallen steadily in the 2000s while the percentage of liberal democracies has been on the rise until 2006. Our account therefore neither supports Diamond and Zakaria's respective descriptions of the aforementioned gap nor their gloomy predictions about its likely increase. On the contrary, the combination of free and inclusive elections and the inadequate respect for political liberties and the rule of law has been rather uncommon. As such, these electoral democracies have not established themselves as a new, stable version of democracy.

If we are to talk about a gap, it is more appropriate to refer to a gap between minimalist democracies and liberal democracies, that is, between democracies in which the elections are competitive but somewhat flawed while political liberties and rule of law are not respected, on the one hand, and democracies in which citizens enjoy such rights and elections are beyond reproach, on the other. Such a gap operates both on the electoral and liberal dimensions in the sense that the former set of countries falls short in both contexts without ending up in the set of autocracies (cf. Møller 2007, 2008; Møller & Skaaning 2010). Bearing this in mind, the pessimists' general interest in the gray zone probably has more to offer than their more particular description of the gap. We return to this issue at the end of the chapter.

From the global to the regional level

It goes without saying that the global tendencies marking the entire period are important for anyone interested in understanding the third wave. However, equally obvious is the danger that the view of the forest will blind us as to the contours of the individual trees. One and the same global development may involve very different regional developments. It is entirely conceivable that the gains in the proportion of democracies have been owing to specific parts of the world, while other parts have by and large been immune to the third wave of democratization; there could actually be democratic setbacks in certain regions over the period.

Likewise, it is possible that the gap between electoral and liberal democracy actually *is* in existence – a possibility that is rather interesting in light of the discussion above – but only in certain regions. In the subsequent section, we therefore investigate the extent to which the global development is reflected on the regional level. In this connection, we also scrutinize whether, on the regional level, there seems to be a basis for separating out a fourth wave. The structure is set by our following the third wave from its source in Southern Europe via South America and on to South and East Asia, Eastern Europe, Sub-Saharan Africa, and the Middle East.

Western Europe

It is pertinent to begin with the most democratic of the regions between which Freedom House distinguishes: Western Europe. As argued in Chapter 4, it was here and in the overseas European settler colonies that democracy emerged in its modern form, and it is from here that it spread to the most remote corners of the world in the 20th century. Even in Western Europe, however, the third wave of democratization is recognizable. Needless to say, the vast majority of Western European countries were already democracies in the 1970s. In fact, there were only two groups of exceptions: the autocratic regimes in Portugal, Spain, and Greece, and small principalities such as Monaco, Liechtenstein, and Andorra.

As Figure 6.2 shows, all of these countries have since spurned their non-democratic credentials. This is hardly surprising, as Huntington's point is precisely that the Southern European democratizations triggered the third wave. But there is also another interesting, positive development. In the course of the period, many Western European countries undergo a democratic deepening by joining the set of liberal democracies. The other forms of democracy virtually disappear, owing to two major shifts. The first takes place towards the end of the 1980s, the second at the beginning of the new millennium. As such, Western Europe clearly drives a non-negligible part of the global increase in liberal democracies.

North and South America

Moving our focus to the Americas, the USA and Canada are liberal democracies throughout the entire period. However, they are not really what we are interested

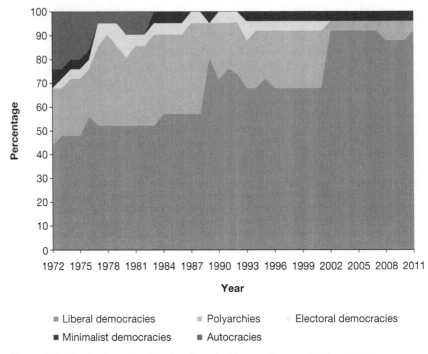

Figure 6.2 Distribution of political regimes in Western Europe, 1972 to 2011

in here. We therefore ignore the 'lower layer' in the liberal democracy category in an attempt to identify the onslaught of the third wave in this region, where it began to make inroads with the democratization of Ecuador and Peru in the late 1970s.

The decrease in autocracies is clearly outlined in Figure 6.3. Whereas the autocratic category included more than 40 percent of the countries in the region in the 1970s, at the time of writing preciously few countries are found here. Only Cuba has continuously been under autocratic rule, whereas Honduras, Haiti, Venezuela, and Nicaragua have lately joined this group again. Today, the Americas is therefore the second most democratic region in the world. Notice, more generally, that the spike in the share of democracies is the result of an incremental development (Peeler 2004; Smith & Ziegler 2008) that over time produces a rather equal distribution between the democratic types, including quite a number of liberal democracies: Costa Rica, a number of small island states in the Caribbean, and more recently also countries such as Chile and Uruguay.

Finally, it is worth noting that Latin America witnessed the emergence of a considerable number of electoral democracies in the 1980s and 1990s (cf. Smith & Ziegler 2008). These were the countries which O'Donnell (1993) took note of when advancing his thesis that a relatively stable subcategory of democracies was in ascendancy; that is, countries with free and inclusive elections which were seemingly not on the road to liberal democracy. In this sense, the data arguably

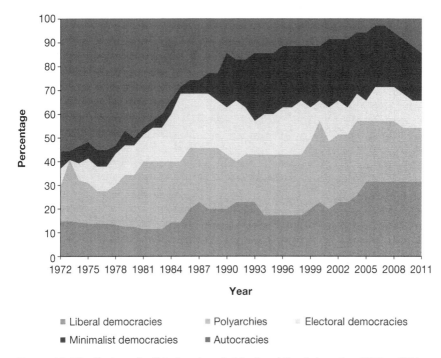

Figure 6.3 Distribution of political regimes in North and South America, 1972 to 2011

support O'Donnell's analysis of Latin America more than is the case with the global analyses of Diamond and Zakaria. Even in this part of the world, however, the electoral democracies dwindled sharply in the 2000s. They have therefore not established themselves as stable regimes, as O'Donnell had predicted. Instead, the minimalist democracy category is again where we find most gray zone democracies.

South and East Asia

The third wave of democratization has also left its clear marks on South and East Asia. This region includes two European settler countries, namely Australia and New Zealand. These two countries belong in a league of their own, as they are both liberal democracies during the entire period while Japan has continuously been a polyarchy. Towards the end of the period, however, the set of liberal democracies also includes a number of Pacific Island states, whereas South Korea and Taiwan have become polyarchies.

Compared with the global distribution, South and East Asia remains a region with relatively many autocratic regimes, including very repressive regimes in China, Myanmar, and North Korea, and less repressive ones in Malaysia and Singapore (cf. Croissant 2004; Shin 2008). Nonetheless, Figure 6.4 illustrates that the proportion of autocratic countries has declined steadily since the end of the

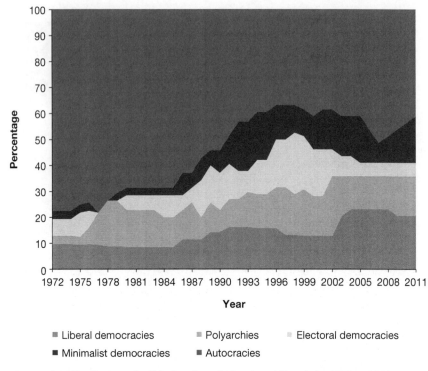

Figure 6.4 Distribution of political regimes in South and East Asia, 1972 to 2011

1970s, from almost 80 percent to less than half of the countries at the end of the period. We also see the earlier encountered tendency that electoral democracies mustered quite a high proportion in the 1990s, but that it is subsequently the minimalist democracies that dominate in the gray zone between autocracy and liberal democracy. Finally, the big increase in democracies began prior to 1989, although it was seemingly reinforced by this juncture, whereas the big increase in liberal democracies occurred in the 2000s.

Eastern Europe

We now move to a part of the world that was hit very suddenly by the wave. As late as the close of the 1980s there were no democracies in this area, which was referred to collectively as the Eastern Bloc, and which included only communist countries. Yet things were about to change. The Brezhnev Doctrine, which entailed prompt intervention against forces·that could potentially undermine an established communist regime, was abandoned by the Soviet leadership towards the end of the 1980s. It was replaced in 1989 by what was humorously referred to as the Sinatra Doctrine, according to which the communist countries were set free to 'do it your way' (Arias-King 2005). After this, democratization spread like wildfire.

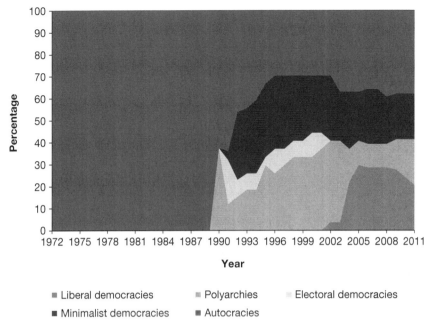

Figure 6.5 Distribution of political regimes in Eastern Europe, 1972 to 2011

The Eastern European region witnessed anything but a gradual development (Mason 1996; Møller 2009) (Figure 6.5). The juncture in 1989 to 1991 was followed by a democratic explosion as almost 70 percent of all of the countries became democracies. It is necessary to keep in mind that the number of countries increased dramatically over the course of the period – from around nine to 29 (not including Mongolia) – as a result of the collapse of the Soviet Union, the disintegration of Yugoslavia, and the division of Czechoslovakia (Mason 1996: ch. 3).

This is probably the region in which the arguments in favor of operating with a fourth wave are the strongest, not least because the upheavals in the immediate aftermath of 1989 to 1991 were superseded by a remarkable stabilization in the late 1990s and the 2000s. Whereas the minimalist democracies dominate the first years, the polyarchies and liberal democracies slowly began making inroads. At the same time, one can identify a consolidation among the autocracies. The total share of the non-democratic countries is by and large stable after the mid-1990s. A few countries, Serbia and Montenegro among them, eased into the democratic category. Conversely, Russia left this category after Vladimir Putin took a firm grip on the reins of power. More particularly, in East-Central Europe, the liberal democracies have made progress, while Central Asia and parts of the Caucasus are marked by repressive rulership. In that sense, the post-communist countries moved towards the extremes after the communist breakdown, a pattern which 'locked in' rather quickly (Kitschelt 2003: 49).

Sub-Saharan Africa

We now turn our attention to Sub-Saharan Africa. As Figure 6.6 demonstrates, this region was largely populated by autocracies as recently as the end of the 1980s (cf. van de Walle 2002: 66–67). In fact, there was a negative development in the 1980s as the percentage of democracies withered from more than 10 percent to slightly above 5 percent.

In the course of the 1990s, however, the democratic wave began to make itself felt in Africa south of the Sahara (Bratton & van de Walle 1997; van de Walle 2002). Almost half of the countries in this region could therefore be found among our four types of democracy in the late 2000s, although a significant decline, including countries such as the Central African Republic, Madagascar, Mozambique, and Nigeria, moving back into the set of autocracies, has recently been registered. This development underlines the importance of the 1989 watershed in general and shows that it had salient effects outside of the post-communist setting – thus lending some support to the fourth wave thesis. Other than that, considerable differences persist vis-à-vis the other regions we have dealt with. In the case of Sub-Saharan Africa, there is a salient predominance of minimalist democracies. The other aspect of this development is that it is almost impossible to find examples of genuine liberal democracies on the African continent (van de Walle 2002). In fact, Cape Verde is alone in this category. However, we do find a number of polyarchies towards the end of the period: Benin, Ghana, Mauritius, Namibia, São Tomé & Príncipe, and South Africa. Even though it generally makes sense to talk about democratic progress in the post-Cold

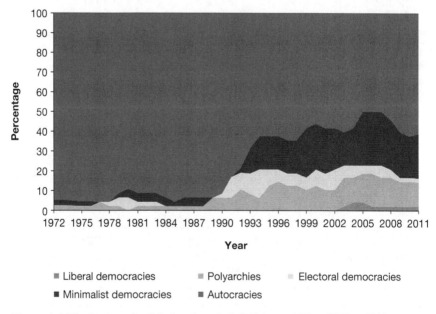

Figure 6.6 Distribution of political regimes in Sub-Saharan Africa, 1972 to 2011

War era, the Sub-Saharan Africa region has by and large been unable to democ-ratize in depth, and today it is the gray zone region *par excellence.*

The Middle East and Northern Africa

The final region we examine is the Middle East and Northern Africa. It is no coincidence that we have reserved this region for last. This chapter follows the third wave around the world – from the early beginnings in the 1970s via the new momentum it gained in the 1980s to the almost total flooding in the 1990s and 2000s. However, the Middle East and Northern Africa have remained virtually untouched by the wave (Stepan & Robertson 2003; Bellin 2004; Diamond 2010: 93). Until the Arab Upheavals, which began in January 2011, no new democracies had entered and gained foothold, as is clearly illustrated in Figure 6.7.

At the very beginning of the period, Lebanon was a democracy but a devastating civil war soon changed this. Hence, Israel has been the only democracy, but even Israel has not attained status as a liberal democracy according to our tallying. At times, Israel has been wallowing among the group of electoral democracies but most of the time it has been situated in the set of polyarchies. Notice also that the Arab Upheavals have had little impact so far. At the time of writing, only Tunisia has left the autocratic camp as it became a minimalist democracy in 2011.

In sum, while the Middle East and Northern Africa generally did not really stand out from Sub-Saharan Africa, Eastern Europe, and most of Asia in terms of the

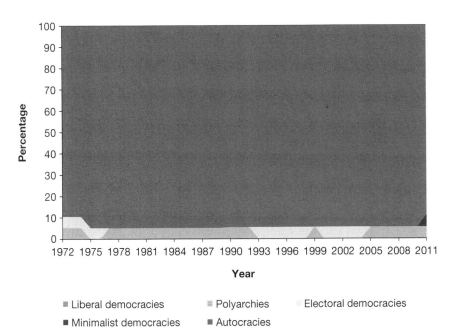

Figure 6.7 Distribution of political regimes in the Middle East and Northern Africa, 1972 to 2011

share of democracies until the third wave of democratization, the area now stands out as an autocratic island in an increasingly democratic sea. In this connection, it seems appropriate to take a brief detour to one of the hot topics of recent years, namely the American-led military intervention in Iraq. Our overview shows that the overthrow of Saddam Hussein in Iraq clearly did not trigger the domino effect that many politicians and some researchers had predicted (cf. Snyder 2003; Mearsheimer 2005).[3] In other words, there were no democratic revolutions in adjacent regions of the Middle East and North Africa as a reaction to the occupation. Instead, both before and after the intervention, the status quo has ruled, and both periods therefore stand in sharp contrast to the developments in the rest of the world. The Arab Upheavals may mark the end of this impasse but it is still too early to tell.

A reverse wave in the offing?

What does the broader picture look like if we attempt to tie the preceding observations to the debate about gray zone democracies, including the claim about a gap between electoral and liberal democracy? Did the democratic pessimists have cause for their assessments in the first place? And have recent developments confirmed their fears?

Our answer to both questions is a conditioned 'No'. We have already demonstrated that there was never any significant gap between electoral and liberal democracies. In addition, even though there was at least a noteworthy ratio of electoral democracies during the second half of the 1990s when Diamond and Zakaria carried out their analyses, this tendency no longer exists. On the other hand, the minimalist democracies obviously dominate among the new democracies. This lends some credence to the general idea of a gray zone. Quite a few countries have left the autocratic camp without proceeding all the way to the set of liberal democracies. Nonetheless, we have witnessed a positive development over recent decades, even after the optimists have had to yield to the pessimists in the literature (see Table 6.1).

Most recently, however, this situation has changed. As reported in Table 6.1, during the period from 2005 to 2011 we have witnessed a marginal decline in both the number and share of democracies: four countries and two percentage points, respectively. This decline has meant that the overall proportion of democracies is presently back at the same level as for 1995. It was around that time that the pessimists began their warnings. However, as the number of democracies was actually slowly increasing up until 2005, the latest one-and-a-half decades have rather been characterized by a standstill than a decrease. Furthermore, and importantly, the distribution of countries among the different types of democracies reflects a democratic deepening since the mid-1990s as both the number and share of liberal democracies are obviously much higher now than back then.

The literature on democratization has not overlooked the setback after 2005. According to some of the researchers who introduced the democratic pessimism in the 1990s, we are witnessing the dying gasps of the third wave. In the late 2000s,

Table 6.1 Number and share of countries linked to political regime types, selected years

	1972	1988	1995	2005	2007	2009	2011
Autocracies	108	98	76	69	72	78	78
	(72)	(59)	(40)	(36)	(37)	(40)	(40)
Minimalist democracies	6	8	34	37	33	31	33
	(4)	(5)	(18)	(19)	(17)	(16)	(17)
Electoral democracies	5	14	18	7	10	8	7
	(3)	(8)	(9)	(4)	(5)	(4)	(4)
Polyarchies	13	22	33	26	26	27	28
	(9)	(13)	(17)	(14)	(13)	(14)	(14)
Liberal democracies	18	23	30	53	52	50	49
	(12)	(14)	(16)	(28)	(27)	(26)	(25)

Note: Percentages in parentheses.

Arch Puddington (2008) and Larry Diamond[4] (2008) predicted a turnaround in the near future. Puddington's article bears the telling title *Is the Tide Turning?*; Diamond's, *The Democratic Rollback*. The backdrop of these writings was that the average Freedom House scores of political rights and civil liberties globally had developed in a negative direction in both 2006 and 2007. It was the first time in one-and-a-half decades that there was such a decline two years in a row, and the scores for 2008 to 2011 have continued this trend. According to the pessimists, this is merely the beginning. Diamond's (2008) diagnosis was that no less than 50 democracies are in danger: a handful of Asian countries, most of the countries in Latin America, and virtually all of the new democracies in Sub-Saharan Africa. Diamond was particularly alarmed by the negative development in a number of populous and strategically important countries: Russia, Venezuela, Nigeria, and Thailand.

Nevertheless, our descriptive analysis provides some ammunition for arguing that one should not be overly pessimistic on behalf of democracy in today's world. As reported in Table 6.1, the recent decrease is still relatively minor. Moreover, if we base our conclusions on the POLITY IV dataset – in the way we did in the previous chapter – there is even less reason to be pessimistic. Here, the proportion of democracies is much higher throughout the 2000s than in the mid-1990s, and there are as many democracies as ever in recent years. The regional developments also feed into this discussion. Most importantly, East-Central Europe and most of Latin America have proven resiliently democratic in the 2000s. The latter region is particularly interesting. In the 20th century, Latin America could be seen as a kind of democratic bell-wether. When waves were in the ascendancy, democracy made great strides; when reverse waves set in, autocracy quickly re-emerged. This change-ability now seems a thing of the past, although recent developments in Venezuela, Nicaragua, and Honduras may be said to slightly question this interpretation.

Why have the democratic gains after 1989 to 1991 proved so resilient? Arguably, democracy as a principle of legitimate political rule is still peerless.

Indeed, no alternative seems to be forthcoming. Here lies the great contrast with, for example, the interwar years, in which communism and fascism offered just such alternatives. According to Puddington (2010), only China presents some kind of an alternative but this autocratic regime has so far not really lent itself to export. This indicates that the democratic wave is more robust than the pessimist has allowed. When democracy can so obviously be on the defensive – Puddington (2010) lists the financial crisis, the wars in Iraq and Afghanistan, and the flourishing of China and Russia – and still broadly hold its own, it is difficult to envisage an actual backlash looming. It is probably for this reason that Puddington (2010) has recently turned much less alarmist. His new view seems to be that the present democratic wave is relatively robust (see also Diamond 2011). Somewhat paradoxically, the historically rather unique resilience in the face of crisis may be the most important conclusion to draw based on the marginal fall in the proportion of democracies that we have seen lately.

Conclusions

In this chapter we have attempted to provide a more elaborate overview of regime developments since the early 1970s. In doing so, we have attempted to investigate two separate issues. The first is the claims of the democratic pessimists, discussed above. The second is the empirical support for distinguishing between a third and a fourth wave of democratization.

Regarding this second issue, the disaggregated analysis made for yet more nuances to the picture painted in the previous chapter. In a majority of the examined regions and on the global level, we did in fact identify an important change in the dynamics around 1989 to 1991. However, it was the thinner types of democracy, in particular minimalist democracy, which spread the most after 1989. Only a decade later, from the late 1990s onwards, was the development followed by a large increase in liberal democracies. These developments indicate that the third wave contains more undercurrents than just that postulated by the fourth wave thesis, which might be taken as an argument against dividing the wave into two.

Other than that, the regional overviews have shown that the third wave has made significant onslaughts in all parts of the world, with the sole exception of the Middle East and Northern Africa; but we have also seen that most regions distinguished themselves somewhat from the global picture. If we attempt to capture this analytically, two important differences must be taken into consideration. The first concerns the dynamics of the democratic transitions and stability, while the second is tied to the relative distribution between the various types. On the global level, we see a gradual development, the consequence of which has been that authoritarian regimes remain the largest group, that the second-largest category is that of liberal democracy, and that this category is followed by minimalist democracies. This gradualist development is visible in most regions, although significant exceptions are also found. East-Central Europe and Sub-Saharan Africa, both of which practically democratized via a 'big bang' logic, are the most remarkable, but the development in Western Europe also proceeded by leaps and bounds rather than incremental steps. The global–regional differences are far greater as regards the relative distribution. Western Europe makes up one end of the spectrum, as it consists almost solely of liberal democracies. The Americas, where autocracy has been close to being an extinct species, follows. At the other end of the spectrum are the Middle East and Northern Africa. South and East Asia and Sub-Saharan Africa are also characterized by quite a few autocracies but in the former the share of liberal democracies and polyarchies is much higher than in the latter.

Finally, we have seen that the lack of rough-and-ready progress in the development of liberal democracy has led a number of scholars to sound the alarm. In this connection, we have argued that one should think twice about the possible advent of a significant democratic rollback. Processes of democratization have usually been messy, with lots of movement back and forth. In a long-term perspective this bumpy road has led to a more democratic world, but it has done so haltingly and with more than occasional setbacks. The one-and-a-half decades after 1989 – showing a remarkable increase in the number of democracies – thus stand out as relatively exceptional. Seen in this light it is not too surprising that this trend has recently changed. Furthermore, as Renske Doorenspleet (2000: 400–401) points out, the general absence of past reverse waves of democracy may be taken as a warning against expecting the advent of an actual large-scale decrease. Periods of seeming democratic crisis have instead been characterized by "trendless fluctuation". Possibly, we have entered yet another of these periods, just as was the case following the end of Huntington's second wave. However, we now move our focus away from descriptive overviews to theoretical explanations of democratization and democratic stability.

Part III

Causes

Democracy – how and why?

7 Modernization theory

In the first two parts of this book we have discussed what the concept of democracy covers, we have accounted for the development that brought about the return of democracy in the 19th century, and we have described the trends of democratization over the past 200 years. We have now come to the third part, where we wrestle with the most important attempts at explaining processes of democratization and democratic stability. This chapter is about the relationship between socio-economic development and democracy. A brief detour to East Asia helps set the stage. As late as the 1980s, the three Asian tigers – South Korea, Taiwan, and Singapore – appeared to be shining examples of how increased wealth, comprehensive investments in education, and the subsequent cultural changes could easily be reconciled with an autocratic regime. For this very reason, the three countries were used to challenge the most predominant theoretical account of democratic growth, namely modernization theory, according to which socio-economic development and democracy go together. The three tigers were taken to provide evidence that democracy did not necessarily follow economic development (see Fukuyama 2010: xiii) – at least not in East Asia.

Then, in the 1980s and 1990s, South Korea and Taiwan turned their backs on autocracy and today the two countries are instead marshaled as evidence that modernization actually erodes authoritarianism from within and paves the way for democracy. The East Asian course of events thus reflects the ups and downs in the standing of modernization theory over the past half century. First, the stock of the theory was at a premium, then it fell under par, and most recently it has received a new injection of capital (see Ross 2001: 357). But why have we seen these fluctuations? This is the main question to be answered in this chapter.

Lipset's perspective

As part of the systematic development of modernization theory in the late 1950s and early 1960s, Seymour Martin Lipset (1959) wrote his ground-breaking article, 'Some Social Requisites of Democracy'. Lipset's premise was that there is a positive relationship between democracy and socio-economic development. According to Lipset (1959: 75), this claim can be traced all the way back to Aristotle and summarized in the dictum: "The more well-to-do a nation, the greater the chances that it will sustain democracy."

To make sense of this association, Lipset draws attention to a number of mechanisms leading from economic development to democracy. The most important of these relates to the level of education, which typically increases with prosperity. Access to higher education promotes norms for social and political tolerance while simultaneously reducing misinformation and myths. Moreover, increased prosperity contributes to the class struggle developing from a zero-sum to a plus-sum game. The working classes therefore have a strong incentive to abandon their revolutionary plans and instead pursue a gradualist strategy. "Only those who have nothing to lose ever revolt," as Lipset (1959: 83) quotes Alexis de Tocqueville. Finally, socio-economic development strengthens both the middle class and civil society that are normally carriers of democratic values.

Can these theoretical expectations be corroborated empirically? Lipset assesses the relationship by examining Europe (and the USA, Canada, New Zealand, and Australia) and Latin America. In both areas, the relatively democratic countries are on average wealthier, more industrialized, have a higher level of education, and are more urbanized than the relatively non-democratic countries. Against that background, Lipset concludes that the level of socio-economic development is decisive for democracy.

Modernization theory and its critics

Lipset's modernization theory set the agenda for the emerging literature on the determinants of democracy; indeed his 1959 article arguably inaugurated this new field of research. What is more, as we document below, the relationship postulated by modernization theory has proven to be rather robust. However, due to the very circumstance that Lipset's theory has been agenda-setting, it has also raised numerous objections. In order to understand these objections, it is necessary to proceed in a roundabout way. The criticism has not just been directed towards Lipset's article; it has also targeted the classical tradition, which modernization theory draws upon. The fundamental logic of modernization theory already pervades much of the economic and political sociology of the 19th century (Fukuyama 2010). Karl Marx directly emphasized how capitalistic production (basis) found its political expression (superstructure) in bourgeois democracy, although he viewed this as a caricature of democracy, because the masses did not have any genuine influence. Émile Durkheim pointed out how economic development led to new patterns of cultural organization – just like a biological mechanism changes as a result of evolution – and Max Weber's works were devoted to capturing and elucidating the roots of the rationalization processes which created the modern West.

More particularly, the famous contrasts of 19th-century sociology – "status/contract; mechanical/organic solidarity; *Gemeinschaft/Gesellschaft*; charismatic/bureaucratic-rational authority" (Fukuyama 2010: xi; cf. Mills 1959) – are meant to capture the changes produced by modernization processes. These contrasts follow from the process of structural differentiation which, according to the classical sociologists, in particular Weber and Durkheim, came to characterize the

West, and which has been summarized in nine staggering developments (Holmes 1979: 115–116, fn. 7):

1   The privatization of religion.
2   The rise of territorial states with increasingly bureaucratic administrations.
3   The emergence of rational capitalism.
4   The specialization of science on the basis of rigorous quantitatively-hypothetical-experimental techniques.
5   The release of art from civic and religious functions.
6   The democratization of mass politics through representative institutions and the eventual stabilization of a universal franchise.
7   The shrinkage of the basic kinship unit to the small and increasingly one-generational nuclear family.
8   The birth of universal-compulsory education.
9   The positivization of law or the shift in the basis of legality from immutable 'natural law' to formal procedures for changing legal codes in an orderly way.

Historically, the first of these structural differentiations is the split between religious and secular power in medieval Christendom (see Chapter 4), one of the "most crucial steps toward the clear differentiation between the polity and total society, toward the proliferation of quasi-autonomous social domains" (Holmes 1979: 125). But the process further increased via what Weber described as the rationalization of the West, including bureaucratic, religious, and economic rationalization (see Weber 2003 [1927]: 312; also Collins 1986: 69).

These processes of structural differentiation, and Durkheim's holistic logic in particular, were – as the name indicates – the point of departure for Gabriel Almond's post-World War II work on 'structural-functionalism' (see Almond & Coleman 1960; Almond & Powell 1966). Almond's grand collaborative project consisted of developing an analytical framework based on systems theory, which could be applied to developed and developing countries alike. In that sense, this body of theory is obviously infused by a modernization perspective, as the conditions in the developed countries are regarded as the end-point towards which the developing countries will logically move. Meanwhile, the perspective was also becoming popular within economics. Most famous is Walt Rostow's (1960) *The Stages of Economic Growth: A Non-Communist Manifesto*, which attempted to flesh out an alternative to Marxist development theory. Rostow portrayed economic development as a linear process which was possibly sparked by external factors (the diffusion of technology), but which was otherwise endogenous to a given society and could be set in motion anywhere.

Generally speaking, modernization theory, classical and modern alike, is thus imbued with developmental optimism. The various versions of modernization theory conceived in the 1950s and 1960s directly or indirectly rest upon the premise that all countries will eventually follow the Western itinerary towards prosperity and democracy. This is the point that many critics have dwelled upon.[1] An examination of this criticism better enables us to understand why decisive aspects of modernization theory – including Lipset's perspective – have subsequently been revised.

The revisionists of the 1960s

Anthropologists were among the first to react against the developmental optimism of modernization theory. Samuel P. Huntington (1971) summarized these reactions with the term 'modernization revisionists'. The fundamental charge of the revisionists was that the dichotomy between modern and traditional is misleading, for two reasons. First, economic development can strengthen – or perhaps even lead to the 'rediscovery' of – traditional institutions. Second, the traditional institutions often encourage modernization.

More specifically, the revisionists noted that even though economic modernization since World War II reached the most remote corners of the world (albeit to varying degrees), it did not necessarily undermine traditional social institutions such as tribal mentality, ethnicity, the patron–client relationship, and caste relations. For example, Lloyd and Susanne Rudolph (1967) provided a large-scale analysis of the development of India before and after independence. Their somewhat startling conclusion was that modernization had actually reinforced, not weakened, the country's elaborate caste system. Moreover, they argued that this reinforcement of the caste system was paradoxically part of the explanation for India's surprising democratic success. The free elections had politicized the caste system in such a manner that the castes had organized themselves as vehicles for achieving political influence through the party system. In the short run, this strengthened the traditional values in society and contributed to counterbalancing individualism. At the same time, however, this mobilization ensured increased participation in the elections and facilitated political stability, which in turn helped explain why India's impoverished peasant society was able to maintain a democracy despite what modernization theory would predict (cf. Randall & Theobald 1998: 48–52).

Others have noted that modernization and democratization alike often led to reactions in the form of political, ethnic, or religious mobilization. The Russian Revolution in 1917 has been taken to provide evidence of the former. The Tsarist efforts to modernize from above facilitated a communist reign of terror, made possible by a brief political opening in 1917. Another well-known example of ethnic mobilization is the Nigerian civil war in the 1960s, which many researchers have attributed to the post-war modernization process (Randall & Theobald 1998: 54–61). Finally, the Iranian Islamic Revolution has been explained along the same lines. Having assumed power in 1925, the Pahlavi Dynasty launched a large-scale modernization program strongly inspired by Kemal Atatürk's reforms in Turkey. The strains of this forced modernization process enabled Ayatollah Khomeini to carry out the Islamic Revolution of 1979. The Shah was overthrown and replaced with a clerical regime, which was unprecedented in Shi'ism. According to the revisionists, this development was a blatant example of modernization supporting and redefining traditional institutions (Randall & Theobald 1998: 62–70). More generally, one may argue that political Islam, or Islamism, should be viewed as a reaction to modernization. According to this interpretation, 20th-century Islamism (the movement is often dated back to the establishment of the Egyptian Muslim Brotherhood in 1928) is basically a corollary, or even offshoot, of the Western modernization process.

Seen from the higher ground, these theoretical reactions to modernization theory sparked a much-needed dialogue between anthropologists and political scientists. Many of the messages from anthropology were in fact picked up by political scientists. Since then, it has become standard for political scientists to point out how development does not necessarily imply that developing countries will re-create themselves in a Western image. While people may well be drinking Coca-Cola and watching MTV in the most remote corners of the globe, diversity still prevails under the globalized surface. "The essence of Western civilization is the Magna Carta not the Magna Mac . . . [and] the fact that non-Westerners may bite into the latter has no implications for their accepting the former," as Huntington (1996: 58) has put it.

Nonetheless, it is important to emphasize that modernization revisionists also – in their own way – can be situated within the modernization paradigm. While they did indeed raise objections about the developmental optimism inherent in modernization theory and about its focus on a single path to prosperity and democracy, economic and political development was, nevertheless, also the trigger in their analyses.

Huntington and political (dis)order

In the 1960s, Huntington initiated another action against modernization theory. Whole-hearted modernization theorists expected that all of the developing countries had begun their respective journeys towards prosperity and democracy; and that decolonization was the first step on this journey. This, however, was not how Huntington (1968) saw realities when glancing at the world in the 1960s (see Munck & Snyder 2007: 221). Instead of progress and stability, he saw chronic underdevelopment, political decay, conflict, and lawlessness. Huntington con-cluded that these detrimental developments piggybacked the efforts to modernize. Independence and access to new technology facilitated a violent politicization, which the weak political institutions in the developing countries could not channel. The result was conflict and poor governance.

Against this background, Huntington reached the rather simple conclusion that only strong political institutions could enable developing countries to navigate the waters between the Scylla of modernization and the Charybdis of tradition. Above all, well-organized parties were needed to channel mobilization in the political arena under orderly conditions. Conversely, whether or not the political institutions were democratic was unimportant. According to Huntington's (1968: 1) dictum: "The most important political distinction among countries concerns not their form of government but their degree of government." In the communist countries in the Eastern Bloc as well as the democratic countries in Western Europe and North

America, the level of government was high because the political institutions were solid. These two groups of countries therefore had more in common than they had respectively with countries in the third world with a low degree of government, whether or not these were democratic. Differently put, democracy and development did not necessarily go hand in hand. Huntington's challenge to Lipset and others was that they could actually work at cross-purposes (see also Randall & Theobald 1998: 86–119; Fukuyama 2010).

Dependency theory and bureaucratic-authoritarian regimes

Huntington at least accepted that development could occur if only the political conditions were auspicious. A far more radical critique came from the so-called dependency theorists. The challenge here, which drew upon Marxist theory in general and Lenin's writings (1999 [1916]) about imperialism in particular, was that modernization theorists ignored the structure of the international economic system (Randall & Theobald 1998: 120–165). The high level of development in the Western world rested on the underdevelopment of the rest of the world. Basically, the center exploiting the periphery was what enabled the continued development of the West. Moreover, the periphery, that is, the developing countries, did not stand any chance of making a dent in this asymmetrical dependency relationship because they were locked into an unequal economic system as the suppliers of raw materials. The Western countries had a privileged market access and used their economic muscle and the existing institutions to maintain this imbalance (Frank 1966; see also Wallerstein 1974, 1980, 1989; Cardoso & Faletto 1979). Thus, dependency theory may be perceived as the polar opposite of modernization theory, at least as regards the expectations about the future of the developing countries. The message is that the periphery is unable – economically as well as politically – to develop due to the asymmetrical dependency. In this sense, this is developmental pessimism through and through.

Guillermo O'Donnell (1973) developed a more refined critique, which shared some of the assumptions found in dependency theory. In a ground-breaking analysis of what he referred to as the 'bureaucratic authoritarianism' of South America, he drew attention to a conspicuous paradox. A number of South American countries failed to maintain democracy as they underwent modernization processes. Instead, autocracy piggybacked on modernization. More specifically, the examples here are Brazil in the period from 1964 to 1985, Argentina in 1966 to 1970 and again in 1976 to 1983, Uruguay in 1973 to 1985, and Chile in 1973 to 1990. O'Donnell notes that these instances of democratic breakdown were also the wealthiest South American countries, which is at odds with Lipset's theory. According to O'Donnell, this was no coincidence. This is where he draws upon dependency theory as he outlines three consequences of modernization in countries that are locked into structural asymmetry with the Western world (cf. Mahoney 2003a: 153).

First, countries in such a situation of dependency will have great difficulty moving up the ladder of development by shifting from producing low-quality primary products to high-quality industrial products. A partial shift may occur under protectionist policies, where industry becomes able to produce relatively unsophisticated consumer goods. But balance-of-payment problems and inflation will eventually render it necessary to convert production in the direction of goods of higher quality. This requires a more market-friendly tack from the government as well in order to ensure the requisite foreign investments. Second, O'Donnell argues that the working class is strengthened considerably during the protectionist phase, politically as well as economically. But the same class is the first and principal victim when the government pursues more liberal economic policies. It therefore takes to the streets. The ensuing strikes and protests exacerbate the economic situation, which is already dire enough to warrant the new, market-friendly approach. Third, the protectionist phase, where the state controls economic privileges, paves the way for technocrats making advances in the private sector as well as the state apparatus, including the military.

This combination sets the stage for an unholy alliance between the technocrats in the private and public sectors. When crisis hits – and the democratic right to protest exacerbates it – the technocrats will carry out a coup d'état. The result is a bureaucratic-authoritarian regime; that is, a technocrat-led autocracy, which is capable of hard-handedly suppressing any opposition but is nevertheless marked by some measure of respect for rules. The most fascinating aspect of the story is that it is an intermediate level of modernization that strengthens the non-democratic coalition and creates the crisis leading up to the reintroduction of autocracy. According to O'Donnell, this is why the most prosperous South American countries were subjected to bureaucratic-authoritarian rule in the 1960s and 1970s, meaning that modernization in these countries has had the opposite effect to what Lipset would have expected.

A glance at the exceptions

The best theoretical objections to modernization theory are characterized by the fact that they build on empirical exceptions. O'Donnell's study of the relatively wealthy South American autocratic regimes provides a telling example. As such, we have already touched upon several of the prominent failings of modernization theory. However, it still seems worthwhile to gather the threads by providing an overview of the possible deviants.

A general challenge to Lipset's thesis may be found by going back in time to the period immediately after the return of democracy in the 19th century. Democracy first struck root in the most developed countries in Northwestern Europe and the English-speaking settler colonies (i.e., Australia, Canada, New Zealand, and the USA). But that does not change the fact that many Western countries introduced and maintained democracy at a – by today's measures – low level of socio-economic development (Rustow 1970: 352; Ertman 1998: 475–477). In these cases, one may argue that prosperity first came after the introduction of democracy, not the other way around. At the same time, it is worth noting that many of the Western democracies proved resilient during periods of deep economic crisis. This is an important observation, as it has been argued that not only a low absolute level of economic development – the focus of modernization theory – has been lethal for democracy; short-term changes in the form of poor economic performance, such as inflation and negative growth rates, have been said to undermine regime legitimacy and therefore democratic stability (Lipset 1994: 7–10). What is more, this relationship appears to be especially strong in poor countries (Przeworski et al. 2000).

The political developments in interwar Europe are occasionally used to support this point about the fragility of democracy during crises. However, not all democracies broke down during the Great Depression. Thomas Ertman (1998: 475–477) thus points out that what is surprising about the interwar political situation is not that some European democracies fell but rather that so many survived. Ertman expressly grounds this point in modernization theory as he points out that the Western European countries were relatively poor in the first place and furthermore hit by the 1930s depression. All of these examples appear to challenge Lipset's notion of a fast and firm nexus between modernization and democratization. More generally, it is striking that so many Western countries could democratize and retain democracy despite low levels of development while almost all of the relatively modernized Latin American countries underwent democratic collapse after World War II. Bearing this in mind, it is possible to argue that the connection between the level of modernization and democracy has had a different character in different periods and in different areas. More specifically, much indicates that unique characteristics of the Western countries enabled democratization and democratic survival at lower levels of development than elsewhere (see, e.g., Weber 2005 [1904/5]; Hintze 1975 [1931]; Downing 1992; cf. ch. 4).[2]

However, exceptions are also found outside of the West in more recent periods. We have already described O'Donnell's South American deviants. Argentina, Chile, and Uruguay constitute a particular problem, as democracy collapsed in these countries despite their relatively high levels of socio-economic development. But three other groups of countries have also deviated from the general tendency. The first group consists of a number of oil-rich states concentrated in the Middle East. Countries such as Kuwait, the United Arab Emirates, Saudi Arabia, and Libya achieved high standards of living after the oil crisis in the 1970s. However, this rising affluence produced no democratic dividends. Insofar as the Middle Eastern oil exporters made political changes during this period, they shifted even further away from democracy by consolidating their respective versions of autocracy, which incidentally has not changed much since.[3]

The other group consists of the aforementioned developing countries in South and East Asia which achieved rather high levels of development before democratizing, while the third group consists of impoverished countries outside of the West that have been able to democratize and in some instances have seemingly consolidated democracy despite a lack of modernization. This group includes countries such as Botswana in Sub-Saharan Africa and Mongolia in Asia. Most of the countries in this category are, however, small island states and/or former British colonies, two conditions which have been emphasized in the literature as encouraging democracy (cf. Dahl & Tufte 1974; Clague et al. 2001; Anckar 2008). The island states (e.g., Jamaica, Trinidad & Tobago, Mauritius, and Micronesia) do not require a major power apparatus and are also often quite homogeneous, while former British colonies have adopted the British constitutional model and – because the British were (oftentimes) good at decentralizing – had relatively efficient public institutions when attaining independence. The most significant exception to all of these theories is therefore to be found in India's impoverished post-colonial democracy. India is indeed a former British colony, but it is neither an island nor of limited size, and is generally something of an enigma for democratization literature (Lijphart 1996).

The revival of modernization theory

Modernization theory has thus met constant (and fierce) criticism, and the various exceptions provided the critics with plenty of ammunition in the 1960s, 1970s, and 1980s. However, it is worth noting that most large-scale statistical analyses have found a robust association between the level of modernization and democracy (Diamond 1992; Burkhart & Lewis-Beck 1994; Epstein et al. 2006; Wucherpfennig & Deutsch 2009; Boix 2011).

Many of the deviant instances have also disappeared. The development in three regions is particularly interesting. As already mentioned, the most highly developed South American countries – Argentina, Brazil, Chile, and Uruguay – have had a rather unstable political experience since World War II; in fact, for the entire 20th century. They democratized relatively early on, but one or more military coups followed in every case. This lack of stability would appear to have subsided. Since the last wave of (re)democratizations in the 1970s and 1980s, democracy has held its ground. The relatively affluent autocratic regimes O'Donnell referred to simply do not exist any longer. As regards the former Eastern Bloc, the collapse of communism is to some extent a test of modernization theory in itself. For the time being, this test has fallen out to the advantage of the theory. Thus, the Central and Eastern European countries that boasted the highest levels of development in 1989 have managed best – democratically speaking – since throwing off the yoke of communism. Finally, except for Singapore, the Asian tigers mentioned at the beginning of this chapter have also changed their ways recently, in accordance with what modernization theory would predict (more on this below).

Neo-modernization theory

In the 1990s, Adam Przeworski and a group of collaborators set out to disentangle the threads of modernization theory once and for all. Things did not quite work out this way, as the analyses of Przeworski et al. (2000), collected in *Democracy and Development: Political Institutions and Well-Being in the World, 1950–1990*, have also subsequently been criticized (see, e.g., Boix & Stokes 2003; Epstein et al. 2006; Acemoglu et al. 2008, 2009; Boix 2011). The study is nevertheless interesting because it is so meticulous and has had so much influence on the field.

Przeworski and a group of PhD students collected a dataset that was intended to enable them to re-test the modernization thesis. Working with a minimalist conception of democracy, the initial conclusion was that there is a very strong and positive co-variation between modernization, as measured in terms of GDP per capita, and democracy. However, they argued that this relationship could have two different causes. First, it may be a result of modernization increasing the probability that a given country democratizes. It is this 'endogenous' explanation that is ordinarily presented under the banner of modernization theory. Second, there is the possibility that the level of wealth has no impact on the actual transition to democracy but instead only on the subsequent prospects for democratic survival. As Przeworski et al. (2000: 101) emphasize, this 'exogenous' explanation actually fits Lipset's original formulation, which precisely stated that wealthier countries are more likely to *sustain* democracy.[4]

Crucially, both causal relationships over time produce one and the same cross-spatial relationship between the standard of living and the political regime, although the logic is fundamentally different. This point builds on the well-established methodological issue that a relationship established across space (i.e., by comparing countries with one another) cannot readily establish a relationship across time (i.e., within the very same countries in the course of a specific period of time) (see Bartolini 1993).

Based on statistical tests of the two hypotheses, Przeworski et al.'s conclusion is unambiguous. It is above all the exogenous explanation – that is, the claim that modernization first and foremost has significance for the durability of democracy – which finds support, while the endogenous does not appear to have much to it (Przeworski et al. 2000: ch. 2). In short, the standard of living is not decisive for whether or not a country democratizes. The transition to democracy may be owing to many other factors such as war, the death of a dictator, negotiations between the regime and the opposition, external pressure, or simply popular uprising. But when the countries have first chosen the democratic path, the prospects for the survival of democracy are much greater in the developed countries whereas democracy often collapses in impoverished countries. Other than that, the findings of Przeworski et al. (2000: ch. 2) challenge both Huntington's and O'Donnell's works, dealt with above. Regarding Huntington, high economic growth actually stabilizes democracy rather than destabilizing it. Regarding O'Donnell, they basically show that his theory was built on the few outliers to the exogenous modernization relationship, in particular that of Argentina, by far the most affluent country to ever experience a democratic breakdown.

This version of modernization theory is sometimes referred to as neo-modernization theory. As should be fairly obvious, it is a rendering of the otherwise so very structural theory which is more open to the importance of agency in the transition to democracy. At the same time, it is less vulnerable to existing exceptions. A wealthy but undemocratic country such as Singapore, for example, poses no problem, as this affluent city-state has yet to democratize. However, on the basis of the analyses of Przeworski and collaborators, the expectation is that democracy would be safe should this happen. The same argument may be used in connection with the countries with a wealth of natural resources, especially oil. Here, however, the logic is less convincing, as another explanation is beckoning, namely the thesis about the so-called resource curse.

The resource curse

"No taxation without representation" was one of the famous slogans during the American Revolution. The American rebels demanded political rights in return for taxation, a demand that points back to a general historical mechanism which deserves some elucidation. In the early 1970s, Douglass North and Robert P. Thomas (1973) published a captivating little story about the emergence of the Western market economy. Their report revolved around the structure of the state apparatus, and they set about describing it in clear terms. They characterized the state as a *quid pro quo*, that is, a trade-off between the rulers and the ruled. The government sells – also in our day – law enforcement and social services to the citizens for hard cash. Basically, the state is an overgrown mafia organization that provides protection in exchange for protection money (see also Tilly 1984).[5]

Implicitly at least, North and Thomas' analysis may be said to draw upon the financial sociology (*Finanzsociologie*), which Rudolf Goldscheid (1958 [1925]) and Joseph A. Schumpeter (1991 [1917/1918]) formulated roughly 100 years ago (cf. Levi 1988). Goldscheid and Schumpeter attempted to diagnose the societal development by investigating how the state finances its activities. According to Schumpeter, the advent of the modern state was a consequence of a trade-off between rights and taxes. Without effective taxation, the European rulers could not survive in the anarchical international system of the late Middle Ages. But in return that had to give in to the privileged corporate groups of society in various ways. Taxation gave these upper strata a bargaining chip with which to systematically keep the state on a leash. In this mutual dependence – termed by Schumpeter (1991 [1917/1918]: 106) a "common exigency" – we find the origins of political representation as well as civil liberties.

Schumpeter's ideas have been dusted off and discussed in recent decades in an attempt at explaining why oil-rich countries – particularly those concentrated in the Middle East – so stubbornly refuse to introduce electoral rights, political liberties, and the rule of law. This is the so-called 'resource curse theory' or 'the paradox of plenty' (Karl 1998), which postulates that large deposits of natural resources can inhibit economic, political, and social development. Michael Ross (2001, 2012) has emphasized how the elite in today's oil-rich countries provide for themselves via two factors that did not play a role in the European state formation process: natural resources and development aid (see also Krasner 2005). The technical word is 'rentier states'; that is, state apparatuses that build on rents and where the authorities are therefore independent of their subjects' tax payments.

Besides severing the historical connection between taxation and rights and allowing the regime to bolster its support via patronage, at least two additional mechanisms have been emphasized in this literature. First, oil-induced economic growth does not advance the cultural and social changes which spur democratic development (see below). Second, oil revenues support the creation of a repressive apparatus which may be used to keep a lid on opposition forces. The theory about the resource curse is thereby able to account for at least parts of the Middle Eastern exception, as oil has functioned as an autocratic stabilizer. Seen in this light, the Middle Eastern outliers may actually serve to corroborate the modernization thesis. To quote an observation by Lipset (1959: 70) from the very article that sparked modernization theory,

> A deviant case, considered within a context which marshals the evidence on all relevant cases, often may actually strengthen the basic hypothesis if an intensive study of it reveals the special conditions which prevented the usual relationship from appearing.

More particularly, the resource curse theory contributes to exposing how the dependence of the rulers on the tax revenue paid by the ruled constitutes one of the mechanisms behind the relationship between modernization and democracy – and that the absence of this dependency has serious consequences for the prospects for democracy.[6] We now delve further into these mechanisms.

The mechanisms revisited

Despite its age, Lipset's proposition on a relationship between socio-economic development and democracy is alive and kicking. As already mentioned, even Przeworski et al.'s revision has recently taken flack. Most scholars seem to agree that the exogenous explanation holds water, as wealthy democracies virtually do not break down. However, recent analyses indicate that besides democratic stability modernization also encourages endogenous development in the form of democratic transitions (Boix & Stokes 2003; Epstein et al. 2006; Boix 2011).[7] For example, Carles Boix and Susan Stokes (2003) find a weak endogenous effect even in the period analyzed by Przeworski et al. (i.e., 1950–1990), but then go on to show that a much stronger endogenous relationship appeared during the period prior to 1950. This is indeed where we would expect to find it, as the distribution of regimes was already correlated with income in 1950, meaning that a post-1950 investigation would miss the formative modernization processes.

The question about the causal mechanisms underpinning such a relationship has been subjected to intense discussion. Tellingly, Boix and Stokes (2003: 518) expressly criticize Przeworski et al. for having no such mechanisms on offer. More generally, modernization theory has long suffered from being treated like a kind of 'black box' explanation. Researchers have demonstrated the general relationship but have had very little to say about the connections leading from modernization via the political actors to the political regime. This has presumably contributed to critics having a relatively easy time criticizing it. The few actual exceptions serve to pinpoint mechanisms via which modernization can foster processes of de-democratization, which was the objection raised by both the revisionists and scholars such as Huntington and O'Donnell. This critique has also been used in attempts to open the black box. The theory about the resource curse offers a good example. However, the connection between natural resources and political repression may above all be understood as a negative scope condition for modernization theory, as it underlines that modernization processes promoting democracy must come from below and provide citizens with economic and political muscle.

What about the more positive mechanisms? Only in the more recent decade have systematic efforts to lay these bare been carried out. The result of this body of research is that the black box has finally been pried open, at least to some extent (cf. Robinson 2006). According to Boix and Stokes (2003: 540), for example, democracy is caused by a set of societal changes brought about by development – especially increasing levels of equality – rather than by income in itself. This fits well with Lipset's effort to expose the causal mechanisms in his original article. As we have already described, Lipset mainly attributed the relationship to lower levels of inequality and increases in tolerance and moderation. The recent attempts to elucidate the mechanism to a large extent follow in Lipset's footsteps. A number of scholars have used a micro-economic approach to contribute to this research agenda. The argument may be summarized as follows:

> The reason why modernization is important in this model is that it is assumed to close the income gap between the elites and the masses, tempering the masses' interest in extensive redistribution and the elites' fear of it. Suppressing the masses' demands for democracy then becomes more costly than conceding democracy and so the elites concede democracy.
>
> (Welzel 2009: 85)

Rooted in this tradition, Boix (2003) and Daron Acemoglu and James Robinson (2006) emphasize that autocratic regimes cater to the interests of high-income groups. The elite accordingly oppose electoral rights because they are afraid democracy will lead to an increase in economic redistribution.[8]

However, the various contributions to modernization theory based on micro-economic approaches do not fully agree about which form the relationship takes. Whereas the relationship in the view of Boix (2003) is linear, Acemoglu and Robinson (2006: 35) argue that in situations with low inequality, the demand for democracy is limited, and in situations of high inequality, the elite have much to lose and therefore opt for repression, meaning that democracy is unlikely in either case. The probability of democratization is thus highest at a medium level of inequality. Thus, Acemoglu and Robinson expect the relationship between inequality and democracy to take on an inverted U-shape (cf. Ziblatt 2006: 320).

Przeworski (2005) has also recently contributed to this debate. Invoking his earlier empirical findings, he does not attempt to explain democratic transitions but only to explain why rich countries tend to be stable democracies.[9] Supposing that people dislike physical insecurity and risks, Przeworski proposes that when income increases, the gap between the well-being of people oppressed under an autocratic regime and electoral losers becomes larger, meaning that the elite's risk of losing safe income under democracy exceeds the potential gains of overturning democratic rule.

Interestingly, Przeworski (2005: 265) claims that basically the same relationship can be deduced by assuming "that people have preference for democracy, independent of income." This alternative interpretation provides a natural link to the alternative 'cultural' model suggested by Ronald Inglehart and Christian Welzel (2005, 2009). Critical of the micro-economic focus, Inglehart and Welzel emphasize that the masses' preference for democracy is neither constant nor always high. Rather, they argue, there is much variation in the cross-cultural demand for democracy.

However, Inglehart and Welzel do suggest that socio-economic development plays an important role through three stages. Socio-economic development influences the capabilities and security of the mass public. This leads to changes in values, which in turn have effects on the political regime type. This argument draws on Inglehart's (1977, 1997) earlier research on 'post-material' values. Inglehart's ground-breaking point, formulated in the 1970s with the Western countries in mind, was that the political opinions were largely a function of whether or not one has experienced economic hardships at an early point in one's life, the so-called 'scarcity hypothesis'. The development from a society of want, where the population is first and foremost occupied by attaining safety and food, to a wealthy society, promotes 'emancipatory' or 'self-expression' values such as gender equality (vs. patriarchy), tolerance (vs. conformity), autonomy (vs. authority), and freedom of expression (vs. security).

According to Inglehart and Welzel (2005, 2009), this is quite obvious when comparing the attitudes in wealthy and impoverished countries at specific points in time or the attitudes in the same countries before and after a development from poverty to wealth. This alternative causal mechanism connects macro-level structural developments – socio-economic development and democratic development – through a micro-level actor-centered linkage (see Figure 7.1; cf. Coleman 1990), as is also the case for the micro-economic approaches described above.

However, Inglehart and Welzel (2009) stress how the modernization logic is not to be understood as a one-track, straight and narrow path that is slavishly followed by all countries. At least partly accepting the insights of the modernization revisionists, Inglehart and Welzel state that modernization does not automatically mean that countries re-create themselves in a Western image.

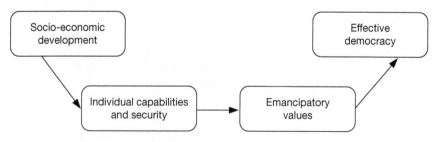

Figure 7.1 Inglehart and Welzel's causal model

History cannot be ignored, and the value-related changes are therefore filtered through an often fine-meshed cultural filter, meaning that the modernization processes will have different effects in, for instance, Muslim countries compared with Protestant or Catholic countries. To elaborate, it is not modernization in itself that creates the self-expression values. It is only in countries where socio-economic development is of such a nature that it is followed by cultural developments that it has a positive impact in terms of democracy. This explains why the superficial increase in the standard of living in the Middle Eastern petro-states has not led to any democratic development worth mentioning; the emancipatory values have simply not made inroads.

Even so, Inglehart and Welzel (2009) emphasize that fundamental modernization processes have a tendency to promote democracy wherever they occur. The speed will vary, but the direction remains the same. Inglehart and Welzel (2009) accordingly argue that there is reason to take heart in the formidable economic development in China in recent decades. In the longer term, the Chinese Communist Party will encounter great difficulty resisting the pressure to democratize simply because the new middle class will demand it, just as we have witnessed in South Korea and Taiwan in the 1980s and 1990s.

Finally, based on the Inglehart and Welzel research agenda the outlined relationship tends to be stronger for thicker than for thinner types of democracy. This is in fact a very important point for Inglehart and Welzel, and it is worth elaborating, as it may be said to have a more general relevance for modernization theory, and because it ties the discussion to our earlier distinctions between different definitions of democracy. Parts of the democratization literature contain the argument that, since the end of the Cold War, electoral democratization has been increasingly unconstrained by structural factors such as the level of modernization (Levitsky & Way 2010: 19; Schmitter 2010). Inglehart and Welzel, however, point out that the proliferation of third wave democracies, in spite of low modernization levels, has only tended to produce what we have termed minimalist and electoral democracies. The level of modernization is as relevant as ever as soon as we use a measure of what they term effective democracy by qualifying the electoral definitions with the rule of law (Alexander et al. 2012) – that is, by adopting definitions that are broadly similar to our concept of liberal democracy.

Conclusion

We are left with the impression of a relationship between socio-economic development and democracy which has proven quite durable in the longer term. Today, only few deny that modernization means something for the survival of democracy (but see Robinson 2006; Acemoglu et al. 2008, 2009). In fact, we can directly establish a threshold for when democracy is secure. Przeworski and Limongi (1997: 165) thus observe that:

> The simple fact is that during the period under our scrutiny or ever before, no democracy ever fell, regardless of everything else, in a country with a per capita income higher than that of Argentina in 1975.

More generally, Przeworski and Limongi point out that only five democracies have ever collapsed in countries that were at least half as prosperous as Argentina in 1974: Uruguay in 1973, Surinam in 1980, Chile in 1973, Fiji in 1987, and Greece in 1967. In other words, a country must be impoverished before democracy is in danger.

A number of recent analyses indicate that modernization also promotes democratic breakthroughs. This endogenous explanation is weaker than the exogenous explanation, however, as we cannot establish thresholds or predict anything about when a democracy breaks down. It is nonetheless possible to illustrate this point by returning to the East Asian tigers. In 1950, South Korea, Taiwan, and Singapore were level with developing countries in Sub-Saharan Africa. By the late 1980s, they had achieved a level of development almost resembling that of the Western European countries. As mentioned in the introduction to this chapter, the Tigers were – back then – often referred to in order to support the claim that democracy is a luxury that developing countries ought to wait to introduce; a well-ordered autocracy was emphasized as being better able to ensure long-term economic growth because it does not have to cater to the short-term interests of the population or the whining and bickering of elected politicians. This has been the 'Asian values' political blueprint which Singapore's dictator, Lee Kuan Yew, has forwarded as a deliberate alternative to the Western democratic model. Singapore has in fact maintained a de facto party (civilian) autocracy since 1959. However, the course of events has been strikingly different in South Korea and Taiwan. Things already started rumbling in South Korea in the 1980s, and the government in Seoul chose to hold free elections in 1987. Taiwan followed suit in the 1990s, and at the time of writing, Singapore is the only country to have maintained Lee Kuan Yew's autocratic ways.

In general, it has been something of a merry-go-round. In the 1950s and 1960s, the South and East Asian tigers fit modernization theory like a hand in a glove. They were impoverished autocracies. In the 1980s, they had suddenly become exceptions, as they were relatively modernized but remained autocratic. Finally, South Korea and Taiwan were 'brought into line' with their modernization level as a result of the political reforms of the 1980s and 1990s. This development in many ways serves as a mirror for the status of modernization theory. There have been repeated exceptions to Lipset's relationship between modernization and democracy. But they have always been rather few, they have become even fewer over time, and more recent work within the genre, such as that centered on the resource curse, has served to account for the most wayward cases. Regardless of how it is measured, modernization and democracy tend to go hand in hand – today as well as in the 1950s, when Lipset formulated the proposition. And even the recent proliferation of minimalist democracies does not really change this fact as the level of modernization remains crucial as soon as we substitute thinner for thicker definitions. In the next chapter, we shall see how modernization theory has also sparked a distinct focus on the social forces which have historically fought over regime change.

8   The social forces tradition

The historical relationship between socio-economic modernization and democracy is so robust that any plausible explanation of democratization must be based upon it. More particularly, a convincing explanation of democratization must explain why economic development and democracy go hand in hand. This is the premise for Dietrich Rueschemeyer, Evelyn Huber Stephens, and John Stephens' (1992) *Capitalist Development and Democracy*. However, Rueschemeyer et al. argue that the then existing interpretations of modernization theory failed to satisfy this requirement. As we described in the previous chapter, Lipset's version of modernization theory finds the causal link in factors such as higher levels of equality, the growth of the middle class, and the emergence of democracy-friendly values, partly due to increased access to education, all of which are understood to be driven by economic development.

This rendering of modernization theory is thus virtually devoid of a conflict perspective. Apart from the general focus on the middle class, the post-World War II modernization theorists did not distinguish between social classes and their respective interests in democratization. Instead, they conjured up the image of a harmonic, seamless, and virtually inevitable development towards democracy, as increased prosperity facilitates the social, cultural, and political reshaping of society. According to Rueschemeyer et al. (1992: ch. 2), this perspective does not fit with the fundamental premise of political development: that rights form in the wake of conflicts between rulers and their subjects, meaning that political change is generally the result of secular conflict between social classes. To quote Charles Tilly (2002: 123), rights are "historical products, outcomes of struggle" (see also Rustow 1970: 353–355, 362).

Historically, the right to vote has either been conquered by the masses or granted by the rulers (Przeworski 2009). In the former case, this has happened due to uprisings, coups, or revolutions. In the latter case, where the suffrage was further extended, the change was at least partly due to fears of such uprisings. This is nicely conveyed by the conservative argument for expanding the right to vote formulated by Lord Grey in connection with the expansion of suffrage in Great Britain in 1832: "reform to preserve." According to Rueschemeyer et al. (1992: ch. 3), all of this points towards the class struggle as the locus in which to find the causal mechanism underpinning the relationship between modernization and democracy.

This claim serves to set the stage for the comparative historical analyses of social forces and their impact upon the respective routes to democracy and autocracy. These explanations are almost always based upon secular class conflicts, particularly between the aristocracy, bourgeoisie, peasants, and the working class. This should not be equated with the micro-economic approaches described in the previous chapter, as the comparative historical analyses within the social forces tradition[1] are always contextual, meaning that they operate within specific historical scope conditions. To keep as many of these scope conditions as possible constant, we only discuss analyses dealing with the democratization occurring in Europe in the 19th and early 20th century.

What the focus on class conflict means is that large parts of the social forces tradition explicitly or implicitly operate in the shadow of modernization theory, as the whole point is to analyze the way in which economic development shifts the balance of power between the social forces in general and the classes in particular; which in turn contributes to the oscillation of the political pendulum. The underlying explanatory factor thus remains modernization, and the theories continue to attempt to explain democratization and/or democratic stability. As opposed to modernization theory, however, the class-based analyses are indebted to the Marxist notion that the economic basis determines the political superstructure via the mechanism referred to as class struggle – with the important nuance that forces and structures not directly related to socio-economic development have also been emphasized in some of the major works rooted in this tradition.

Class struggle as the driver of regime change

Just as with modernization theory, the social forces tradition draws upon some of the major breakthroughs of 19th- and 20th-century sociology, including those of Karl Marx and Max Weber. As an independent discipline, however, it is a relatively new field. Barrington Moore Jr. (1991 [1966]) sparked it in the mid-1960s with his publication of *Social Origins of Dictatorship and Democracy*. Moore wrote against the backdrop of classical modernization theory and the notion that all countries – independently of contextual factors – take the beaten path from modernization to democracy. Instead, Moore (1991 [1966]: xiv–xv) argues, there are multiple paths to modernization, determined by the relationship between the classes.

Recall at this point that the comparative historical analyses of social forces to some extent rest upon the Marxist coupling between the economic base and political superstructure. A number of scholars have expressly concluded that Moore carries out a (neo-)Marxist analysis (Rothman 1970: 62; Femia 1972: 40–41; Skocpol 1973). This point is understandable, since Moore traces both the ideology of the dominant classes and the political structure to the mode of production and also seems to argue that the ruling class always exploits subordinate classes, thereby basically making cultural factors epiphenomenal (Moore 1991 [1966]: 486). Nevertheless, it is important to note that Moore extensively revises

Marx's structural perspective. Moore thus emphasizes the causal importance of timing in the commercialization of agriculture and does not address the working class at all. In fact, one of his important points is that the communist revolutions occurred in predominantly agrarian societies, which Marx's class analysis cannot account for.

In continuation of Moore's work, a field of research has been developed which James Mahoney (2003a: 151–152) calls 'structuralism'. Structuralism emphasizes the various combinations of social structures, state structures, and international structures establishing the framework surrounding the actors' (particularly collective actors in the form of social classes) strategies and actions. This focus on structures pervades all of the works we discuss in this chapter, thus demonstrating Moore's seminal importance. Three other crucial features of comparative structural analyses of social forces and democracy should be highlighted (cf. Mahoney & Rueschemeyer 2003: 6). First, the aim is to shed light on actual causal relationships. Second, these relationships are always grounded in historical processes. Third, the studies usually deal with a relatively limited number of countries.

The latter two points require further elaboration. Beginning with the number of countries, the analyses of the relationship between class struggle and democratization mostly deal with Western Europe in the period from the French Revolution to World War II. It is hardly any mystery that Western Europe is at the center of attention for the social forces tradition. The general endeavor is to assess the impact of modernization from the class conflict perspective, and until World War II Europe and the former European settler colonies in the Americas and Oceania were virtually alone in exhibiting actual modernization and the associated shifts in the class structure (cf. Luebbert 1991). More generally, comparative historical analyses are somewhat idiosyncratic in the sense that they often do not aim to generalize beyond the cases dealt with (Mahoney & Rueschemeyer 2003: 7–8; Skocpol 1984: 376). As far as the historical processes are concerned, sequencing (i.e., the timing of factors) is attributed important explanatory potential. Moore shows that *when* an event occurs is often decisive for what kind of impact it will have (see also Tilly 1984: 14; Rueschemeyer et al. 1992: ch. 2).[2] Finally, it is important to note that the origins of democracy or autocracy are often traced further back in time than is the case with modernization theory proper. For example, Moore delves all the way back to the end of the Middle Ages, even though his objective is to account for the emergence of democracy, fascism, and communism in the 20th century.

No bourgeois, no democracy

In *Social Origins of Dictatorship and Democracy*, Moore addresses the question as to why Great Britain, the USA, and France were able to combine capitalism and democracy, whereas capitalism in Germany, Italy, and Japan went hand in hand with fascism in the interwar period. And, along these lines, why did Russia and China end up pursuing a communist path to modernization?

As indicated by the book's subtitle, *Lord and Peasant in the Making of the Modern World*, Moore finds the answer in the patterns of landholding. His general thesis is that the impact of industrialization upon society is determined by the encounter between the agrarian classes and the ascending bourgeoisie.[3] This encounter crystallizes into three routes. The first runs via that which he refers to as bourgeois revolutions – the English Civil War (1642–1651) and subsequent Glorious Revolution (1688–1689), the French Revolution (1789–1799), and the American Civil War (1861–1865) – which weakened the landowning aristocracy and strengthened the middle class, thereby paving the way for democracy. Second, Moore outlines an alternative capitalist route along which modernization was set in motion from above via an alliance between a strong landowning gentry and the bourgeoisie (with the latter as the 'junior' partner). The result here is fascism. The third route involves a scenario in which the bourgeoisie is insignificant, the rural elite is strong, and the revolutionary potential of the peasantry is high. Capitalism never gains a proper footing, and the peasants support a communist revolution.

Moore's analysis differs from the classical versions of the modernization literature for the simple reason that he has a sense of how modernization processes can have different characteristics and consequences. That said, his explanatory factors are somewhat vague, particularly in the actual country analyses. His three alternatives cannot be derived systematically from a set of explanatory variables that vary between the three respective routes. Tellingly, the literature contains considerable disagreement about how his analysis is actually to be understood (see, e.g., Femia 1972; Skocpol 1973; Stephens 1989; Mahoney 2003a: 137).

Nevertheless, widespread agreement exists that the work contributes to the formulation of two general hypotheses concerning the relationship between class structure and democratization (Mahoney 2003a: 138–139). According to the first hypothesis, a strong middle class is a necessary condition for democracy. In the words of Moore (1991 [1966]: 418) himself: "No bourgeois, no democracy." Democracy succeeded in Great Britain, France, and the USA for the very reason that the bourgeoisie avoided becoming the junior partner in an alliance with the landowners against the peasants. The second hypothesis proposes that the rural elite has traditionally posed the greatest barrier to democracy. According to Moore, the suppression of the peasants by this class paved the way for fascism in Germany and Japan, where the rural elite allied with the emerging bourgeoisie, and for communism in Russia and China, where the peasants revolted.

Ever since Moore's magisterial work was published, other researchers have lined up to test these explanations. Generally speaking, these studies have tended to challenge Moore's claims more than they have validated them. As regards countries that Moore himself did not study, the results are rather mixed. Countries such as Switzerland and Austria appear to support Moore's model, while the pathways of other countries obviously do not (Huber & Stephens 1995; Mahoney 2003a; Stephens & Kümmel 2003).

Moore (1991 [1966]: xiii) himself maintained that smaller countries had limited value as test material, as they usually copy the political destination of the larger countries. However, it is the new analyses of Moore's own countries – Great

Britain, the USA, France, Germany, Italy, Japan, Russia, India, and China – that have exposed the greatest problems. First, the English landowners were in fact overwhelmingly strong before and after the 17th-century revolution. Hence, it is difficult to interpret English democratization as the product of a dominant bourgeoisie. Second, and more problematically, a number of researchers have argued that the middle class has not been a steady guarantor of democracy. The bourgeoisie surely led the way in establishing civil liberties and the rule of law and delimiting the political influence of the landowners. However, when it comes to the extension of suffrage to the lower classes they have often been hostile, simply because it has not always been in the interests of the bourgeoisie (Mahoney 2003a: 138–145). In sum, Moore's model has a number of major shortcomings. However, works inspired by his reintroduction of the comparative historical research agenda have taught us much about the emergence of democracy (Mahoney 2003a: 137–152). The rest of this chapter describes some of these theoretical and empirical advances.

Democratization in 19th- and 20th-century Western Europe

The working class as the driver of democracy

Göran Therborn was one of the first to revisit Moore's core propositions and come up with an alternative. Like Moore, Therborn (1977) finds the source of democracy in industrialization and the subsequent capitalist development. Nonetheless, he eagerly emphasizes that it is the working class – not the bourgeoisie – that is responsible for the final breakthrough to modern democracy.

In order to understand Therborn's argument, we must pay attention to his definition of democracy. Therborn envisions a representative government and suffrage being extended to the entire adult population. Furthermore, the votes are to be weighted equally, the voters protected from intimidation by the state apparatus, and the electorate is to enjoy freedom of speech and assembly.[4] More generally, Therborn (1977: 10) operates with a number of different regime types. The most important are: actual 'dictatorship', where elections and the parliamentary principle[5] are obviously absent; 'exclusivist authoritarian' regimes which are characterized by limited suffrage and not the parliamentary principle; 'democratic exclusivist' regimes which are marked by limited suffrage but where the parliamentary principle is beginning to make inroads; and finally, 'democracy', which fulfills all of the criteria described above. In relation to the definitions presented in Chapter 3, a democratic exclusivist regime largely corresponds to that which we refer to as minimalist democracy whereas Therborn's definition of democracy corresponds to polyarchy.

Consequently, Therborn's treatment of the dependent variable differs from that of Moore. While it is somewhat vague as to precisely what Moore understands by democracy, he would most probably be ready to accept the criteria linked to a minimalist democracy.[6] This is first and foremost a consequence of Moore conceiving of democracy in relation to clear-cut alternatives such as fascism and communism. Therborn's definition is therefore much more demanding than Moore's definition, and his critique follows logically from his distinction between various types of democracy. Therborn argues that the grand bourgeois revolutions Moore describes did not lead to genuine democracy – but rather, at most, to a democratic exclusivist regime. While the bourgeoisie were responsible for a liberal constitution and, in time, for the parliamentary principle, they were not the driving force when it came to extending the right to vote to the entire population.

At the same time, Therborn writes against modernization theory. He emphasizes that democracy does not emerge from a calm and peaceful process initiated by increases in wealth, education, urbanization, and a larger middle class. Prior to World War I, only three capitalist countries could be characterized as democracies: Australia, New Zealand, and Norway. It was not until after World War I that universal suffrage and the parliamentary principle spread to a significant number of countries. According to Therborn (1977: 21), there is a simple reason why this is the case. The working class was the only consistent bearer of democratic values, and the demand for soldiers and industrial production resulting from the war meant that the working class found itself in a powerful position. In this way, the growth of the working class accounts for the relationship between modernization and democracy. However, the labor movement unto itself did not have the strength required to bring about democracy. As Figure 8.1 illustrates, the power of the labor movement had to be combined with one of four components to be effective.

One possibility was external pressure in the form of the military defeat of the autocratic regimes. This situation occurred in Austria, Finland, Germany, Italy, and indirectly in Sweden. In Norway and Belgium democratization instead resulted from pressure exerted by the working class combined with national mobilization in the form of the economic, ideological, and not least military integration of the general population for the national effort. In the third pathway, represented by the Danish case, the working class forged an alliance with the independent farmers. Finally, the last opportunity consisted of the working class allying with parts of an internally divided ruling elite. This occurred in France, the

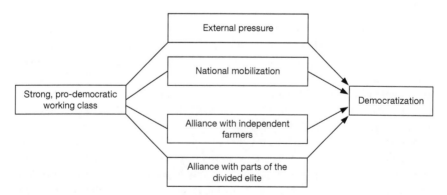

Figure 8.1 Therborn's paths to democratization

Netherlands, and Great Britain, and could only come about in the event that the lower classes were not perceived as posing a threat.

Taken together, although the working class could not bring democracy about on its own – it is a necessary but not sufficient condition – it played the absolute lead role in the performance on the modern breakthrough of democracy. According to Therborn, the sole exception to this rule is found in Switzerland, where democratization took place without a strong working class. Therborn's criticism of Moore offers a clear example of how definitions often have considerable influence on the conclusions. Therborn actually confirms Moore's fundamental idea when arguing that the bourgeois revolutions led to democratic exclusivist regimes. Yet, he arrives at a different overall conclusion because he is operating with a thicker definition of democracy.

A critical defense of Moore

John D. Stephens (1989; Rueschemeyer et al. 1992: ch. 4; Huber & Stephens 1995; Stephens & Kümmel 2003) has continued where Moore and Therborn left off. Stephens largely defends Moore's claims but also draws inspiration from Therborn and modifies both of them on important points. First, Stephens argues that Moore underestimates the significance of the working class in the final phases of democratization. Second, he argues that Moore paints an excessively positive portrait of the role of the bourgeoisie. Stephens (1989) reaches these conclusions after analyzing the Western European countries that democratized in the period from 1870 until 1920, including Germany, Austria, Italy, and Spain, where democracy collapsed in the interwar period. As Stephens disagrees with Moore that the development in the smaller countries was determined by the developments in the larger neighboring countries, he deals with a broader sample of Western European countries. His analysis also differs from Moore's work in that it focuses on a period that is closer to the outcomes that Moore was attempting to explain. In fact, Stephens continues Moore's work by initiating his analysis in the period where Moore finishes his, namely the mid-1800s (Stephens 1989: 1020). Finally, he attempts to account for both the transition to democracy and its subsequent stability.

Stephens' definition of democracy corresponds to Therborn's (i.e., polyarchy), except for the fact that he delimits the requirement of universal suffrage so that it does not necessarily cover women. Against this background, Stephens (1989) concludes that the working class played a central role in the introduction of democracy – not so much in the early phases, where it was relatively weak, but all the more so in the later phases of democratization, where the working class constituted the only consistent advocate of suffrage extensions. Industrialization endowed the working class with unprecedented power, and the balance of power tipped in its favor in many countries prior to World War I. Like Therborn, Stephens thus rejects Moore's claim that the bourgeoisie was the most important driving force behind democracy. Great Britain and France were the only countries in which the bourgeoisie played a purely positive role for the ultimate introduction of democracy; that is, the development from an exclusivist constitutional democracy to equal and universal suffrage. In most countries, the bourgeoisie were against giving the working class a share in democracy. Nonetheless, democratizations proceeded for the most part without any revolutionary break, which Moore (1991 [1966]: 505–506) otherwise regarded as a necessary condition.

Stephens (1989) thus accepts much of Therborn's analysis. Yet he also argues that Therborn has a tendency to exaggerate the importance of the working class. Recall that Therborn holds Switzerland forth as the sole exception to the thesis about the working class as the motor power of democratization. Stephens qualifies this by referring to the case of Norway, where the working class cannot be credited with democratization, as a coalition of independent farmers and the middle class carried the load. Moreover, it was not so much the pressure from below that led to the repeated expansion of suffrage in Great Britain. Finally, the trajectories to democracy in Denmark and Sweden owed more to the independent farmers and middle class than to the workers. That said, the working class according to Stephens constitutes a very important driving force behind the achievement of universal suffrage in the European countries. Only France, Switzerland, Norway, and Denmark were completely democratic prior to 1918. The final breakthrough in the other countries analyzed by Stephens resulted from the social distortion in the wake of World War I. Basically, the ruling classes were weakened while the working class was strengthened, causing the political pendulum to oscillate (Stephens 1989: 1066).

Stephens also investigates the subsequent stability of democracy. Examining the democratic breakdowns in the interwar period, he reaches the following conclusion: a strong rural upper class is a necessary requirement for such breakdowns. In countries where the large landowners had been weakened, democracy was safe. Even though the rural elite in Great Britain was strong, the introduction of commercialized agriculture meant that its needs were less labor-intensive and suppressive. Italy, Spain, Germany, and Austria, on the other hand, were marked by an alliance between the rural upper class, the state, and the bourgeoisie, which led to the reintroduction of autocratic regimes. As opposed to Moore, however, Stephens (1989: 1066–1070) emphasizes that Austria was actually the only country in which the rural upper class was considerably stronger than its alliance partners. Nevertheless, Stephens broadly agrees with Moore's second main thesis: that the large landowners have historically been the enemy of democracy *par excellence*.

Rueschemeyer, Huber Stephens and Stephens have elaborated on these points and supplemented the analysis with other cases from Latin America and the Caribbean as well as the settler colonies in the USA, Canada, New Zealand, and Australia. Even though Rueschemeyer et al. (1992) add a number of explanatory factors, such as international influences and the strength of civil society, they claim to have uncovered a relatively simple causal mechanism connecting modernization and democracy. In a nutshell, industrialization (and capitalism) strengthens the working class and weakens the large landowners. As the working class is clearly interested in extending electoral rights to the lower strata of society, this process leads to modern democracy, albeit often via a sidestep or two.

This leads us to one of the strongest generalizations in democratization theory, namely that modern democracy requires a capitalist mode of production (a market economy), where the means of production are owned by private individuals or associations. In *The Road to Serfdom*, Friedrich August von Hayek (1944) has provided a classic treatment of this issue. He describes a number of ways in which a planned economy undermines liberal democracy. Conversely, Schumpeter (1974 [1942]: 284) expressly argues that planned economies are in principle compatible with (minimalist) democracy.

Subsequently, the democratization literature has widely acknowledged the assertion that a market economy would appear to be a necessary condition for democracy (Lipset 1994: 2–3; Dahl 1998: ch. 13). It is, however, not a sufficient condition for democracy. It is possible to combine a capitalist system with an autocratic regime, whereas achieving democracy in the absence of capitalism would appear well-nigh impossible. This proposition also finds empirical support, as there are no examples of full-fledged planned economies which have also been democratic (see Friedman 1962: ch. 1; Sartori 1987: 399–449; Berger 1992: 9). A number of researchers have also noted that modern capitalism reinforces the bourgeoisie, which according to Moore is the *sine qua non* of democracy. This is where Rueschemeyer et al.'s intervention differs. While they accept the general focus on capitalism, they direct attention from the bourgeoisie to the working class:

> It was neither capitalists nor capitalism as such but rather the contradictions of capitalism that advanced the cause of political equality. Capitalism contributed to democracy primarily because it changed the balance of class power in favor of the subordinate interests.
>
> (Rueschemeyer et al. 1992: 302)

To sum up Rueschemeyer et al.'s explanation: modernization (*qua* industrialization) created a strong and cohesive working class, which would fight to get enfranchised politically. It was the consequent class struggle – rather than the 'harmonic' mechanisms outlined by Lipset – which ultimately paved the way for equal and universal suffrage, and hence for thicker types of democracy.

Elite calculations, middle-class pressure, or joint projects?

The analyses carried out by Therborn and Rueschemeyer et al. have influenced the field considerably, but their respective conclusions have not been accepted unconditionally. For example, Ruth B. Collier (1999) has added a number of important nuances in *Paths toward Democracy*. Collier goes to the root and investigates the role of the working class in a number of different periods of democratization in Western Europe and South America.[7]

Collier (1999: 19–21) points out that a focus on the working class alone does not get us very far. It is necessary to understand the interplay between the various classes and the strategies pursued by the elites. Against this, Collier (1999: 14–16) asserts that the role of the working class has been exaggerated in the analyses of the first wave democratizations. She begins by clarifying which actors have had a genuinely democratic agenda and played a decisive role in pushing through democratic reforms. Here, it is important to note that she only attempts to explain democratization and not the subsequent democratic stability. Collier (1999: 24) understands democratization as the introduction or expansion of political institutions guaranteeing (1) constitutionalism, which limits the arbitrary exercise of power by the state apparatus, (2) elections characterized by comprehensive suffrage and competition, and (3) an elected legislative assembly that is relatively independent of the executive. Based on this framework, Collier (1999: 35) identifies three paths to democratization during the first wave in Western Europe:

1   *Middle-class democratization.* This path was traversed by Denmark in 1849, Greece in 1864, France in 1848 and 1875 to 1877, Portugal in 1911 and 1918, and finally by Spain in 1868, 1890, and 1931.
2   *Elite-driven democratization.* This path was followed by Switzerland in 1848, Great Britain in 1867 and 1884, Norway in 1898, and Italy in 1912.
3   *Democratization as a result of joint projects.* This path was taken by Denmark in 1915, Finland in 1906 and 1919, Sweden in 1907 to 1909 and 1918 to 1920, the Netherlands in 1917, Belgium in 1918, and Germany in 1918 to 1919.

In the case of the middle-class democratizations, it was first and foremost liberals and/or republican movements that fought against monarchs and the privileged aristocratic elites. These movements demanded – on behalf of the middle class – suffrage extensions as well as the introduction of constitutionalism. The aim was primarily to guarantee civil liberties and representation to the middle class. In several cases, however, the liberal agenda also included demands for equal and universal suffrage (for men). Elite-driven democratization usually occurred as a by-product of party politics, as the elite-dominated parties sought increased support among the previously excluded segments of the population, including the working class. The best-known instances are probably the ongoing competition between the Whigs and Tories in 19th-century Great Britain. For example, the Conservatives under Benjamin Disraeli extended suffrage in 1867, expecting to receive the lion's share of the new votes. In such instances, democratization was a project carried out by political insiders seeking to fortify their own respective positions.

The two first forms of democratization were both extensively dominated by political elites. In the great majority of cases, the working class was non-existent, indifferent, split, or outright hostile towards democratization. The only partial exceptions were France in 1848, Great Britain in 1884, and Norway in 1898, where the working class (or parts of it) played a minor role by supporting democratization. Division within the labor movement was in fact the most frequent reaction when elite calculations were the basis for reforms. The working class was aware that the elites were extending suffrage for their own sake. However, it was not yet sufficiently organized to be able to reach agreement about how to assume a position in relation to it. The two elite-dominated paths are distinguished from one another in one important respect. In connection with elite calculations, it was insiders who pushed reforms through in order to ensure votes for themselves. Middle-class democratizations, on the other hand, were carried out by outsiders pushing for reforms. In the latter instances, actual revolutions or coups often ensued (cf. Weyland 2009).

The third path was radically different, as the lower classes had their say. These joint projects typically occurred towards the end of the first wave of democratization. They were characterized by pro-democratic socialist parties and trade unions playing a prominent role. In most cases (Finland in 1906 is an exception), the working class was already partially included and represented. Occasionally, the socialist party was even the largest party and/or part of the government when new political reforms were pushed through. Even in these cases, the working class was merely one of multiple coalition partners. In countries such as Sweden, Belgium, and Germany, the working class was particularly dominant in such coalitions, while it was the junior partner in other cases. Collier (1999: 78–79) here points out a tendency in the literature to exaggerate the significance of World War I in relation to the influence of the working class. In several cases, the reforms had already been carried through or were at least on the political agenda before the war. Other classes in society also became more democratically inclined as a result of the war. Furthermore, part of the impact usually attributed to World War I should rather be ascribed to the Russian Revolution (1917).

Where does this leave us? There is definitely a place for the working class in Collier's account, but it does not occupy nearly as prominent a position as with Therborn and Stephens. To some extent, however, the difference is again a result of the respective definitions. Collier wants to explain each and every movement towards democracy, including developments occurring long before actual polyarchy or liberal democracy made inroads. As we have already argued, the middle class was indeed important for 19th-century democratizations, while the working class primarily became important in the final reforms of the 20th century, where the democratic project was completed. But these differences in relation to the focus only explain the overall difference up to a point. For even in the late phases of the democratizations, Collier argues that the working class was not necessarily the decisive driving force, even though it fought for democratization relatively consistently during this period (not so in Latin America, however). Finally, it is important to note that Collier, unlike Stephens, does not attempt to explain democratic breakdowns. This leads us to a discussion of the determinants of democratic survival and autocratic revival in the interwar period (cf. Berg-Schlosser & Mitchell 2003; Skaaning 2011).

Conflict over democracy: Europe in the interwar period

The Wall Street stock market collapsed on October 29, 1929. The Roaring Twenties were over, the Great Depression lay ahead. The economic crisis of the 1930s proved fatal for many European democracies. The totalitarian movements of the day – fascism, Nazism, and communism – made advances at the expense of democracy because they promised to provide work, order, and food to the hungry and insecure masses on the Continent.

That is the conventional interpretation of the history of the enigmatic 1930s. But just because this story has been repeated time and again does not necessarily mean that it holds water. A historical retrospective shows that the relationship between economic crisis and democratic breakdown is not as clear as it is often made out to be (see Luebbert 1991: 307–308; Bermeo 1997a; Ertman 1998). The well-known story about the disheartening political impact of the economic crisis builds first and foremost on the German case (Bermeo 1997a: 3). The Nazi takeover occurred – conveniently enough for the theory – when the economy hit rock-bottom. But the crisis of the 1930s actually had a greater impact in a number of other European countries, several of which managed to retain their democratic credentials (Luebbert 1991: 307–308; Bermeo 1997a). More specifically, countries such as the Netherlands and Norway were hit just as hard by the economic crisis as were the instances of breakdown. In both of these countries, unemployment was probably higher than in Germany (and Austria), and the crisis branched out to all aspects of society (Linz & Stepan 1996: 80). Nevertheless, the non-democratic movements gained very limited support. The Netherlands are telling in this context, as the country played host to one of the worst recessions in Europe. Thousands of Dutch laborers went so far as to cross the German border to find work in their great neighbor to the East. Nonetheless, the Dutch fascists never won more than 9 percent of the popular vote in the various elections held over the course of the decade. As in Norway, the Dutch simply avoided falling for the totalitarian temptation – crisis or not.

Moreover, democracy had broken down in a number of European countries *before* the crisis gained momentum. Mussolini had already seized the reins of power in 1922; in Spain, Primo de Rivera established his dictatorship the year after; and Poland, Portugal, and Lithuania had also all left the democratic fold in the mid-1920s (Luebbert 1991: 307–308; Bermeo 1997a). As an effect obviously cannot occur prior to the cause, this further weakens the account of the detrimental effects of the economic crisis on democratic breakdown. These events form the backdrop for two recent contributions within the genre of the social forces tradition, namely that of Gregory Luebbert (1991) and that of Thomas Ertman (1998). Both are at odds with Stephens' argument as to what ensures the survival of democracy (or fails to do so), and both provide alternative explanations for the results.

Liberal hegemony, red–green alliance, or fascism

The first of these two accounts distinguishes between three different regime types, which consolidated in Western Europe during the interwar period. Great Britain, France, and Switzerland combined a free market economy with democracy, and these three countries were therefore instances of 'liberal democracy'.[8] In Denmark, Norway, and Sweden, democracy went hand in hand with a mixed economy – in which the market was heavily regulated – a combination constituting 'social democracy'. Finally, Spain, Germany, and Italy developed a combination consisting of a corporatist economy and autocracy referred to as 'fascism'. This diversity is what Luebbert (1991) seeks to explain in *Liberalism, Fascism, or Social Democracy*. His book provides an exciting answer to the two following questions: Why did the tripartition between liberal democracy, social democracy, and fascism develop in the interwar period? And why was it Western Europe in particular that served as the background for this tripartite division?

Beginning with the latter question, Luebbert argues that Western Europe alone had the necessary level of modernization to realize and sustain these regime forms. In doing so, he draws a direct comparison between Western and Eastern Europe. According to Luebbert (1991: 3–4), during the interwar period the entire area between Czechoslovakia and the Soviet Union came to be characterized by a fourth regime type, which he labels 'traditional dictatorship'. This regime type is primarily to be understood with fascism as the frame of reference. In the 1920s and 1930s, many European democracies fell apart, but they did so in one way in the East and in another way in the West. In Italy, Germany, and to some degree Spain, the democratic institutions were completely destroyed, and totalitarian regimes destroyed independent parties and trade unions. In countries such as Poland, Lithuania, Romania, and Bulgaria, parliaments, parties, trade unions, and elections continued, but only as a kind of window dressing. They were hollowed out by dictators who exercised the real power (e.g., Pilsudski in Poland). Nevertheless, these dictators did not suppress civil society in the same manner as was the case with fascism.

According to Luebbert (1991: 259), this difference was no coincidence. Eastern Europe was lacking the level of modernization necessary for liberal democracy, social democracy, and fascism alike. In virtually the entire area, over half of the population was employed in agriculture, and the domestic economy was not commercialized. Furthermore, the Eastern European countries were a patchwork of ethnic, religious, and linguistic groups. This brings us back to Luebbert's question of why the Western countries moved along three different paths in the interwar period. The answer may be summarized in two points (cf. Luebbert 1991: 7–8):

1 An alliance between the liberals (middle class) and the labor movement prior to World War I was both a necessary and a sufficient condition for liberal democracy. The British case – where the Labour Party was closely interwoven with the liberals – offers the best example of such *lib-labism*. The point is that the labor movement was established under the auspices of what Luebbert refers to as liberal hegemony. After World War I, Britain was therefore unable to introduce social democracy.

2 The absence of such liberal hegemony was a necessary condition for the other two regime types. In this situation, the alliances forged by the family farmers made the difference. Alliances with the workers resulted in social democracy. This 'red–green' cooperation was the recurring pattern in the Scandinavian countries. In the cases where the farmers felt threatened because the socialists

began mobilizing support among the rural laborers, they instead entered into alliances with the middle class. Here, the consequence was fascism, a result found at the time in Germany, Italy, and Spain.

Luebbert thus presents a class analysis in the pure sense, as the classes – workers, family farmers, and the urban middle class – have firm interests, and the relations between them determine the political development. In fact, in a very categorical formulation Luebbert (1991: 306) claims that "One of the cardinal lessons of the story I have told is that leadership and meaningful choice played no role in the outcomes." Another way of saying this is that the classes sought entirely to realize their economic interests via the political superstructure. After a conflict, this led to a specific political-economic regime that attended to the interests of the *Gründer* classes: the working class in social democracy and the middle class in liberal democracy.

Luebbert's explanation definitely has much to offer also in terms of its edge. For example, he rejects Moore's proposition that a strong rural upper class is an effective barrier against democracy. Luebbert (1991: 308–309) argues that fascism came about as a result of an alliance between the farmers and the middle class. He also emphasizes that the rural nobility was unable to manipulate the votes cast by the other classes in interwar Western Europe. Luebbert illustrates this point with references to how the Nazis enjoyed greater support in areas populated by independent farmers than in the regions where the rural laborers were subjected to powerful landowners (see also Mahoney 2003b: 364–365).[9]

But Luebbert's work is not devoid of problems. First, the Netherlands and Belgium do not fit his model well (Kitschelt 1992: 1029). According to Luebbert, these two countries were not characterized by liberal hegemony prior to World War I. Yet a subspecies of liberal democracy developed in the interwar period, where religious parties forged compromises together with the working class. Second, as Ertman (1998: 497) has stressed, Luebbert's analysis begs a particular question: What determined the relative strengths of the respective classes and of liberal hegemony in the first place? Luebbert's own suggestion seems to be that the ethnic, religious, and linguistic cleavages were decisive. If such differences divided the middle class, it was not strong enough to embrace the labor movement prior to World War I. There is undoubtedly something to this. As Ertman notes, however, this explanation is at best inadequate. This takes us to Ertman's own contribution to the understanding of the situation.

Party systems and civil society

Based on a critical examination of the explanations provided by Rueschemeyer et al., Collier, and Luebbert, Ertman (1998) concludes that they, each in their own way, present relatively convincing explanations of the emergence of democracy in the period between 1848 and 1920. But none of them provide a satisfactory explanation as to why so few of the Western European democracies collapsed in the interwar period. He therefore introduces an alternative model.

Ertman's take on the issue may seem slightly odd, as attention is normally directed towards why so many democracies broke down in the interlude between the world wars. Ertman's argument for turning the question on its head is that doing so is a corollary of using modernization theory as a yardstick. As mentioned in the preceding chapter, according to contemporary standards, the Western European countries were relatively poor during the democratizations of the 19th century and in the interwar period. In the latter period, they were additionally subjected to a dramatic economic crisis in the form of the Great Depression. According to Ertman (1998: 475–477), what is truly remarkable is therefore that so *few* Western European democracies fell during this period.

Ertman anchors his account in Luebbert's focus on the capacity of the democratic parties to hold on to their voters in a period of crisis. However, he does not subscribe to Luebbert's point about liberal hegemony, which he argues cannot be demonstrated empirically. For example, Ertman (1998: 496) points out that countries such as Denmark and Norway actually set the scene for alliances between laborers and the liberals (farmers) before World War I, which smacks of 'lib-labism' and liberal hegemony. The Danish Social Democrats thus collaborated in elections with first the Liberals (farmers) and later the Social Liberals (typically smallholders). Nevertheless, the Social Democrats in the Scandinavian countries proved strong enough after the war to be able to implement their desired model. Against this background, Ertman asserts that Luebbert is (to some degree) making the pieces of his puzzle fit together by categorizing the countries in classes with and without liberal hegemony prior to World War I depending on how things unfolded *after* the war.

Ertman goes on to argue that the only way to arrive at a better understanding of the development in the interwar period is by bringing civil society into play. One of the crucial differences between the crisis-plagued democracies of the interwar period and democracies in contemporary developing countries is that civil society was blossoming in the former. The fate of democracies should therefore be understood in the intersection between the civil society and the party system.

A number of scholars have emphasized civil society's beneficial impact on democracy (cf. Putnam 1993; Warren 2000). But others have stressed that civil society is not an unmitigated blessing for democracy (cf. Berman 1997; Bermeo 1997a: 14–15). Ertman uses this latter observation to point out that we cannot simply assert that democracy survived in countries with vibrant civil societies. Germany and northern Italy, where the fascists and Nazis enjoyed the greatest support, could boast of some of the most vibrant civil societies (Berman 1997). Germany was indeed the Mecca of voluntary organizations. It is not without reason that there is an old saying that if more than two Germans got together, they would start laying down formal rules of organization.

Yet if we introduce the party system as a necessary requirement for a strong civil society to have a positive effect on democracy, we are suddenly able to solve the great equation of the interwar period. Only in the countries characterized by a decisive, competitive party system prior to World War I – that is, only where the parliamentary principle had gained ground – did a vibrant civil society lead to the survival of democracy after the war (Ertman 1998: 499–500). Benelux, the Scandinavian countries, France, Switzerland, and Great Britain exemplify this combination (see Table 8.1). In contrast, democracies failed if political life did not revolve around the party system prior to World War I (i.e., where the parliamentary principle had no solid foothold), and this despite the presence of a vibrant civil society, as was the case in Italy and Germany.

Furthermore, the revival of autocracy also became a reality where political activity revolved around the party system before World War I but where a vibrant civil society never emerged. In these instances – Portugal and Spain – patron–client structures hollowed out democracy from within. And where none of the components conducive to democracy existed (e.g., in Russia), the democratization process was even doomed beforehand. To elaborate upon the last point, Ertman (1998: 476) argues that Central and Eastern Europe were moving along totally different paths than those of Western Europe because the basic conditions here were radically different. New states were being formed against the background of the gradual reduction of the Ottoman Empire in the Balkans and the collapse of the Austro-Hungarian and Russian Empires in 1917 to 1918. It is therefore meaningless to examine whether their political life rotated around democratic competition in the period leading up to World War I. For this reason, Ertman also excludes relatively 'Western' countries such as Austria, Finland, Ireland, and Czechoslovakia. It is worth noting that the three latter countries do not fit his argument, as they maintained democracy during the interwar period despite lacking a (national/independent) democratic party system prior to World War I. Ertman's analysis is therefore not the final word to be uttered in this case.

Table 8.1 Explanatory typology of Ertman's account

| | | Well-established party system before World War I | |
		Yes	No
	Yes	Democratic survival (Belgium, Denmark, France, the Netherlands, Norway, Switzerland, Great Britain, Sweden)	Democratic breakdown (Italy, Germany)
Strong civil society			
	No	Democratic breakdown (Portugal, Spain)	Democratic breakdown (Russia)

Conclusions

As already mentioned, one of the most important premises for science is that empirical results hinge on definitions (Sartori 1970). The examination of historical comparative analyses within the social forces tradition in this chapter clearly illustrates this point. Whether it is the bourgeoisie or the working class that appears to be the main driving force behind democracy thus depends upon what lies in the term democracy.

Neither Luebbert nor Ertman devote much attention to spelling out their respective definitions of democracy. This is because they are primarily interested in explaining whether democracy could stand the distance in the interwar period, where universal suffrage (at least for men), the parliamentary principle, and political liberties were associated with the democratic regime almost without exception. But it makes a big difference for the work of all of the other scholars discussed in this chapter. If we are closest to what we term minimalist democracy, then the middle class/bourgeoisie was often the driving force. On the other hand, if one seeks to explain the final drive in the direction of electoral democracy characterized by the introduction of universal suffrage, the working class played a more important role.

Next, it makes a big difference whether one is merely seeking to explain democratization or whether democratic stability is also included in the equation. Stephens, who investigates both, concludes that the two things have different causes. Similarly, the choice of empirical scope is of great importance. We have attempted to account for the latter by only scrutinizing analyses of Europe in the period between the French Revolution and World War II. Even here, however, it proved decisive whether one – like Moore – includes only the major countries or whether one also includes the small Western European countries, possibly supplemented with the new states in East-Central and Eastern Europe.

Finally, it is striking that even though various researchers – Ertman being the most notable exception – promote a relatively unadulterated class analysis, the predominant conclusion is that factors other than the strength of the classes are also decisive. Elite calculations, the party system, and civil society represent three of the most important additions. To sum up these points, we can note that most democratic progress occurred when different classes forged alliances.

Taken together, the focus on the social forces and class constellations has received much attention since Moore's pioneering work. We now know that the class structure played a decisive role for democratization in Europe in the 19th and 20th centuries. Shifting the focus to a more particular level, there is widespread agreement that the middle class was decisive for the establishment of the rule of law, political liberties, and limited suffrage in the first part of the process, while the working class played an important role when suffrage was subsequently extended to the general population. At the same time, there is (despite Luebbert's objections) widespread agreement that the large landholders have consistently been the enemy of democracy. Finally, a recurring theme in this chapter has been that the historical comparative analyses operate with modernization theory as the frame of reference. Here, two points are important. First, it would not be wrong to say that the overall causal chain is virtually identical in the two approaches. Modernization is thus also directly or indirectly a background variable in the analyses of class struggle and democracy. The significant difference consists of the causal mechanism being essentially different. The message in the analyses covered in this chapter is that economic change (of the basis) changes the class structures, which in turn has an impact on the political regime (the superstructure).

The thrust of the class analyses is thereby simultaneously aimed at modern-ization theory. The point in most of the analyses discussed is that the impact of modernization basically depends upon the class structure, upon the timing of the structural changes, and upon mediating factors such as the party system and civil society. This is to say that democracy is born of secular conflict between the classes. It does not simply descend from the heavens as the result of a painless modernization process. Moore (1991 [1966]: 28–29), for example, argued that the gradual English development involved massive violence against the peasants as a result of enclosures of agricultural land (the commons) in the period between 1500 and 1800,[10] a course of events which Marx (2007 [1867]) in *Capital* (*Das Kapital*) calls "the parliamentary form of the robbery." Luebbert has also argued that certain class constellations led to autocracy rather than democracy and that any kind of regime serves the interests of a particular class. And Ertman has demonstrated that even the most vibrant civil society could not prevent democratic collapse if the party system was still in its infancy. Consequently, one may argue that these comparative historical analyses are more realistic than modernization theory. The other side of the coin is that it is difficult to generalize their findings to a broader selection of countries – not to mention periods (cf. Bellin 2000). This might appear somewhat paradoxical, since they pretty much exclusively emphasize structural conditions, which the actors respond to more or less automatically. Collier offers the only partial exception, as she softens things up by focusing on the strategic reflections of the elite, which is the focal point of the following chapter.

9 Transitology[1]

Does democracy require fertile soil to sprout and strike root, or can it also grow and survive in a context bereft of favorable structural conditions? The democratization literature features very different answers to these questions. The theories emphasizing the importance of modernization and class struggle for democratization processes answer 'Yes' to the first question and therefore 'No' to the second. Transition theory – or transitology, as it has also been labeled – adopts the opposite answer to the first question and also, more implicitly, to the second.

Transitology may be traced back to Dankwart A. Rustow's (1970) groundbreaking article, "Transitions to Democracy: Toward a Dynamic Model". Rustow broke with the dominant democratization theories, which emphasized structural conditions for democracy, as presented in the previous chapters. Rustow's alternative was a narrower focus on the transition process itself, the general points being, first, that the causes of the transition were likely to differ from the causes of the functioning of democracy, and, second, that no socio-economic prerequisites for a transition could be identified (Rustow 1970: 342, 352; see also O'Donnell & Schmitter 1986: 65).

Towards the end of the 1970s, new ammunition was provided to this perspective when Juan Linz and Alfred Stepan (1978) published their four-volume work, *The Breakdown of Democratic Regimes*. They rejected that the democratic collapses in interwar Europe and in Latin America after World War II had been inevitable; a position that otherwise had a strong standing at the time. Linz and Stepan emphasized that in several – if not most – cases, it was the decisions made by the key actors more than the structural circumstances that determined the outcome of the struggle between democracy and autocracy (see also Bermeo 1997a; Cappoccia 2005).

The breakthrough of transitology

However, transition theory first began to receive considerable attention in the 1980s when the third wave of democratization broke through the dikes in earnest (Haggard & Kaufman 1997: 72). A number of researchers continued where Rustow had left off, advocating a more optimistic perspective on democratization, which allocated greater maneuvering room to the actors (Di Palma 1990: 1–13).

Bold proclamations were made that democracy did not require particular structural conditions (cf. Carothers 2002: 8). This was actually a more radical position than Rustow's, as he had described national unity as a necessary condition, emphasized the importance of collective social forces, and underlined that a transition at the minimum lasts a generation. As such, his theory was much more structural than what came to be known as transitology in the 1980s and 1990s.

According to the transitology perspective, it was first and foremost the actors' strategies in the transition process itself that were understood as being decisive. In short, the idea was that it is possible to establish democracy even though the structural conditions are unfavorable, as long as the actors make the right decisions (Karl 2005: 4). Perhaps it is more correct to say that the transitologist was unapologetic in maintaining that we must – from a normative perspective – *assume* that democratization can occur in the face of even severe structural constraints. As Gerardo Munck (2011: 4) points out, the reasons behind the transitology emphasis on actors' choices were thus "largely political rather than purely scientific," a rejection of structural determinism termed 'thoughtful wishing' by Abraham Lowenthal, one of the driving forces behind the 1986 project.

Seen through this lens, the emergence and popularity of transitology may to a large extent be understood as a reaction to the circumstance that the structural accounts did not offer specific instructions to democrats in the struggle against autocratic rulers. In the wake of the democratization processes in the Southern European countries in the 1970s – and particularly after the end of the Cold War – the opposition forces in a number of developing countries took the lead and rallied their forces against autocratic rule. The rest of the world faced the following question: Bearing the structural accounts in mind, should these movements merely be regarded as ripples on the surface because these countries were ultimately lacking the necessary conditions to democratize – or at least to sustain democracy? Few researchers, politicians, or others interested in promoting democracy were ready to accept this pessimistic perspective. As Myron Weiner (1987: 862) formulated the general mood: "Perhaps it is time to recognize that democratic theory, with its list of conditions and prerequisites, is a poor guide to action."

For two of the founding fathers of transitology, Guillermo O'Donnell and Philippe C. Schmitter, the new perspective also represented a personal break with their own theories from the 1970s. Back then, they had pointed out that a number of structural factors played a decisive role for political development (Munck & Snyder 2007: chs 9 and 10). But the four volumes under the common heading *Transitions from Authoritarian Rule* (O'Donnell et al. 1986), which they edited together with Laurence Whitehead, had a major impact in focusing research on democratization away from the structuralist perspective towards more dynamic causes. Especially O'Donnell and Schmitter's (1986) concluding volume, *Tentative Conclusions about Uncertain Democracies*, in which they reflected on the major findings, was agenda-setting. It replaced the structural and deterministic accounts with a much more contingency-oriented perspective focusing on agency.

In a nutshell, transitology ascribes independent and decisive significance to the agents. Transition processes are characterized by a number of strategic choices which O'Donnell and Schmitter (1986: 66) believe have a great impact on the final outcome. While they avoid rejecting the long-term impact of structural factors, they emphasize the significance of the short-term political calculations which cannot be derived from the underlying structural factors (O'Donnell & Schmitter 1986: 5; cf. Karl & Schmitter 1991: 270–272). O'Donnell & Schmitter thus reiterate both Rustow's general insights that the causes of transitions differ from those sustaining democracy (O'Donnell & Schmitter 1986: 65) and his more particular argument that when analyzing transitions a focus on political action is inescapable.

The mode of transition as key factor

There is a considerable heterogeneity within the discipline of transitology. The most obvious point of consensus concerns the postulate that the mode of transition is decisive for the development of democracy in two ways. First, it bears upon whether a transition away from an autocratic regime results in democracy at all. Second, it impacts upon the extent to which such a democracy will be able to consolidate. However, in spite of the claims forwarded by both critics and proponents of transitology (see, e.g., Carothers 2002), the perspective does not include any assumption about transitions always leading to democracy. O'Donnell (2002: 7) has subsequently emphasized "that there was nothing predestined about these transitions . . . their course and outcome were open-ended and uncertain." Recall in this connection that O'Donnell and Schmitter's book was *not* entitled *Transitions to Democracy* but *Transitions from Authoritarian Rule*, indicating that though the actors' choices were seen as crucial for the character of the transitions, the long-term outcome of these choices was perceived as nebulous.

Among the many versions of transition theory (see, e.g., Share 1987; Mainwaring 1992; Munck & Leff 1997), it is natural to begin with O'Donnell and Schmitter's seminal perspective. O'Donnell and Schmitter (1986: 6–7) define a transition as the interval between one political regime and another. In this phase, the old political rules of the game no longer apply, while the new rules have yet to be decided. The whole situation is marked by uncertainty and contingency with respect to the outcome. The agents are therefore free to make choices that have unintentional (and possibly also unwanted) consequences for the future. These choices create new rules, which then lock in. One can say that the transition gives the agents opportunity to directly or inadvertently 'select' institutions that subsequently 'freeze' and limit the opportunities for choosing a new course.

According to O'Donnell and Schmitter, in the instances where democratization carries the day, the transition period may be divided into two phases. The first consists of a liberalization of the authoritarian regime; that is, a process in which political liberties such as freedom of speech and association are introduced and expanded. The second phase is marked by actual democratization. More specifically, the fundamental democratic procedures, institutions, and rights such as suffrage, party competition, and – decisively – competitive elections are introduced.

Karl and Schmitter's transition typology

O'Donnell and Schmitter do not really define the different types of transitions. This is somewhat surprising considering the centrality of the term. Much subsequent work has been devoted to this issue, however, and the transitology literature therefore contains a number of definitions and applies a range of different classification principles (see Table 9.1). Needless to say, there is consensus about the importance of identifying the main actors in the transition. What is more, there seems to be agreement with respect to drawing a general distinction between the autocratic incumbents and the opposition, both of which can be further subdivided into hard-line hawks and moderate doves.

In contrast, there is disagreement as to whether one should emphasize the strengths and positions of the agents involved (Share 1987; Huntington 1991; Mainwaring 1992) or their strategies (Karl & Schmitter 1991; Munck & Leff 1997). Nevertheless, this difference does not run that deeply, as the strengths and strategies of the involved agents in many ways represent two sides of the same coin. In most cases, the strategy chosen will be determined by how strong a group feel compared to their counterparts.

Among the many contributions within this literature, we focus on the influential version of transition theory of Terry Karl and Philippe Schmitter (1991), two of the founders of transitology. As seen in Table 9.1 and Figure 9.1, Karl and Schmitter focus on the specific combinations of agents and strategies in the transition process. They construct a typology and formulate a number of hypotheses about the significance the various modes of transition have for the subsequent democratization process. The first dimension of the typology reflects which actor is the driving force behind the changes. Here, Karl and Schmitter distinguish between the masses and the elites. The second dimension reflects the strategy of the main actors and distinguishes between whether the transition between regimes results from a compromise between the most important actors or against the background of unilateral exercises of power. By combining these two dimensions, Karl and Schmitter construct four ideal-typical modes of transition (see Figure 9.1). They point out that if a combination of elites and masses triggers the transition and/or external actors participate in the process, the transition is categorized in the area between the ideal types (Karl & Schmitter 1991: 275).

Insofar as the transition is primarily a result of the elite actors reaching a compromise, we are dealing with a pact. The transition to democracy in Spain

Table 9.1 Classification principles in transition typologies

	Share	Huntington	Mainwaring	Karl & Schmitter	Munck & Leff
Main actors	X	(X)	(X)	X	X
Relative strength	(X)	X	X		
Strategy				X	X

Note: X indicates that the typology covers the respective principles. An (X) means that the principle is somehow included, but only indirectly or secondarily.

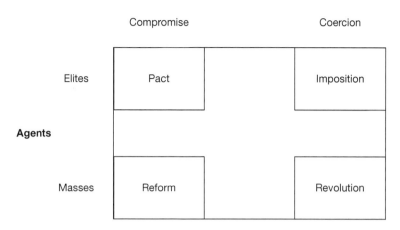

Figure 9.1 Karl and Schmitter's transition typology

following Franco's death in 1975 has been regarded as the prototype of such a pact (Share 1987). But the South African transition to democracy in 1994 also constitutes a good example, as the process was characterized by compromises and elite management, including the fact that the previous ruling elite escaped serious punishment but agreed to the establishment of a 'Truth and Reconciliation Commission'. As summarized by Michael Bratton and Nicolas van de Walle (1997: 178; cf. Barkan 2000: 239):

> The ruling whites conceded ANC's core demand of free elections . . . and the principal black opposition group accepted rules of proportional representation for elections, job security for white civil servants, and an amnesty for security forces that admitted to crime under the old regime.

If the masses are mobilized from below and reach a compromise with the former incumbents without resorting to violence, we have an instance of reform rather than a pact. Illustrating this type of transition, in the years leading up to the dissolution of Yugoslavia there was a strong popular movement in Slovenia spearheading a non-violent campaign aimed at introducing independence and democratic reforms. As a result of this pressure, the Slovenian Communist Party set a reform process in motion, paving the way for multi-party elections in 1990 and independence the year after (Bunce 2003: 172; Karatnycky & Ackerman 2005: 40).

The third type of transition, namely imposition, covers the cases in which elites push a regime change through from above. Taiwan's transition fits this category, as the Kuomintang Party, which held power firmly during autocratic rule, controlled the introduction of the democratic reforms. The process began in 1986 and followed the party's own schedule. First, martial law was repealed, and certain political liberties were introduced. Political parties were then allowed to function, and the first democratic elections followed in 1991. The direction and speed of the process were controlled by the Kuomintang rather than the opposition. The Taiwan transition was thus both set in motion and carried out by the ruling elite (Rigger 2000: 141; Shin & Lee 2003: 41).

Finally, the transition may be categorized as a revolution if the masses take to the streets and press change through despite resistance offered by the ruling elite (Karl & Schmitter 1991: 275; cf. Karl 1990: 8–9). Madagascar set the stage for such a scenario at the beginning of the 1990s. President Ratsiraka's autocratic rule was challenged from August 1990 to July 1991 by increasing unrest in the form of comprehensive strikes, demonstrations, and violent clashes with the security forces. When he refused to accept the civilian demands for democratic reforms, half a million citizens marched on the presidential palace, resulting in a clash leaving 100 dead and more than 300 injured. The pressure from the popular protests ultimately forced Ratsiraka to begin work on a new democratic constitution (van de Walle 1995: 129; Sandbrook 1996: 71).

Karl and Schmitter's transition types may initially seem well suited to distinguishing between different courses of events. However, Valerie Bunce (1995: 113) has – correctly – criticized them for not setting out specific criteria for when a transition belongs to one category and not another: When can an agreement be understood as a pact, and how much and in which phases do the masses have to participate before it is a revolution? This lack of clarity has contributed to confusion and disagreement about the classification of specific transitions. Nancy Bermeo (1997b), for instance, questions the widespread understanding of the transition in Spain in the 1970s as an elite-controlled compromise (i.e., a pact). She emphasizes that the course of events was characterized by numerous incidents of political violence and mass strikes; indeed, she points out that there have not really been any peaceful transitions in the third wave of democratization. This leads to a crucial question: Does the mode of transition have any independent effect on the subsequent democratic development?

The relationship between the mode of transition and democratic development

According to O'Donnell and Schmitter (1986: 39), it is often propitious for the development of democracy if the opposition refrains from inciting a revolution from below. Indeed, it is best if uncertainty is reduced via a pact with the authorities. A pact is:

> an explicit, but not always publicly explicated or justified, agreement among a select set of actors which seeks to define (or, better, to redefine) rules governing the exercise of power in the basis of mutual guarantees for the 'vital interest' of those entering into it.
>
> (O'Donnell & Schmitter 1986: 37)

Karl (1990: 11) adds that pacts are comprehensive, inclusive, and primarily rule-making in the initial stages, as opposed to narrower agreements such as managerial accords that are partial, exclusionary, and about concrete policies. Pacts are not based on consensus regarding the objectives. The driving force behind the compromises is the fundamental unpredictability ('contingency') characterizing many transitions. Inspired by John Rawls' (1971) writings in political philosophy about the 'veil of ignorance', where one is hypothetically unaware of one's own negotiating position – and supported by arguments drawn from game theory – Adam Przeworski (1991: 87) has presented an interesting account of why this situation is likely to result in democracy. The great uncertainty concerning one's own position of power will force the competing elites to choose a so-called 'maximin strategy'; that is, to pursue the change that provides the best possible conditions for the weakest party, since that might ultimately prove to be oneself. If you do not know whether you are the strongest or the weakest, you have an obvious interest in stability, guaranteed basic rights, and opportunities to police the rulers.

A compromise between the power elites logically reduces the potential for conflict, has an impact upon the balance of power, and sets new political processes in motion. In the longer term, democratic institutions ensure these elements best. Somewhat paradoxically, pacts therefore lead to democracy via non-democratic means. Transitologists actually point out that it is possible to realize 'democracy without democrats' because pacts are in practice exclusive agreements that are typically negotiated by a limited number of exclusive, elite groups in a closed process. From the perspective of transitology, however, this is a necessary evil that is legitimized by the improved chances of establishing and consolidating democracy under such conditions. There are certain requirements for a pact to have a positive effect. Transition theory emphasizes three specific characteristics facilitating democratic development (cf. McFaul 2002):

1   A pact should preferably limit the political agenda. The actors should focus on reforming the political regime without simultaneously introducing extensive economic reforms. If the prevailing economic system is not subject to excessive reform – especially the property rights, which are typically to the advantage of the authorities – elites will be more inclined to go along with democratization. That is to say, they will go along with surrendering political power in exchange for retaining their economic power.
2   A pact should ensure a relatively equal distribution of goods between the parties. This promotes the willingness to engage in compromises among the elites about the fundamental institutional rules of the game, thereby reducing the incentive for open conflict in the form of a coup or a revolution.
3   The masses and any possible extremists on either side (i.e., uncompromising democrats/autocrats) are preferably to be excluded from influence. A stable transition to democracy is more likely if matters can be taken care of among the elites and in the event that the negotiation parties are moderate instead of extremist. Karl (1990: 8) even argues that "*no* stable political democracy has

resulted from regime transition in which mass actors have gained control, even momentarily, over traditional ruling classes." Or as Michael McFaul (2002: 218) has laconically stated: "mobilized masses spoil the party."

While Karl and Schmitter (1991: 269) are somewhat vague when it comes to operationalizing their four ideal-typical modes of transition, they are quite explicit when it comes to coupling them to the prospects for consolidating democracy. They expect that a pact between the authorities and the opposition will best promote the consolidation of democracy, while the next-best mode of transition consists of an imposition; that is, a transition led by the incumbent elite. Conversely, if the mode of transition is characterized as a reform involving compromise in which the protests of the masses play a decisive role, the likelihood of democratic consolidation is lower. This is because the elite, with its ties to the previous regime, cannot control the process alone as in the case of imposition. Unacceptable demands from the masses become more likely, and with them the likelihood of democratic reversals increases. Revolutionary transition is, however, an even worse option. If extremist masses set the agenda, the prospects for the establishment and stabilization of a democratic regime are not good. The message is thus, "put the pact in gear and go," as Charles Tilly (1995: 365) has sarcastically written.

Interestingly, Schmitter had grown increasingly more convinced about his perspective during the period from when he kicked things off in 1986 until he and Karl formulated a common position five years later. In the mid-1980s, O'Donnell and Schmitter (1986: 66) were not quite as assertive regarding the blessings of pacts; they argued that if guarantees and rigid rules lead to significant dissatisfaction and procedural deadlocks, the shortsighted pact can hamper democratic consolidation. In the longer run, a paradox may emerge, as pacts contributing to a transition to democracy can work to the detriment of the consolidation of democracy. The problem is that excessive elitism, prior agreements, exit guarantees,[2] and a lack of democratic competition, which is often an important element in pacts, can undermine democracy. In the absence of a strait-jacket, however, excessive division and competition can develop between the parties, which may inhibit political and economic performance and legitimacy. This dissatisfaction can ultimately lead to a military coup or a revolution (O'Donnell 1992).

O'Donnell and Schmitter also argue that socio-economic pacts increase the chances for the survival of the new democracies. In a later article, Karl and Schmitter (1995: 969) defend this ambivalence by stating that their "approach is quite explicitly possibilistic – not probabilistic or deterministic – in epistemology and design." However, this maneuver, referring to the relationship between transition type and democratic development as possible rather than probable or manifest, does not solve the problem. In fact, one may argue that it undermines the scientific status of transition theory, to reuse Lowenthal's term, making it 'thoughtful wishing' rather than a rigorous theoretical framework. If one cannot use it to deduce firm predictions about causes and effects, the theoretical propositions cannot be falsified. Logically, one must therefore at least talk about the probability of a certain phenomenon taking place if one is to live up to the requirement that it must be possible to test a theory meaningfully. The ambiguity should rather be solved through a more detailed specification of the relationships, including the underpinning causal mechanisms, and through subsequent empirical testing. In this light, Schmitter's resorting to the notion of possibilism is all the more surprising as transitologists have in fact presented falsifiable hypotheses about the transition to democracy.

Elite transformations and democratic regimes

Michael Burton, Richard Gunther, and John Higley (1992) have developed a theoretical framework connecting an elite perspective with democratic consolidation, which may be seen as a close kin to transition theory. They begin by defining elites as persons capable of exploiting their strategic positions to exercise significant influence on political outcomes. Their primary claim is that the extent of the control of the elite over social groups and their capacity to obtain agreement about decisive issues and to obligate their respective supporters in relation to agreements is decisive for democratic consolidation and stability (Burton et al. 1992: 8–10). Hence, democratic consolidation requires that past discrepancies between elite groups are replaced by broad consensus about the value of democratic institutions and procedures (Burton et al. 1992: 3).

In countries where authoritarian government and political instability are the norm, transformations that the elites themselves have set in motion are therefore the most significant – and possibly the only – path to democratic consolidation. Elites that have been split in the past must reach agreement as regards the norms and fundamental rights that are to form the framework for future political practice. There are two ways of obtaining the necessary consensus. One of these, 'elite consensus', is possible where previously divided and hostile elites suddenly change the relationships between them. This typically occurs when they negotiate a compromise that effectively puts a lid on the worst discords and establishes agreement about the rules of the game (Burton et al. 1992: 13–14). To illustrate this, Burton et al. point to Costa Rica (1948), Colombia, and Venezuela (both 1957–1958), which are actually the only countries in Latin America that have continually been democracies – to a more or less liberal degree – throughout the 1960s, 1970s, and 1980s (cf. Peeler 1985).

The other way an elite transformation can ensure democratic consolidation is through 'elite convergence'. This is a more gradual process than elite agreements. Basically, a process unfolds over years – in some cases several decades – during which rivaling elites make tactical decisions which gradually lead to consensus among the elites. One can distinguish between two consecutive sequences. First, there will be groups from the rivaling elites that engage in amicable collaboration aimed at mobilizing voters. After these groups have won several elections in a row, thereby establishing a firm grip on the governing power, the most important elite group outside of the coalition will become frustrated by not having any influence. It will therefore form a political alternative and choose to take up the fight within the parliamentary arena by participating in the elections – instead of challenging the democratic rules of the game, the opposition accepts them. This adaptation will often be followed by a moderation of the ideological positions of the political parties (Burton et al. 1992: 24–25). When agreement is reached at the elite level, the outcome will be a consolidated democracy. Burton et al. mention the development during the Fifth French Republic, established in 1958, as a good example of elite convergence. This process, which gradually led to agreement about the structuring of the government, culminated in the 1980s with a socialist president and a conservative prime minister who enjoyed majority support in the parliament. This phenomenon has subsequently been labeled 'cohabitation'.

Independent explanatory power?

The transition and elite transformation theories are rather enticing as it seems a priori convincing for the strategic choices made by the elites to have independent leverage for the development of democracy. However, both explanatory currents have met critiques that emphasize fundamental weaknesses, and questions have been raised regarding their contribution to the explanation of democratic development.

Elite transformation theory is burdened by two interconnected problems. First, the explanation may be said to have some tautological elements, as the acceptance of the democratic rules of the game represents the essence of what the theory is intended to explain, namely democratic stability. In gist, the elite support democracy by acting democratically. As Andreas Schedler (2001: 78) has commented, it is hardly surprising that "democracy will last if all major actors expect it to last." Moreover, it is unclear which circumstances have motivated the elite groups in society to carry out a transformation from being conflict-prone to seeking consensus in connection with the preferred form of government. There is, in particular, a lack of attention devoted to why it often proves impossible to reach agreement about democracy. To be sure, it should be mentioned that the empirical studies that have applied this theoretical framework have often provided good descriptions of what has ultimately led to successful or failed incidents of elite agreements or elite convergence. Nonetheless, the theoretical perspective would be more convincing if it included systematic considerations as to how specific preferences and the distribution of resources fit together. This would increase the chances of providing the predictions necessary for testing the theory. Moreover, tightening things up in this manner would make it clearer how the elite account could be integrated with structural explanations.

Turning attention to transition theory, two general problems again present themselves. On the one hand, the explanatory power tends to be fairly low. No strong, systematic relationships between the mode of transition and the actual transition to democracy and consolidation of the same have been identified, especially if we look beyond the very short term. Along these lines, with reference to Latin America, Maria Tavares de Almeida has argued that "After twenty years, it is difficult to sustain that the mode of transition was an important variable to explain the limits and pitfalls of democracy" (quoted in Karl 2005: 39). Extending the perspective to the rest of the world does not significantly improve the support for transition theory as represented by the hypotheses forwarded by O'Donnell, Schmitter, and Karl (Viskum 2009). Insofar as the transition forms coincide with democratic development, this seems to be the result of an overlap between the mode of transition and the background structural conditions. This can either mean that the explanation of the transition serves as a tie between the outcome and a number of background conditions or that we are confronted by an outright spurious relationship.

To illustrate this point, consider McFaul's (2002) attempt at explaining the regime development in the Eastern Bloc following the collapse of communism. His explanation is one of the few examples of a transition theory with considerable explanatory power. McFaul begins by rejecting the transition theories referred to above, which had been developed against the background of developments in Southern Europe and Latin America. His main objection is that the best democratic performance among the post-communist countries is represented by those that went 180 degrees against the recommendations made by O'Donnell and Schmitter about not setting economic reforms on the agenda, ensuring equal distribution of goods between incumbents and opposition, and keeping the masses calm. In Karl and Schmitter's terminology, reform and revolution have, according to McFaul, proven superior to imposition and pact strategies in the post-communist setting, which is completely at odds with the predictions made by transitology.[3]

On this basis, McFaul (2002) fleshes out an alternative theory. He proposes that it was the ideology of the challengers and the balance of power in relation to the communist authorities that determined the subsequent outcome (see also Easter 1997). In the cases where the balance of power tipped towards the democratic opposition, the outcome was – using our conceptualization (see Chapter 3) – polyarchy or liberal democracy, as in Czechoslovakia and Poland. Where the incumbent elites were strongest, a new autocracy was installed, as in Turkmenistan and Uzbekistan. Finally, the outcome was a form of minimalist democracy or sustained and often violent conflict in countries where there was a relatively equal balance of power, as in Albania and Ukraine. Scrutinizing McFaul's empirical ordering of the countries on the basis of their respective modes of transition, it becomes clear that his actor-centered division reflects the expectations that could be deduced from a focus on the countries' prior structural conditions in the form of resource allocation, mobilization capacity, and the predominant values at the time of the transition. As Herbert Kitschelt (2003; Kitschelt et al. 1999: 29–31) has pointed out, however, these conditions were largely the result of the histories of the respective countries that had found expression in different forms of pre-communist political and economic organization, which were then largely reproduced during the communist era. More particularly, on the eve of the collapse of communism, the balance of power appears to stand in a cause-and-effect relationship with the background structural factors (see also Chapter 11).

This does not mean that McFaul's categorization of cases and the connection between the balance of power and regime outcome do not hold water. But the qualification raises questions regarding his claim that historical patterns and former regime types do not display much co-variation with the post-communist regime development (McFaul 2002: 239). With very few exceptions, a clear and rather meaningful connection between the historical legacy on the one side and the transition form and development of democracy on the other can be identified (Bideleux & Jeffries 1998; Janos 2000; Darden & Grzymala-Busse 2006). Moreover, as we elaborate in the next section, the former regime type has also been linked systematically to both autocratic stability and the chances of democratization.

Former regime type and the prospects for pacts and democracy

Linz and Stepan (1978) were not only among the first to criticize the structuralist bias in democratization studies and to direct attention to the critical choices of key actors; they were also among the first to systematically modify the transitological perspective (Linz & Stepan 1996). Drawing on their distinctions between totalitarian, post-totalitarian, sultanistic, and authoritarian regimes (outlined in Chapter 3), they argue that the mode of transition to a large extent depends on the kind of autocratic regime that is to be replaced.

Table 9.2 shows that in times of transition, the prospect for pacts is highest if the autocratic regime is authoritarian or post-totalitarian, whereas they are very difficult – indeed, next to impossible – in the case of totalitarian and sultanistic regimes. What is more, the chances that democratic consolidation will be achieved follow the same hierarchy, meaning that this is easier with an authoritarian and post-totalitarian past than with a totalitarian or sultanistic legacy.

Turning the research agenda upside-down, Barbara Geddes (1999) focuses on a necessary but not sufficient phase before a democratic transition; that is, autocratic breakdown. Based on game theoretic elaborations of elite interests, she constructs

Table 9.2 Former regime type and the possibilities for pacts

Authoritarian regime	Totalitarian regime	Post-totalitarian regime	Sultanistic regime
As civil society can be relatively developed and some moderate opposition can exist, pacts between moderates from the ruling elite and the opposition are possible.	As there is no space for an independent civil society or an organized political opposition or moderates among the ruling elite, pacts are not possible.	As there is often a collective leadership and room for a moderate wing as well as incipient opposition and civil society groupings, pacts are possible if the incumbents believe that elections are necessary and that they have a chance to win.	As civil liberties and the rule of law are lacking and personalistic penetration characterizes the whole polity, pacts are virtually not possible.

Source: Based on Linz & Stepan (1996: 57).

a number of propositions on the resilience of different forms of autocracy. In line with her expectations, Geddes (1999: 37) finds that single-party regimes tend to have the longest average time span (about 23 years), whereas personalistic regimes tend to have a shorter duration (about 15 years), while military regimes break down after only nine years on average. Using the distinctions provided by Geddes, Jason Brownlee (2009) has moved beyond the study of autocratic stability by examining if there is any systematic relationship between former regime type and perspectives for democratization once an autocratic breakdown has happened. He finds no indications that the frequency of breakdown is significantly different between the various forms of autocracy but shows that the prospects of subsequent transitions to democracy are indeed impacted by regime type (Brownlee 2009: 516).

However, Axel Hadenius and Jan Teorell (2007) reach a different conclusion, when they use their own distinctions between autocratic regime forms (see Chapter 3). They argue that autocratic regimes differ not only in their endurance but also in their propensity to democratize. Their main finding is that multi-party autocracies – besides being the most unstable regime type – are most likely to experience democratic transitions. Hadenius and Teorell (2007: 154) take this as a "hopeful sign for the future of democracy" since multi-party autocracies have become the most widespread type of undemocratic rule (but see Brownlee 2009: 520). In this way, they write into the debate on the impact of holding elections under autocratic rule. While some scholars argue that (insufficiently competitive) elections tend to impede democratization (e.g., Gandhi 2008; Schedler 2010), others claim that elections under these circumstances generally facilitate democratization (e.g., Lindberg 2006; Howard & Roessler 2006). The former group often points to the direct and indirect legitimizing role of elections, the latter to the opportunities for the opposition to organize and campaign (cf. Lindberg 2009). In an attempt to test the effect of elections under the circumstance of autocracy, Brownlee (2009: 531) reaches the following conclusion:

> Elections have not provided oppositionists an independent mechanism for ousting incumbents, but where the opposition is able to perform strongly, competitive elections augur well for chances the successor regime will meet the minimum standard for democratic governance.

This result sounds rather convincing. Indeed, it is hardly surprising that elections per se have no significant effect on the chances of democratic transitions nor that the likelihood is significantly higher if the opposition has a stronghold. Moreover, the blurred borderline between such regimes and minimalist democracies in Brownlee's study (and that of Hadenius and Teorell) means that the second finding may be partially tautological.

In retrospect

A number of prominent scholars have argued that the structural factors that used to heavily condition the advent of electoral competition have done so increasingly less over recent decades, at least since the end of the Cold War (Levitsky & Way 2010: 19; Schmitter 2010). In a recent retrospect, Schmitter (2010: 18) sums this view up nicely when observing that during the past 25 years, "Democratization has proven far easier to accomplish in the contemporary historical context than I had at first thought it would be." If true, this observation would lend support to the basic postulates of transitology. However, there is a catch. Schmitter is keen to add that the ease of democratization seems to owe to the fact that it has been much less consequential than under prior waves of democratization. It has, so to speak, merely created small ripples outside of the political arena as regards social and economic consequences. The old elites have not had to fear increased redistribution. In large parts of Latin America, for example, they have not even had to respect the civil liberties of ordinary people. The only expense has been that one group has had to yield to the other in connection with regular elections. Democracy has therefore been accepted in the very circles that formerly (especially in Latin America) often undermined it via coups. O'Donnell (2010a, 2010b) broadly concurs with this observation (see also Munck & Snyder 2007: 294–295, 326). Przeworski (2009), too, has emphasized that the new democratizations may well have led to political equality but not to economic redistribution.

It may seem slightly paradoxical that O'Donnell, Schmitter, and Przeworski are behind this charge against the recent democratizations. As described above, an important premise for the transition theories they were involved in creating was that democratization can only genuinely succeed if a pact ensures that the economic privileges of the upper class are not endangered as a result of their having to renounce their political privileges. In that sense, it is tempting to conclude that the development in particularly Latin America – but also in other regions affected by the third wave (e.g., Nodia 1996: 22) – has merely confirmed their analytical points about the potential of pacted transitions. But it was probably their hope that such backroom deals, which had been necessary in the short term, would eventually pave the way for redistribution and that democracy in general would prove to present the solution to more than merely 'the problem of tyranny' (Huntington 1991: 263). For example, Schmitter (2010: 22)[4] and O'Donnell (2010a: 31) emphasize how the derived effects of the new status quo have led to disenchantment among citizens. O'Donnell (2010b), in particular, argues that democracy is in a state of crisis in the sense that even convinced democrats are disappointed about its effects. This disappointment is amplified in many new democracies by widespread political corruption and misgovernment.

We return to some of these issues in Chapter 13. What is important here is that these thoughts make for coupling transitology to our distinction between thinner and thicker types of democracy. What Schmitter (2010) and O'Donnell (2010b) are basically observing is that democratization has only been relatively unconstrained by structural conditions – indeed, more unconstrained than they had imagined back in the 1980s – if we maintain a thin definition of the concept. Tellingly, much of O'Donnell's (1993, 2001, 2007, 2010a) work over the past two decades has revolved around the observation that the more demanding attributes of democracy, such as civil liberties and the rule of law, have not been piggybacking on the introduction of electoral competition.

Conclusion

In the aftermath of the third wave's initial erosion of autocracies in Southern Europe and Latin America, transition theory was welcomed by academics and practitioners alike; not only because the perspective offered a stimulating, novel take on regime change but also because it supported the growing optimism on behalf of democracy in structurally unpropitious countries.

All told, the assumption that the transition period is a process in which the background structures are next to unimportant is problematic. A diagnostic example is the flagrant inconsistency in a book by one of the most persistent proponents of transitology, Giuseppe di Palma, with the catchy title *To Craft Democracies*. After having lambasted structuralist explanations and appraised transition theory in the theoretical part of his book, the empirical examination makes di Palma (1990: 156) concede that "Even when we favored explanations that focus on the transition and its strategies, these in turn have begged for their own explanations – often of a deeper historical and structural nature." Kitschelt (1993) makes a similar observation with regard to some of Przeworski's influential work within the genre. Stephan Haggard and Robert Kaufman (1997) are, similarly, able to argue convincingly that the power position and basic values of the agents to a great extent depend upon the long-term socio-economic development.

What is more, the definition of democracy has important bearings on the validity of the transition paradigm. It seems fair to conclude that agents' choices have so far not seemed to pave the way for the development of inclusive citizenship rights and the rule of law. It is electoral competition that has made inroads in the most unexpected of places. Only in this sense has democratization proved easier than anyone had anticipated back in the 1980s. This means that it is only what we term minimalist and possible electoral democracy – not polyarchy and liberal democracy – that has made inroads where the structural conditions are inauspicious. More generally, these debates strongly indicate that it is necessary to integrate agency-oriented and structure-oriented accounts precisely due to their considerably overlapping explanatory power. This question is fundamentally about whether we ought to perceive various explanations as supplements or alternatives to one another. We return to this coupling of multiple explanations in Chapter 11. But first we address an explanatory dimension often neglected by transitology and other approaches, namely the impact of international factors.

10 International factors

It is normal to conjure up an image of democracy waxing and waning along with shifts in the *Zeitgeist*, that is, the spirit of the age. Consider the democratic explosion that took place in the wake of the victories of the democratic countries after the two World Wars and the end of the Cold War, or the numerous democratic collapses in the interwar period, influenced by the attraction of communism, fascism, and nazism. Indeed, we can go all the way back to the great liberal revolutions in 1830 and 1848 to 1849, when the spirit of revolution could be felt throughout Europe and parts of Latin America (Weyland 2009, 2010). In addition, democracy has sometimes been established as the result of actual occupations, as in Japan and West Germany after 1945. Against this background, it may sound paradoxical that the transition theories that dominated the democratization literature in the 1980s and early 1990s showed little interest in the impact of *inter*national factors (Levitsky & Way 2010: 37–38). The message was that transitions emerge from within, regardless of whether we are dealing with transitions to or from democracy. Juan Linz (1978) accordingly argued that democratic collapse had domestic causes, and Guillermo O'Donnell and Philippe Schmitter (1986: 19) insisted on maintaining a domestic focus when analyzing transitions to democracy. To quote their uncompromising claim:

> we assert that there is no transition whose beginning is not the consequence – direct or indirect – of important divisions within the authoritarian regime itself, principally along the fluctuating cleavage between hardliners and softliners.[1]

As we noted in the previous chapter, O'Donnell and Schmitter's focus on the internal dimension was based on experiences from the regime changes in Southern Europe and Latin America in the first phase of the third wave of democratization in the 1970s and 1980s. In other words, their trenchant domestic emphasis was based on events in a particular place and time, not analytical postulates about the necessary logic of transitions across space and time. When the wave flooded Central and Eastern Europe in late 1989, the limitations of the domestic focus became readily apparent. The transitions in the former communist countries were not triggered by internal conflicts between hard-liners and soft-liners (although the outcomes of the transitions were oftentimes affected by such cleavages). Instead, they occurred the moment it became clear that Moscow was no longer protecting the single-party communist regimes in the satellite states (Przeworski 1991: 5). The international dimension also played a decisive role in the events that followed. For example, the possibility of gaining EU membership stabilized the democracies in Central and Eastern Europe, while the post-Cold War international environment – characterized by a 'Western liberal hegemony' (Levitsky & Way 2002) – paved the way for new political openings elsewhere, particularly in Sub-Saharan Africa (Bratton & van de Walle 1997).

It is in these empirical developments that we find the seeds of one of the great theoretical shifts of the 1990s, namely the increasing emphasis on international influences. Compared with the analyses of the 1950s, 1960s, 1970s, and 1980s, the exploratory thrust in international factors only came to the forefront after these changes[2] – but since then the impact of international factors has become broadly accepted. Most telling, perhaps, is the fact that Schmitter has made clear that the domestic emphasis he arrived at together with O'Donnell in 1986 is no longer valid for students of democratization:

> I do not think O'Donnell and I were mistaken when we said that the processes of democratization we were analyzing were fundamentally driven by domestic, not international, forces. The situation is different now. Today, when a country democratizes, it gets invaded, not just by NGOs, but also by the European Union, The United States Agency for International Development (US AID), and all these different democracy promotion programs. They commit substantial resources, and they meddle in the internal politics of democratizing countries in ways that were unthinkable in the late 1970s and early 1980s, when we were studying the Southern European and Latin American cases. So now I am working on the international dimension of democratization.
>
> (Munck & Snyder 2007: 329–330)

The interplay between internal and external factors

The fact that Schmitter now focuses on the internal dimension does not mean that he has thrown out the transitology baby with the domestic emphasis bathwater. Instead, the point is that it has become commonplace to combine different perspectives on democratization in one and the same explanatory model to overcome a general problem addressed by Robert Putnam (1988: 427) in his work *Diplomacy and Domestic Politics: The Logic of Two-Level Games*: "Domestic politics and international relations are often somewhat entangled, but our theories have not yet sorted out the puzzling tangle."[3]

One of the early attempts to navigate the internal and external dimensions of democratization was carried out by Juan Linz and Alfred Stepan (1996). We reserve a discussion of their important book for the subsequent chapter but note that their explanatory model to a large extent set the stage for the work taking place throughout the 1990s in that it presented a forceful argument for treating the internal and external dimensions alongside of each other. While international factors are still oftentimes treated separately, the underlying premise of the present debates would appear to be that they are to be considered together with domestic factors in the form of the actors' interests and the structural constraints. For example, Georg Sørensen (2008: 98) argues that successful democracy promotion from the outside depends on three domestic conditions:

1   political leaders who are committed to democratization
2   an autonomous, merit-based (i.e., Weberian) bureaucracy
3   a vigorous civil society capable of holding the rulers to account.

Similarly, Christian Welzel (2009: 88) asserts that while domestic elites might well react to external pressure by carrying out certain democratic reforms, this does not necessarily lead them to respect all aspects of liberal democracy. It is only when there is also pressure from below (i.e., from societal groups) that one can seriously expect effective democratization. Hence, external factors rarely stand alone in analyses; most often they are understood to interact with domestic conditions. With this premise in mind, we now present an overview of the most influential international explanations.

Two early attempts to systematize the international influences

One of the first scholars to propose systematic distinctions amenable to empirical analysis was Laurence Whitehead. Whitehead (1996: 3) acknowledges that internal factors often play a decisive role in democratizations. But, he adds, the international context must be included in the equation, whether we are to understand democratic breakthroughs or democratic breakdowns. Against this background, he distinguishes between three categories of international factors:

1   *Contagion.* This factor refers to how countries tend to carry out regime changes in 'neighboring clusters'. In the course of the third wave of democratization, we have seen this first in Southern Europe, subsequently in Latin America, then in Central and Eastern Europe, and finally in Sub-Saharan Africa. The most significant mechanism is the transfer of information about the development in the (neighboring) countries with which the population (and often also the elites) identifies.
2   *Control.* The point here is that external forces can realize ends-oriented regime change by relying on good old-fashioned power politics. This has been seen in Germany and Japan after World War II, in a more moderate version in the course of the de-colonization of the British colonies, and, most recently, in Afghanistan and Iraq.
3   *Consent.* When consent is operating, there is a mutually accepted interplay between the internal and external actors, which can help contribute to democratization.

Geoffrey Pridham (1997: 10–11) addresses the issue from a slightly different angle. In order to deal with the complexity of the impact of the international context, he encourages researchers to distinguish between three categories of external influences:

1 *External background factors* in the form of patterns in the foreign policy of a given country during the prior autocratic regime, pressure to reform, the geostrategic situation, international political economics, special international events, and the fundamental design and development tendencies of the international system.
2 *External actors* in the form of worldwide or regional organizations such as the EU, NATO, IMF, World Bank, and OSCE, foreign governments (great powers or neighbors) as well as NGOs such as parties and civil society groups.
3 *External impacts* in the form of direct intervention – such as invasion or occupation – or political, diplomatic, economic, commercial, moral, and cultural impacts. Moreover, one can distinguish between direct and indirect impacts and whether they are based on coercion or persuasion.

Linkage and leverage

As pioneers of the international approach, Whitehead and Pridham have obviously had a significant influence on the literature, but it would be incorrect to claim that consensus has developed regarding the merits of their distinctions. Conversely, Steven Levitsky and Lucan Way's (2005, 2006, 2010) relatively new perspective has found broad support. The premise for their explanation is the existence of Western liberal hegemony since the collapse of communism. This hegemony entails that the structure of the international system serves to promote democracy. But this does not mean that the consequence will, as it were, be effective democratization. Here, it is necessary to distinguish between 'leverage' and 'linkage'.

Leverage refers to the strength of the democratic countries in relation to the 'receiving countries'; that is, the direct impact of external powers using carrot and stick, respectively, based on the existing, asymmetrical power relations. The influence of the USA in Latin America, which in recent decades has mostly been democracy facilitating but earlier was sometimes democracy impeding, offers a good example (Livingstone 2009). It is also worth mentioning the position of the Western donor countries in relation to recipients of development aid, particularly in Sub-Saharan Africa (Sørensen 1993; Stokke 1995; Wright & Winters 2010). Here we hear an echo of Whitehead's control, as the promotion of democracy is included alongside other priorities such as security, stability, and the supply of oil.

However, according to Levitsky and Way (2006), linkage is far more important. They use this term to refer to the degree of contact to – or even the interweaving with – Western democracies. The ties can be economic (e.g., trade and investments), social (e.g., media, tourism, and education), and political (e.g., treaties), in some circumstances supported by membership of certain international/regional organizations. Linkage is usually rooted in geographical proximity as well as a cultural and/or historical community or fellow feeling. For instance, Latin America has great linkage with the USA, while the African countries do not. Yet the most obvious, recent example of dense linkages is found in another region. We are here referring to the relationship between Western European countries and the East-Central and Eastern European countries. Due to the EU accession process, which kicked off in the second half of the 1990s and led to the enlargements in 2004 and 2007, the EU's leverage over East-Central Europe has been at least as pronounced as US leverage in Central America.

We take up the issue of the external influence of the EU below. The example is merely intended to capture the logic behind Levitsky and Way's model. Their general message is that leverage unto itself is not particularly valuable, as the external pressure must combine with internal support in order to be effective. Only where powerful foreign policy is combined with linkage – that is, integration with the receiving state – will it lead to effective democratization. Phrased in terms of raw power politics, leverage is merely potential power, as an external actor (including a great power) can only have an impact on a country if the country in question finds that failing to live up to the pressure comes at a cost. These costs become a reality if there are important connections (linkages) between the two countries. The leverage available to the external actors is proportionate to the strength of these linkages.

Combining leverage and linkage in this way is both elegant and intuitively relevant, and Levitsky and Way have undoubtedly struck upon a central distinction. Their work has so far culminated in a book that uses these concepts to explain the flourishing of what they term 'competitive authoritarianism'; that is, hybrid regimes in which formal democratic institutions are undermined by authoritarian practices. Levitsky and Way (2010: 20–23) here offer a structural perspective in which leverage, linkage, and the organizational power of authoritarian incumbents are used to explain the trajectories of 35 instances of this regime form in the period 1990 to 2008. The argument is as follows. First, where extensive linkages exist, competitive authoritarian regimes democratize, even in the absence of favorable domestic conditions. Second, where linkage is low, the outcome depends upon the organizational power of the incumbent and, though to a lesser extent, on leverage. If organizational power is high, authoritarianism stabilizes. If, on the contrary, organizational power is low, leverage becomes important. In this case, low leverage means that even poorly institutionalized regimes often survive as authoritarian (Levitsky & Way 2010: 23–24).

In this way, Levitsky and Way (2010) are able to rather resiliently explain which of three paths competitive authoritarian regimes have traversed between 1990 and 2008: towards democracy, stable authoritarianism, or unstable authoritarianism.[4] Their model may be said to accentuate a point we made above, namely that the literature is increasingly prone to combine internal and external dimensions of democratization. What is more, it sheds light on some of the many cases where Western initiatives have petered out, as in Central Asia, South Asia, the Middle East, and Africa. Finally, Levitsky and Way's model has some important implications for the dynamics of democratization, which we return to below.

But one important point of criticism deserves to be mentioned. Particularly when fleshing out the theory, Levitsky and Way (2005, 2006) seemed to harbor a view of linkage and leverage as factors which (if at all effective) by definition exert a positive impact on democratization. As Jakob Tolstrup (2009, forthcoming) has argued, this is problematic. For instance, an international player such as Russia has an obvious hamstrung effect on its 'near abroad' with regard to democratization. More generally, the democracy-constraining influence of a wider number of regional great powers, including China, has been recently acknowledged (Puddington 2008). Levitsky and Way's initial neglect of this seems to owe to the fact that their premise of Western liberal hegemony clouded these points. Yet in their book from 2010, they have made an important concession as they operate with the democracy-inhibiting force of so-called 'black knights'. This goes to show that the 'negative influence' is no longer ignored in the literature.

Overview

Against this background, let us attempt to tie the strands together. Almost two decades after Huntington's contribution, we are faced with a body of literature that contains four different forms of external impacts (cf. Diamond 2008: ch. 5):

1   Diffusion and demonstration effects, including the snowball effect (Huntington 1991; Brinks & Coppedge 2006; Gleditsch & Ward 2006).
2   Sanctions and conditionality, including from international organizations in general and the USA and the EU in particular (Pridham 2000; Vachudova 2005; Levitsky & Way 2005; Pevehouse 2005).
3   Direct intervention or occupation, including military campaigns and phenomena such as the collapse of the Eastern Bloc and decolonization (Huntington 1991; Whitehead 1996).
4   Support for key domestic actors, including support to local parties, civil society groups, and independent media as well as assistance in carrying out and observing elections (Burnell 2000; Carothers 2004; Kelley 2009).

The literature also includes a current emphasizing 'social learning'. The point here is that via diplomacy and exchange – linkages in general – the external agents can convince the local elites to move in a democratic direction. This current is related to several of the aforementioned forms of influence and is therefore difficult to situate as an independent point.

What, then, are the general conclusions in the literature? It is important to tread carefully, but a couple of general observations seem warranted. There have been few direct interventions, and in the post-Cold War period they have often resulted in the opposite of what was intended (Merkel 2008); just compare the examples of West Germany and Japan after World War II with recent events in Iraq and Afghanistan. Conversely, there is reasonable agreement that diffusion has played a decisive role in the third wave of democratization. Daniel Brinks and Michael

Coppedge (2006) found the following trends in a large-scale statistical analysis of the years 1972 to 1996:

- Adjustments in the direction of the global average level of democracy.
- Adjustments in the direction of the regional average level of democracy in most parts of the world.
- Adjustments in the direction of the average level of democracy of the neighboring countries.
- That a positive impact on the level of democracy is associated with being placed in the US sphere of influence.

Finally, the EU appears to be the only international institution that has had genuine success promoting democracy via conditionality. This is elaborated below but first we need to touch upon another point. As we have already mentioned, the literature is peppered with critical voices when it comes to less obligating measures aimed at promoting democracy, as in connection with development aid.

A glance at the skeptics

Consensus exists to the effect that recent decades have been characterized by a general diffusion of democratic norms. In addition, there is widespread agreement about the unique influence of the EU in East-Central and Eastern Europe (more on this below). However, many researchers have been skeptical when it comes to the impact of the softer forms of conditionality and the promotion of democracy. One of the earliest – and most persistent – critics of international democracy promotion has been Thomas Carothers (1991, 1999, 2002). Carothers (1991: 218) advanced the following argument shortly after the fall of the Berlin Wall:

> Problems in Latin America [and other developing countries] such as political violence, the weak rule of law, and the absence of real democratic norms are problems that go to the core of the societies. They represent deep-seated economic and social structures, long-standing political habits, and fundamental cultural patterns. The notion that some modest amount of training seminars, exchange programs, and technical assistance can solve these problems has no logical foundation.

Carothers' criticism must be understood as an internal criticism within the democracy promotion establishment. He is thus working within the field himself, and his general message would appear to be that the promotion of democracy can actually have important consequences. Nevertheless, these consequences depend on the internal structural conditions. Hence, there are limits on the potential to re-create societies from the outside, and Carothers' warnings serve to shore up against naïve optimism that can lead to setbacks for politicians and transnational civil society organizations working to promote democracy. Others have gone one step further. Jean Grugel (2002: 135) argues that the extent of the resources used and the number of programs and missions carried out do not appear to have any direct connection to whether or not democratizations have proven successful. This is basically because effective democratization requires internal support from the political elites, the existence of a vibrant civil society, and a relatively efficient state apparatus. Measures aimed at supporting democracy are often provided on the assumption "that democratization is a matter of relatively straightforward institutional reform, rather than a complex process of transformation requiring socio-economic change, cultural shifts and a redistribution of power" (Grugel 2002: 136).

The most important point of the skeptics is that none of these things can be grafted onto a country from the outside. Foreign aid only helps democracy to strike root if there is a strong, local foundation upon which to build democracy. Further along these lines, Grugel (2002) argues that, in practice, the promotion of democracy often conceals the exercise of power politics in which Western countries 'teach' developing countries – often against their will – how they must organize their internal political affairs. Against that background, it should come as no surprise that the results have often been limited (2002: 136). These disheartening conclusions have gradually made inroads in the literature, to some extent piggybacking on the general consensus about the need to tie internal and external dimensions together. In the following section, we investigate parts of this criticism more closely. This endeavor simultaneously enables us to wrestle with one of the modern classics in the social sciences.

Marshall revisited

In a lecture entitled *Citizenship and Social Class*, T.H. Marshall (1996 [1949]) argued that citizenship rights in Great Britain had been introduced in the form of a three-stage rocket: first, civil liberties (in the 18th century), second, political rights (in the 19th century), and finally social rights (in the 20th century). Since then, a number of researchers have expanded the empirical scope of Marshall's sequence. Seen from the higher ground, it seems fair to say that – with some partial exceptions such as Imperial Germany where at least rudimentary social rights preceded political rights – it characterizes the itinerary of the Western world towards liberal democracy and the modern welfare state (see Bendix 1964; Habermas 1996; O'Donnell 1998, 2001). However, as O'Donnell (2001: 54) and others note, the situation in most contemporary developing countries is strikingly different, as "Political citizenship may be implanted in the midst of very little, or highly skewed, civil citizenship, to say nothing of social welfare rights." In other words, the historical sequence of citizenship rights seems to have changed (see also Diamond 1999; Zakaria 2003; Sørensen 2008). In today's developing countries, political rights (free, inclusive elections) thus precede civil rights (rule of law, freedom of speech, the right to assembly, and private property). As in the Western historical sequence, social rights (the welfare state) still come at the end of the chain – if at all.

This is where the discussion directly relates to the debate about international influences that we have just touched upon. From the literature, we can derive two related reasons why Marshall's 'Western' sequence is likely to differ from that of the contemporary developing countries. The first, which practically has the status of a general premise, relates to that which we have earlier referred to as liberal hegemony (Levitsky & Way 2002). The *Zeitgeist* and the foreign policy pursued by the Western democracies and the general agenda of the international organizations contribute to sustained pressure to democratize. With the exception of great powers such as China and Russia and a number of oil-rich countries, there are very few countries outside of the West that are immune to this pressure (Levitsky & Way 2010: 18). The problem, however, is that the internal structural conditions in most developing countries are not favorable to democratization. As already mentioned, most of the developing countries are characterized by low levels of modernization, weak civil societies, incompetent and corrupt state apparatuses, and cultural norms promoting patron–client structures. In this situation, it is difficult to carry out genuine democratization (Grzymala-Busse & Luong 2002: 536; Møller & Skaaning 2011).

The combination of external pressure and internal limitations has had salient consequences. The literature teems with examples of how the political elites in developing countries play along with the democratic agenda without serious, in-depth democratization taking place (e.g., Nodia 1996: 22; Oxhorn 2003; O'Donnell 2007, 2010a, 2010b; Diamond 2008; Levitsky & Way 2010: 19). Political elites introduce political rights, which are more or less sanctioned, but they are unable and/or unwilling to ensure a broad range of civil rights; and this is even more the case with social rights. In other words, the elites only provide superficial, half-hearted support to the democratic agenda, which therefore is not realized fully. Based on these theoretical writings, we can deduce the following hypotheses. Though the external pressure often leads to minimalist democracy, and at times even to electoral democracy, more demanding regimes in the form of polyarchy and liberal democracy can only become a reality if the domestic conditions are favorable. The same is the case for the social rights associated with the welfare state.

In prior work, we have attempted to carry out a systematical empirical appraisal of these postulates (Møller & Skaaning 2011: ch. 5). Our analyses show that the historical sequence – described by Marshall – has changed, so that the developing countries are faring at least as well (and often better) in terms of electoral rights than civil rights, which in turn are enforced at least to the same extent as (and often more than) social rights.[5] This finding immediately raises the question as to when the sequence changed. The general message in the literature seems to be that Western liberal hegemony made its entry in the wake of the breakdown of communism. Until 1989, two opposed international forces had to be considered: one pressuring for market economy and democracy (from the West) and one for planned economy and one-party autocracies (from the Eastern Bloc). What is more, this very competition meant that the emphasis on democratization was something of a luxury that could not necessarily be prioritized (over security and economic interests) from the Western side. Instead, foreign policy was often led by the maxim: better our dictator than theirs (Moscow's).[6]

The superpower rivalry between the Soviet Union and the USA clearly limited the agenda of regime change and diversity around the world (McFaul 2010). In Latin America, the USA intervened directly or indirectly if crucial economic interests were thought to be at stake and/or if a (potential) government was considered to be too left-leaning and maybe a challenge to alliance relationships. Financial, military, and moral support was frequently offered to autocratic regimes, as exemplified by the interventions in Guatemala in 1954 and the Dominican Republic in 1965, and the support of military coups in El Salvador in 1960 and in Chile and Uruguay 13 years later (Grandin 2004). Under certain conditions, though, the USA did support liberalization attempts, and after the Cold War, US foreign policy shifted in the direction of more emphasis upon the promotion of liberal-democratic practices (Carothers 1999; von Hippel 2000). Nonetheless, trade-offs with other interests have continued to play a significant role, as demonstrated by the US support of autocratic regimes in the Middle East in the 1990s and 2000s (Callaway & Matthews 2008).

However, in the Soviet sphere of influence, limits on democratic development were even more rigid as any type of transition was prevented. Some of the most obvious manifestations of this mantra were the crackdowns of popular uprisings in East Germany (1953), Hungary (1956), Czechoslovakia (1968), and Poland (1956, 1970, 1976, and 1981). Thus, it is not surprising that the 1989 breaking point initiated new patterns of regime change (McFaul 2002; Doorenspleet 2005; Levitsky & Way 2010). Levitsky and Way (2010: 18) describe the effect of this new structure of the international system in the following way:

> These changes in the international environment raised the external cost of authoritarianism and created incentives for elites in developing and post-communist countries to adopt the formal architecture of Western-style democracy, which – at a minimum – entailed multiparty elections.

In Levitsky and Way's (2010: 34) opinion, this implies that the prospects of generalizing across the Cold War period and the post-Cold War period are limited. Even if we should not take the argument this far, one would hypothesize that Marshall's historical sequence changed after the fall of the Berlin Wall, at which time political rights unmistakably came high on the international agenda. Our analysis only to some extent supports this, however (see Møller & Skaaning 2011: ch. 5). The sequences really began changing a decade prior to 1989. Yet we do find some evidence that this trend was further boosted by the end of the Cold War (Møller & Skaaning 2011: 80). That said, the conclusion must be that the efforts to pursue the sequence back in time raise questions regarding the specific expectations that may be derived from the literature, most notably the timing of the onset of the dynamic factor of liberal hegemony. However, none of this changes the fact that, in the latest generation, Marshall's sequence has been replaced by one based on the primacy of political rights.

The EU: in a league of its own?

If we take another look at the 2011 distribution between different types of democracy (as reported in Chapter 3), one specific detail catches the eye. A number of post-communist countries in East-Central Europe obtain the status of either liberal democracy (Czech Republic, Estonia, Lithuania, Poland, Slovakia, Slovenia) or polyarchy (Bulgaria, Croatia, Hungary, Latvia, Romania). This is conspicuous considering that so few recently democratized states can boast such a status. This striking geographical distribution points back to the argument that the most effective – indeed, perhaps the only genuinely effective – international influence is to be found in the EU accession process, which culminated in the two 'eastern enlargements' in 2004 and 2007 (Schimmelfennig & Sedelmeier 2005; Vachudova 2005). As opposed to the Western influence in Sub-Saharan Africa and the strong position of the USA in Central America, the conditionality of the EU would appear to have led ten formerly communist countries genuinely in the direction of liberal democracy.

Otherwise they would not have been able to have been admitted to the EU. For at the meeting of the European Council in Copenhagen in June 1993, it was stipulated that those aspiring to the EU had to be democracies in order to be allowed to begin negotiations for membership. This political criterion[7] was not subject to negotiation, so there was no mistaking the incentive for the candidate countries. For the same reason, many politicians, journalists, and scholars credit the EU for the political and economic merits of the East-Central and Eastern European countries. The situation is not that simple, however. As Milada Vachudova (2005: 25–62) has shown, up to seven[8] of the ten countries – Estonia, Latvia, Lithuania, Poland, Slovenia, Czech Republic, and Hungary – were full-fledged democracies before the EU accession negotiations had started in the mid-1990s, indeed, before the Copenhagen Criteria were formulated. Vachudova calls these countries 'liberal' and compares them to three 'illiberal' East-Central European countries of this period, namely Bulgaria, Slovakia, and Romania.

Vachudova uses this comparison to flesh out two forms of EU leverage: passive and active. Passive leverage is the result of the general attractiveness of the EU. Active leverage results from the negotiation process itself, where Brussels has been able to demand very specific economic and political reforms. Until the mid-1990s, the EU only had its passive leverage to fall back on. Against this background, Vachudova (2005) shows that the political and economic diversity of the early 1990s was very much home grown, as the influence of the EU was only passive during this period. Moreover, she demonstrates that the subsequent uniformity (where all countries went liberal) was due to the active leverage that began with the accession process.

Why did the active influence of the EU prove to be so effective? According to Vachudova (2005: 105–138), three things are worth emphasizing: first, the fundamental asymmetry in the relationship between the applicant countries and the EU. The East-Central and Eastern European countries were much keener to join than the club's members were to open the doors. It would hardly be any great loss for the 'old' member states if the enlargement came to naught. The EU could therefore make demands that were entirely unheard of in the light of the traditional conceptions regarding the sovereignty of the state (cf. Moravscik & Vachudova 2003). Second, and along these lines, the bureaucrats in Brussels were able to enforce the requirements. Third, the EU apparatus used relatively transparent assessments. If there was progress, the countries got pluses, regardless of size or political significance. This merit-based procedure lent a sense of credibility to the accession requirements.

The EU thus played a rather important role in the political and economic transformation of the ten East-Central and Eastern European countries (see also Schimmelfennig & Sedelmeier 2005). Without the accession negotiations, it is doubtful whether the political elites in Bulgaria, Romania, and Slovakia would have changed their illiberal ways in the early 1990s. At the same time, it is conceivable that certain liberal states would have turned their backs on democracy and the market economy if one political faction suddenly became pre-eminent. Nonetheless, Vachudova's (2005) analysis leads us to conclude that even in Central and Eastern Europe, the internal conditions played a very important role for the democratizations (and economic reforms). As Herbert Kitschelt et al. (1999; see also Møller & Skaaning 2009) have shown, most of the eight countries that became EU members on May 1, 2004 were relatively modernized, had historical experience with the rule of law and democracy, and had close ties to Western Europe. In our view, it is among these factors that we must find the explanations for the democratizations in the early 1990s.

In sum, the EU accession process has helped keep the East-Central European countries on the straight and narrow. Moreover, it has led countries such as Bulgaria, Slovakia, and Romania onto a more democratic track the first time around – a tendency that may also be observed among the countries that the EU has touted as potential members: Macedonia, Serbia, Montenegro, Albania, Bosnia-Herzegovina, and not least Turkey. In this manner, the accession process probably distinguishes itself from all other international factors in terms of a deeper impact. The active leverage of the EU is unique because it has an impact on the civil, political, and social dimensions at one and the same time. To use our typology, it has facilitated not only minimalist democracy but genuine movements towards liberal democracy. But, crucially, the soil of East-Central Europe was also fertile for this stately plant.

Conclusion

Not many researchers would today claim that political shifts in the direction of democracy or autocracy solely arise from domestic conditions. To the contrary, the most recent literature teems with theories about how international factors impact upon national developments. This chapter has shed light on this literature. An important theme that has arisen is that one should not overestimate the consequences of the external pressure. First, we have repeatedly emphasized that the new literature on international influences seeks to understand these consequences by combining internal and external dimensions of democratization. Second, on the basis of a number of recent analyses, we have argued that the international influences have tended to have asymmetrical consequences. While they may contribute to spreading minimalist democracy – a development that is strengthened by diffusion via neighboring countries – liberal democracy is not part of the package because it must grow strong from within, which depends on the internal structural limitations.

A final theoretical issue presents itself here. In the above discussion, international influences have by and large been conceived of as a structural factor exogenous to the receiving state. Levitsky and Way (2010), for instance, are unapologetic about this blunt structuralism. The recent literature includes an attempt to bring the domestic actors back into this debate, for example, by analyzing what is termed 'domestic gatekeeper elites'. The main thrust of a recent contribution is that such elites can, even over relatively short stretches of time, alter the degree of linkage with external actors such as the EU and Russia (Tolstrup forthcoming). This addition serves to make Levitsky and Way's theory more dynamic and it is an important research agenda because it promises to shed some light on the often belittled domestic filters of international influences, which – considering the consensus about the need to combine the external and internal dimension – can probably only be neglected at our peril.

Returning to the substantial implications, in light of the above it is not particularly strange that the situation in many of the new democracies is reminiscent of the southern Italian nobleman and author Giuseppe Tomasi di Lampedusa's renowned dictum regarding political change: "If we want things to stay as they are, things will have to change." This is the entire point in his novel *The Leopard*, which describes the inclusion of Sicily in the new Italian state as part of the Italian unification in the 1860s. At the time, Sicily was very poorly prepared to incorporate the rule of law, elections, and economic modernization. The result, which endured over the next many decades, was a modernized façade, and Sicily is still limping after northern and central Italy to this day.

We see virtually the same picture when comparing the established liberal democracies in the developed countries with the new democracies in the developing countries. This may possibly prove to be decisive for the survival of democracy should the *Zeitgeist* shift again, to the disfavor of democracy. The only genuine example of external pressure leading to in-depth democratization may be found in the EU accession negotiations. This exception is rather striking in the sense that the opportunities for the EU to have an impact on these countries via voluntarism are unique. What is more, it is important to keep in sight the fact that the new member states – with Bulgaria and Romania as partial exceptions – have actually had rather favorable structural conditions for democratization. We address this issue in the next chapter where we discuss the possibilities for integrating various types of explanations.

11 Combining agency and structure

In this chapter, we change focus from the clear-cut approaches discussed in Chapters 7 to 10 and instead diagnose the most prominent attempts to combine different explanatory perspectives. In this connection we also discuss why, on the one hand, such integration is so crucial for coherent analyses of democratization but, on the other hand, why it is also so difficult.

A panoramic view of the development within the literature

The approaches discussed in the chapters on modernization theory and the social forces tradition conjure up a picture in which structural drivers – such as the level of modernization or class constellations – are all important for democracy, and in which the actors hold virtually no independent sway over the events. Recall merely Gregory Luebbert's (1991: 306) symptomatic claim that "One of the cardinal lessons of the story I have told is that leadership and meaningful choice played no role in the outcomes." Transitology obviously represents a very different take on the great game of democratization. Here, it is the actors' choices during periods of upheaval that are of the essence – and which can override the effect of structural conditions.

But the contrast is striking in two other ways as well. First, because any attempt to face it forces us to confront the fundamental 'agency-structure problem'; that is, whether social actions are largely determined by structures or whether actors can alter this context in a voluntaristic way (Mahoney & Snyder 1999: 4). Second, as emphasized by Herbert Kitschelt (1992: 1028), because we have here touched upon a more general dividing line within the democratization literature:

> The main theoretical division within this field is drawn between those who seek more 'structural' and 'configurational' explanations, on the one side, and those who focus on the process of change itself – the sequence of events and the strategic moves of the actors.

By drawing such a clear dividing line, Kitschelt is basically saying that no or at least insufficient attempts have been made to combine agency and structure into a coherent explanatory framework.[1] The two approaches simply did not speak with each other, somewhat analogously to the divide separating the quantitative and qualitative approaches in the social sciences (see Mahoney & Goertz 2006). Indeed, to some extent these two divides – one theoretical and the other method-ological – overlap as the structural approaches normally consider a multitude of cases, whereas the actor-centered approaches tend to focus on a few,[2] something that has obvious consequences for the choice of methods (cf. Lijphart 1971). Finally, we find an important difference in the temporal focus of the two different approaches. Whereas structural theories tend to emphasize what Kitschelt (2003) elsewhere terms 'deep' causes, stretching far back in time, actor-centered theories, revolving around contingent choices, tend to emphasize more proximate causes.

However, quite a lot has changed since Kitschelt made the observation cited above. After first being dominated by structuralist perspectives and then voluntarist perspectives, the aim in the democratization literature has increasingly become to integrate agency and structure (Mahoney 2003a: 136). It is interesting to note that just as the prior theoretical divide was reflected in the parallel methodological development, so is the new call for integration. The 2000s have thus witnessed a strong call for combining quantitative and qualitative methods, an agenda that has come to be known as 'mixed methods' (Lieberman 2005; Munck & Verkuilen 2005; Rohlfing 2009). It is probably no exaggeration to say that the present consensus holds that a large-n analysis which is bereft of a convincing micro-level foundation – and preferably a micro-level analysis – cannot establish a causal relationship (Hedström & Swedberg 1996). For this reason, scholars using statis-tical analyses are increasingly prone to complement this with more detailed treatment of illustrative cases.

The general objectives of this chapter are to discuss both some of the particular attempts to reach integrative explanatory frameworks, the reasons for combining structures and actors, and the more general possibilities for doing so. The premise of this discussion is that, as Kitschelt (1992: 1029) emphasizes, agency-based and structure-based explanations need not be competing, meaning that some such integration should be possible. In Table 11.1, we have illustrated our understanding of what an integrative approach implies.

The illustration anticipates the discussion carried out in this chapter. However, at the outset it is important to make clear that, in spite of the stylized simplicity,

Table 11.1 Contrasting voluntarist, integrative, and structuralist approaches

	Voluntarist approach	*Integrative approach*	*Structuralist approach*
Explanatory focus	Actors/choices	←——→	Structures/constraints
Temporal focus	Proximate causes	←——→	Deep causes
Methodological focus	Micro-level exposure of events and processes within cases	←——→	Macro-level matching of conditions and outcomes across cases

Source: Inspired by Mahoney & Snyder (1999: 7).

such integration is staggeringly difficult. Kitschelt's own attempt to do so offers an illustrative example of this. In a number of works, Kitschelt (1993, 2003; Kitschelt et al. 1999) has forcefully recommended that any agency-based explanation must be nested in a more general structural account which constrains the choice set from which actors select, meaning that both structural constraints and micro-level causal mechanisms are appreciated. Indeed, this may be seen as an attempt to formulate a macro–micro–macro causal chain (Munck 2001: 140; cf. Hedström & Swedberg 1996). Yet, in his actual application of this template, Kitschelt arguably slights the role of actors because the historical legacies narrow the actor choices so much that endogenous transformation cannot meaningfully occur (Munck 2001: 142). We return to this issue below.

An early example and some pitfalls

The attempts to systematically combine agency and structure began in earnest in the 1990s. To list some prominent examples, one might be tempted to begin with Samuel P. Huntington's (1991) *The Third Wave*. Likewise, Michael Bratton and Nicolas van de Walle (1997) integrate agency and structures in their *Democratic Experiments in Africa*, and Stephan Haggard and Robert Kaufman (1997) do the same in *The Political Economy of Democratic Transitions*, covering 12 Latin American and Southeast Asian countries. Geoffrey Pridham (2000) also uses the integrative logic in *The Dynamics of Democratization* to account for political regime developments in Southern, Central, and Eastern Europe.

However, if we wish to scale up in importance within the field, Juan Linz and Alfred Stepan's (1996) ambitious effort to synthesize structural, agency-oriented, and international explanations is probably the best starting point. Not only is their *Problems of Democratic Transition and Consolidation* a good representative of the advent of a theoretical focus on integration, the book has in itself provided an impetus for others to follow suit. Linz and Stepan's causal model combines three different forms of influences upon regime transition and consolidation. First, Linz and Stepan identify two general structural 'macro-variables' conditioning democratic development: the prior regime type and 'stateness'.[3] Second, they list three more context-dependent structural factors: international influences, the political economy of coercion and legitimacy, and the constitution-making environment. Third, two agency-centered factors are included, namely the institutional composition and leadership of the preceding regime and the ownership over the transition (i.e., who initiated and controlled the regime change).

The theme pervading Linz and Stepan's book is that the transition to democracy and its subsequent consolidation must be understood as processes of interaction between these factors. However, on one important point Linz and Stepan remain loyal to the transitological perspective, which they helped to shape (e.g., Linz & Stepan 1978). An implicit premise for their model is that the core actors can either be democratically oriented or not. If the former is the case, it seems clear that Linz and Stepan are confident that it is possible to carry through democratization even if the structures are unfavorable. Nonetheless, their model is an obvious attempt to synthesize the different perspectives. At the same time, Linz and Stepan's book offers a good example of how the new focus on international factors, treated in the preceding chapter, has also come to the fore in the recent literature. The book divides the international factors into three different categories: foreign policy, *Zeitgeist*, and diffusion. These three factors can all influence transitions to – as well as the consolidation of – democracy. But Linz and Stepan (1996: 76) emphasize that diffusion is the most important factor for the actual transition, while the *Zeitgeist* and foreign policy (including democracy promotion from the outside) have a bigger impact upon the subsequent developments.

This is all pretty solid. However, the end result is ultimately unsatisfactory because structure and agency are not systematically integrated. The very distinction between 'macro-variables', on the one hand, and context-centered and actor-centered variables, on the other hand, implies some kind of hierarchical relationship. According to Gerardo Munck (2001: 139), "The problem, however, is that Linz and Stepan do not really follow through on this idea by making their hierarchical causal model explicit." One way of doing so would be by systematically distinguishing between variables which are temporally prior to others. This leads us to delve further into the distinction between deep and proximate factors (Kitschelt 2003).

Deep and proximate causes

David Hume (1993 [1748]: 51) once referred to causality as the "cement of the universe" and stated that "the only immediate utility of all sciences, is to teach us, how to control and regulate future events by their causes." While most social scientists would readily agree that we trade in causal relationships, such relationships are often difficult to establish. Fundamentally, doing so requires observing four criteria. First, there must be some kind of systematic co-variation between cause and effect.[4] Second, there should be a theoretical relationship between cause and effect. Third, the cause must come before the effect in time. Fourth, it is necessary to rule out alternative explanations (the *ceteris paribus* clause).

One of these four requirements is particularly relevant for the discussion about combining agency and structure. It is rather commonplace to note that a cause must come before an effect temporally. But a cause can either occur relatively long before or close to the effect in time. This is not trivial. As John Gerring (2001: 142) points out, "The further away we can get from the outcome in question, the better (ceteris paribus) our explanation will be." In a nutshell, the objective of any science is to provide the deepest possible explanation of a given phenomenon. While it is neither possible nor desirable to hark back to the Big Bang, it is nevertheless necessary to attempt to uncover the point of departure or basis of the inquiry. With this in mind, Kitschelt (2003) has distinguished between two different types of causes. First, there are deep causes, which stretch far back in time, are often based on structural conditions, and therefore cannot be affected by actors in the short term. Second, there are proximate causes, which are closer to that which is to be explained and normally either directly consist of the choices made by the agents or phenomena (e.g., formal institutions) that agents can change or manipulate in the short term.

The proximate explanations are characterized by the causal mechanisms often being relatively explicit and they can often explain very much of the variation in the dependent variable. In that sense, the proximate explanations seem to have the most to offer. But Kitschelt's (2003) conclusion is the exact opposite. He argues that the choices made by agents are often so proximate in relation to the dependent variable that the explanation becomes near-tautological and thus uninteresting.[5] To summarize Kitschelt's point, the choices made by agents must be explained, not used to explain. Against this background, he draws attention to the deeper structural characteristics setting the framework for these choices. More generally, Kitschelt (1999: 13) argues that "What social science should explore are *chains of causation*, organized around variables at different levels of causal depth." The proximate steps in this chain should thus not be slighted. Indeed, Kitschelt seeks to offer a solution to the problem of infinite regress into the recesses of history, i.e., that any explanatory model must start somewhere. This solution may be summed up in the slogan 'depth with mechanisms'. In gist, one should not venture further back in time than one's ability to provide mechanisms which explain how the cause has provided the outcome.

The post-communist laboratory

In prior work, we have demonstrated how Kitschelt's template may be used to arrive at a resilient explanation of post-communist regime change (Møller 2009; Møller & Skaaning 2009). The post-communist setting is an obvious place to attempt to combine structure and agency. A number of scholars (Easter 1997; Fish 1998a; Bunce 1999) have pointed out that "this region furnishes an exceptionally promising laboratory for assessing which factors facilitate – or at least accompany – democratization and which do not" (Fish 1998a: 214). The laboratory status derives from two aspects of post-communism. First, the ability to hold a number of potentially relevant variables, such as prior experience with one-party autocracy and a planned economy, constant with reference to the relatively similar starting point in 1989 to 1991. Second, the existence of a massive variation in regime developments in the aftermath of communist breakdown. This great political variation in the 30 post-communist countries is documented by our previous overview of regime development (see Chapter 3). Whereas the whole region was under autocratic rule before 1989, today over 40 percent of the countries are liberal democracies or polyarchies, 20 percent minimalist democracies, and the remaining countries are undemocratic.

However, there has been a tendency to overrate the structural similarities of post-communist countries. The fact of the matter is that deep variables such as the pattern of pre-communist nation- and state-building, the level of modernization, and linkages to the West differ significantly across the post-communist space[6] (Kitschelt 2003; Pop-Eleches 2007; Møller & Skaaning 2009). This, at least, is the point of departure for our attempt to integrate agency and structure in the context of post-communism. Such integration is called for to account for the fact that the post-communist countries have broadly followed three different tracks.[7]

1   The Baltic region and East-Central Europe have covered the distance to liberal democracy/polyarchy surprisingly quickly, which paved the way for full-fledged EU membership in 2004 and 2007.
2   The geographical Eastern Europe together with parts of the Balkan region have developed into instances of electoral/minimalist democracy – or even reverted to autocracy after brief political openings.
3   Further to the east, in the former Soviet republics in the Caucasus and Central Asia, the autocracies almost completely dominate the picture.

At first glance, a set of proximate explanations – emphasizing factors such as the degree of parliamentarianism (Fish 2006), the outcome of the first election (Fish 1998b), and the extent of economic liberalization (Fish & Choudhry 2008) – have shown very high levels of co-variation with these regime developments. Among the former communist countries, successful democratization has generally gone hand in hand with specific values on the three aforementioned political factors. All of the countries in East-Central Europe and the Baltic region have, for instance, introduced parliamentary systems, while this has not been the case in Central Asia or the Caucasus (Fish 2006). This pattern is repeated with respect to the other two variables. In East-Central Europe and the Baltic countries, landslide victories to the democratic opposition were the order of the day in the first elections held following the collapse of communism, and comprehensive economic reforms were implemented immediately thereafter (Fish 1998b; Fish & Choudhry 2008). Russia, Ukraine, and almost all Balkan countries share some – but not all – of these characteristics, while virtually all of the Central Asian and Caucasian republics fall through across the board. Thus, there is an almost perfect overlap with the tripartite division between liberal democracy and polyarchy on the one side, autocracies on the other side, and electoral and minimalist democracies in the middle (see Møller & Skaaning 2009).

What is more, it is possible to show that these proximate variables 'beat' deeper variables, as their co-variation with the outcome is a little higher than that of the deep factors. But looks may, to some extent at least, be deceiving. Based on Kitschelt's framework, such a 'tournament of variables' is an inappropriate way of testing explanatory significance. This is reflected by the fact that the listed agency-based accounts suffer from a fundamental problem. The very premise for the proximate accounts is that the agents can act independently of – or at least break with – the deeper-lying structures (e.g., Fish 1998a: 77–78; 2006: 11–12). This does not fit particularly well with the systematic geographical division character-izing the variables as well as the outcome to be explained. As described above, we exclusively find liberal democracies and polyarchies on the one hand and favorable actor choices on the other hand in the western part of the former communist world. Conversely, the region furthest to the east, Central Asia, is almost exclusively marked by autocracy and unfavorable actor choices. Finally, the region in the middle is characterized by thinner types of democracy and a mix of favorable and unfavorable actor choices.

This systematic geographical diversity indicates that the deeper-lying structures distinguishing the respective subregions from one another have, if not determined, then at least delimited the opportunities available to the political elites following the collapse of communism. According to Kitschelt et al. (1999), two central factors distinguished the Baltic and East-Central European countries from the Balkans and the lands further to the east at the time: the character of the state apparatus and the strength of the civil society. In addition to these deeply historical factors, structural factors such as oil production, proximity to Western Europe, and the level of socio-economic development prior to the collapse of communism may also be included among the structural factors that constrained the actors (see Møller & Skaaning 2009).

These variables also display great empirical co-variation with the outcome, reflected in the fact that the geographic pattern is again obvious. The liberal democracies/polyarchies in East-Central Europe and the Baltic region are characterized by the presence of all of the democracy-inducing structural characteristics, most of the autocracies in Central Asia are characterized by the absence of all of these characteristics, and many of the electoral/minimalist democracies are situated somewhere in between. The result thus clearly indicates that – whether proximate or deep – the more democracy-facilitating conditions we observe, the more democracy. Against this background, it is pertinent to address the question as to whether we can combine the deep and proximate explanations of democratization. One way of investigating this is by setting up a combined typology encompassing all of the explanations. We have done so by constructing, respectively, the deep and proximate explanations as one dimension, where all three characteristics can either be present ('completely present'), absent ('completely absent'), or there can be a mix of presence and absence ('mix'). In other words, we have combined two classifications, each consisting of three classes, resulting in a typology with nine types (or combinations), as presented in Table 11.2 (cf. Møller & Skaaning 2009).

In the table, the regime form in 2011 is also reported. The table indicates that the deep and immediate explanations co-vary rather systematically – both with one another and with the variation between the regime outcomes. Twenty-two of the 26 countries included in our analysis[8] are thus placed along the diagonal of the typology; that is, in the symmetrical combinations consisting of the same value for each dimension. At the same time, all of the liberal democracies except three are placed in the upper-left-hand corner, which specifically indicates an expectation of liberal democracy or polyarchy. Similarly, four of the ten autocracies are placed in the lower-right-hand corner, while half of the electoral and minimalist democracies are found in the center of the typology.

This is where our prior discussion concerning causality makes it possible to couple the deep and proximate causes. The deep structural characteristics are prior to the actor choices. On this basis, the results strongly indicate that the structural conditions have had an impact on the political choices during the transitions in the

Table 11.2 The combined typology of deep and proximate factors

		Proximate factors		
		Completely present	Mix	Completely absent
Deep factors	Completely present	**Czech Rep.** **Estonia** **Croatia** **Hungary** **Lithuania** **Latvia** **Poland** **Slovakia** **Slovenia**		
	Mix	Macedonia	Albania *Armenia* **Bulgaria** *Georgia* *Kyrgyzstan* Moldova **Mongolia** **Romania** *Russia*	*Belarus* *Tajikistan* Ukraine
	Completely absent			*Azerbaijan* *Kazakhstan* *Turkmenistan* *Uzbekistan*

Note: The **bold** text indicates that – in 2011 – a country is a liberal democracy or polyarchy, *italics* that it is an autocracy, and ordinary text indicates an electoral or minimalist democracy.

early 1990s; while the deep variables seem to trigger particular scores on the proximate variables. This can be underwritten theoretically. Factors such as the outcome of the first election, the strength of the legislature (vis-à-vis the president), and the extent of the economic reform process reflect various aspects of that which could be referred to as 'political openings' and 'political mobilization'. It seems highly probable that these phenomena have much to do with structural factors. If a country is modernized, has a vibrant civil society, and close ties to Western Europe – as the case was (and is) in East-Central Europe and the Baltic countries – one would expect a competitive and open political life after a transformation process. If none (or only a few) of these factors are present – as the case was (and is) in the eastern part of the formerly communist world – one would not expect a competitive and open political life (Møller & Skaaning 2009).

To sum up: as the structural characteristics lie outside of the manipulation of the present agents in the short term – and because it makes good sense to carry out a theoretical coupling of the deep explanations with the immediate explanations – it also makes sense to set up a combined causal chain. According to this chain, the deep factors have set the conditions for the immediate choices, and the entire setting has thus led to different transformation processes with respect to the character of the political regimes.

What more general conclusions may be drawn on this basis? Above all else, the illustration from the post-communist setting goes to show that it is possible to integrate the competing explanations into a single, overall model. In this light, it is no coincidence that multiple explanations seem relevant. This is because democracy is the result of a number of different factors in combination with one another – although one should not exclude the possibility of a number of different relationships being spurious or coincidental.

Different ways of combining structure and agency

The post-communist findings reported above represent a crude version of Kitschelt's approach to integrating structure and agency in analyses of regime change. But the manifest regularities notwithstanding, it also falls prey to the problem that the endogenous role of the actors is easily slighted when emphasizing deeper factors. To make the case for this, a more panoramic view of the extant attempts to integrate structure and agency is warranted. We are here in the fortunate situation that James Mahoney and Richard Snyder (1999) have carried out just such an appraisal. Their point of departure is that the increasingly salient tendency to employ integrated explanatory frameworks normally runs up against the agent-structure problem. Virtually by definition, structural approaches thus tend towards an 'over-socialized' version of agency whereas actor-based approaches – infused by voluntarism – tend towards an 'under-socialized' version. The over-socialized position entails that both the identity and the interests of actors are defined by the structures. At its extreme, the actors are not only slighted; there is no room for them at all. Conversely, the under-socialized position entails that the identity and interests of actors are exogenous to the structural constraints. On this basis, Mahoney and Snyder (1999: 10-11) define integrative approaches as the

> use of both subjective evaluations of actors *and* objective conditions as primary causal variables; a focus on temporally proximate *and* remote factors; a methodological concern with case-specific *and* general causes of regime change; and an emphasis on multi-level explanations that span micro *and* macro levels of analysis.

Mahoney and Snyder go on to categorize the extant attempts to carry out such integration in three classes: the funnel strategy, the path-dependent strategy, and the eclectic strategy. Though the general aim is the same, namely to combine structure and agency, the three strategies differ remarkably.

The advantage of the funnel strategy is its simplicity. Such analyses first exhaust the structural variables, increasingly narrowing the focus down to the micro level (cf. the funnel metaphor). The structural variables can here be understood as necessary but not sufficient for the regime outcome investigated; the sufficient variables should instead be found at the micro level in the form of the actors' choices. The deep variables do not systematically constrain this choice set – we do not ask *why* the actors chose as they did – rather they set the stage for the actors. As such, the funnel strategy basically has a voluntarist conceptual basis (Mahoney & Snyder 1999: 14). In terms of examples, Mahoney and Snyder identify a number of the contributions to the Linz and Stepan (1978) edited volume as specimens of this approach. To some extent, Linz and Stepan (1996), discussed above, could also be situated here.

The path-dependent strategy is quite different. In this case it is important to note that we are not speaking about path dependency in the structurally determined way of, for example, Barrington Moore's (1991 [1966]) classical study (Mahoney & Snyder 1999: 16). Rather, the critical junctures which spark the path-dependent sequences must be contingent (unexplainable by extant structural theories). This phase thus privileges the actors, who are rather free to make choices about institutions (cf. Mahoney 2000: 507, 509; Capoccia & Kelemen 2007: 341). Subsequently, however, the ties bind as the path-dependent sequences have deterministic properties. The upshot of this is that the path-dependent strategy tends to emphasize structure over agency. The independent role of the actors is confined to the critical junctures, after which the actors are in thrall to the structural logic. For this reason, the path-dependent strategy has a structuralist basis.[9] Among exemplary applications, Mahoney and Snyder mention David and Ruth Collier's (1991) study of the incorporation of labor in eight Latin American countries, a study which is often claimed to have inaugurated the path-dependent strategy. Among the studies we have discussed under the social forces tradition, Dietrich Rueschemeyer et al. (1992) also belongs here, which further underlines the structural bias of this approach.

Finally, there are the eclectic strategies. The name is revealing, and it is quite obvious that Mahoney and Snyder find little to recommend in this category. In a nutshell, analyses treading this path produce an unsystematic mishmash of structural and actor-based variables. The eclectic strategies are thus bereft of clear mechanisms linking macro-level conditions with micro-level choices, and they do not specify the respective causal weights of actor-centered and structural variables, thereby producing what Mahoney and Snyder (1999: 22) term an "indiscriminate eclecticism". Among prominent examples, Mahoney and Snyder list the framework constructed by Larry Diamond, Juan Linz, and Seymour M. Lipset (1990) in connection with their volume on *Democracy in Developing Countries*. They also mention Huntington's (1991) *The Third Wave*. The merits of Huntington's book notwithstanding, he makes no systematic attempt to integrate the different explanations he identifies (see Kitschelt 1992: 1033–1034; Mahoney & Snyder 1999: 22–24). Instead, he simply adds one after another in the rather indiscriminate way often used by historians, thereby arguably producing an over-determined account.

Subsequent developments

To some extent, Mahoney and Snyder's (1999) discussion ends on a pessimistic note. As should be clear from the summary above, none of the three strategies are able to genuinely balance agency and structure, thus facing the structure agent problem head-on. Among the existing strategies, Mahoney and Snyder view the path-dependent strategy as the most systematic attempt to provide an integrative edifice. Hence, it is probably not so surprising that this approach has witnessed most development over the recent decade (e.g., Pierson 2000; Hall 2003; Capoccia & Kelemen 2007). Other than sharpening the tools available for researchers, the refinements have to some extent remedied the structuralist conceptual basis of the path-dependent strategy identified by Mahoney and Snyder. Tellingly, the present writings on path-dependency are thus much more centered on agency than were those highlighted by Mahoney and Snyder (i.e., Collier & Collier 1991; Rueschemeyer et al. 1992).

Most recently, Giovanni Capoccia and Daniel Ziblatt (2010) have proposed a research agenda on democratization, based on the so-called 'historical turn'. One of the focal points of this intervention is exactly to bring the actors back into historical analyses of democratization. Capoccia and Ziblatt's (2010: 933–934) research agenda is a reaction against the social forces tradition as represented by Moore (1991 [1966]), Luebbert (1991), and Rueschemeyer et al. (1992). Crucially, Capoccia and Ziblatt's (2010: 934) focus on "the historical episodes in which democratic institutions were created or substantially reshaped" is much inspired by the recent work on critical junctures and path-dependency. What is most striking about their research agenda is that they seemingly envisage that the critical junctures, largely determined by actor choices, should be studied in singular cases. Arguably, this make for a voluntarist basis because cross-case regularities, which tend towards privileging structures as explanatory factors, are thereby easily ignored (Møller forthcoming).

Capoccia and Ziblatt's (2010) intervention is thus symptomatic of the increasingly trenchant emphasis on the actors within the study of regime change. As already noted, the aim of this drive is to lay bare the micro-level mechanisms that make the causal relationships work. Nonetheless, one should be wary of not throwing out the baby with the bathwater here. When manifest empirical regularities exist, structural perspectives probably have a competitive edge in elucidating them. Only by understanding macro-level structures is it possible to – in an analytically systematic way – account for the emergence of critical junctures and for the effects of actors' choices during these crucial openings. Partisans of micro-foundations would immediately turn the tables here and claim that until convincing micro-level mechanisms are identified, such manifest regularities, based on structural attributes, tell us little or nothing about causality. The disturbing question, however, is whether it is at all possible to square the circle here. Gerring (2011: 370) puts it well when noting that:

> Of course, one may hope that distal causal relationships could be disaggregated into proximal (microfoundational) causes, and explored piece by piece.

Insofar as macro causal relations are built on micro causal relations, we may learn a lot by scoping down – for example, from democracy to its component parts, from structures to 'cogs and wheels.' Likewise, we ought to be able to aggregate up to macro levels. . . . Yet this presumes quite a lot. While it is true – more or less by definition – that macro-level phenomena are the product of micro-level phenomena, it is not clear that we will actually be able to reconstruct macro-level causal relationships by tracing their micro-level components. Nation-states are composed of citizens, just as a brick wall is composed of bricks, but we cannot observe a nation-state being constructed, person by person.

Conclusions

This chapter has discussed the increasing tendency to seek to combine structure and agency in analyses of democratization. This integrative enterprise came to the fore in the 1990s, and it may be understood as a reaction to prior periods where first structural explanations and then actor-based explanations dominated. Throughout the 1990s and 2000s a number of studies have attempted to combine these hitherto relatively isolated approaches. The methodological concomitant of this is the increasingly popular call for mixed methods analysis, including the endeavor to provide sound micro-level bases for macro relationships.

We have seen that the quest for integration is not an easy one because any-one attempting to do so has to face the acrimonious agent-structure problem. It follows from this that most attempts are burdened by some salient problems, the most general of which is that they either have a structuralist or a voluntaristic bias. The most promising attempt is probably that centering on the concept of path-dependency. While this approach used to have a structuralist bias, some of the more recent variants have been rather actor-centered. This probably reflects the attention increasingly devoted to micro foundations. However, we raise a voice of warning here. Though micro-level mechanisms are obviously of the essence for social science, the search for them should not preclude us from observing macro-level regularities. Such regularities are often quite salient in the study of regime change and, crucially, they tend to point back to deeper structural constraints.

Finally, some more pragmatic advice is pertinent. One of the reasons for the lackluster record of integrating structure and agency in the democratization litera-ture is probably that doing so is hugely difficult, sometimes next to impossible. One analytical device that may facilitate such endeavors is to be found in Anthony Giddens' (1984: 288) notion of 'methodological brackets'. The idea is that one can, in turn, bracket either structures to concentrate on actors or actors to con-centrate on structures. This is helpful to avoid losing focus in the often excessively complicated relationship between structures and actors. The danger of course is that this approach can easily end in an over-socialized and an under-socialized part, which does not add up to an integrative whole. To repeat the main thrust of this chapter, at the end of the day an iterative approach to structures and actors which appreciates their dynamic relationship is desirable for students of regime change. In this chapter, we have solely discussed this in terms of dealing with the causes of democracy. But similar arguments could be made with regard to the consequences of democracy, the issue which we turn to in the fourth and final part of this book.

Part IV

Consequences

Democracy – so what?

12 Democracy and conflict

Part IV hews back to an observation made in the Introduction: that a major reason for the present prominence of the research agenda treated in this book is the increasing focus on the consequences of democracy. In this chapter, we discuss the relationship between democracy/democratization and external warfare and internal conflicts, respectively. In the next chapter we shift focus to economic growth and distribution. In that connection, we also briefly discuss the normative and scientific import of studying democracy's consequences in the first place.

Towards the perpetual peace

The proper place to begin any discussion about democracy and conflict is surely with the most famous such theory, the so-called democratic peace thesis. The thesis may be traced back to Immanuel Kant's (2003 [1795]) *Perpetual Peace*; it was subsequently picked up by Thomas Paine (cf. Waltz 1959 [1954]: 101), and it has experienced a remarkable popularity in recent decades. In a nutshell, the theory attributed to Kant states that what he refers to as 'republics' do not wage war on one another.

Though Kant (2003 [1795]: 490–491) defined a republican constitution mostly in terms of officially sanctioned civil liberties and what we today would refer to as the rule of law, he also stressed that the perpetual peace is sustained by the need of such republics to secure the people's consent to declare war. For this reason, and because Kant's republics have today been superseded by democracies, contemporary scholars coin this relationship as one of democratic peace. Three causal mechanisms are normally used to underpin this retouched version of Kant's theory (cf. Sørensen 2008: 134). First, citizens in democratic countries are deeply enmeshed in democratic norms for how to settle conflicts: using the word as opposed to the sword. Second, citizens in democracies share the same fundamental values, which render their electorates and political elites sympathetic towards one another. Third, citizens in democracies will pressure the politicians not to engage in war, as war disrupts trade, and increases the need for more tax dollars for gunpowder and cannons, both being to the economic disadvantage of the ordinary voter.[1] Or, to use Bruce Russett's (2003 [2000]: 496) version, shared democracy, economic interdependence, and shared membership of international organizations reduce the risk of military disputes tremendously.

This is thus a pure specimen of a theory about the consequences of democracy. The peace thesis states that democracy has entirely different consequences for the relationship between countries than autocracy. While democracies have never had problems getting rough in conflicts with autocracies – two World Wars have been fought on that account, and democracies have repeatedly shown their prowess at waging warfare (Doyle 1986: 1155; Reiter & Stam 2002) – "the more democracies there are in the world, the fewer potential adversaries we and other democracies will have and the wider the zone of peace will be" (Russett 2003 [2000]: 493–494). Indeed, if all of the countries of the world were to become democracies, we could beat our swords into plowshares, since the age of warfare would then definitively be over.

If this sounds almost too good to be true, it will come as no surprise that so it is, at least according to a considerable number of critics. First, historically speaking, the theory is frayed around the edges. It is possible to find historical examples of democracies – at least minimalist democracies – that have waged war against one another. Moreover, the theory is rather weak as regards the point about trade, particularly as the period leading up to World War I was marked by great economic interdependence which nevertheless failed to guarantee peace. Finally, there are also contemporary problems with the theory, problems that point towards the discussion of the second part of this chapter, namely the debate about the conduciveness of the early stages of democratization to conflict. We attend to these points of criticism one at a time.

Historical exceptions

When uncovering the historical exceptions to democratic peace, researchers are ready to venture far back in time. The annals of ancient Greece tell of many wars between democratic city-states. For example, Athens, the mother of all democracies, rarely strayed from an opportunity for a fight with other city-states, democracies included. Indeed, the Athenian use of direct democracy arguably fueled the flames via the ability of demagogues to incite reckless military expeditions and via the practice of condemning defeated generals to death upon their return, which meant they would often be unwilling to withdraw from precarious positions (see Bradford 2001: 87–94). Most famous in this respect is the Sicilian expedition (415–413 BC), part of the Second Peloponnesian War, where the Athenian citizen army sailed to Sicily to test their strength against the Syracuse citizen army. The expedition was incited by the warmongering Alcibiades, against the objections of the moderate statesman Nicias. But Nicias was appointed as one of the generals and was hesitant to retreat once the position in Syracuse became hopeless for fear of being condemned upon his return (Bradford 2001: 89–91). The result was defeat at the hands of the army of Syracuse, after which power in the Greek world oscillated towards Athens's great (and non-democratic) rival, Sparta.[2]

The Punic wars between Rome and Carthage are also sometimes pointed to as contradicting the peace thesis, as both city republics had elected leaders. This challenge to the theory is not particularly convincing, however, as Rome and Carthage were oligarchic rather than democratic. The criticism has more bite when we proceed to the second coming of democracy in the 19th century. The War of 1812 between the USA and Great Britain is often referred to when the peace thesis comes under fire. The American Civil War (1861–1865) was also a conflict between two relatively democratic entities: the North and the South. The same is the case with the Spanish-American war over Cuba in 1898. But, as we shall see below, the various examples from the pre-1914 era ultimately miss the target.

'When goods do not cross borders, soldiers will'

Next there is the problem with the economic component of the peace thesis. The economic link in the theory rests upon the premise that countries that freely trade with one another will have a very strong incentive to avoid military conflict. War brings an abrupt end to trade and will therefore be destructive for the economy in the warring countries. In the 19th century the French economist Frederic Bastiat described the negative side of this relationship with his famous dictum: "When goods do not cross borders, soldiers will."

A small side trip serves to situate the economic dimension within the more general peace theory. What, we must ask, does free trade have to do with democracy per se? Here, it is pertinent to hark back to Joseph Schumpeter's (1991 [1919] classical essay about "The Sociology of Imperialisms". Michael Doyle (1986: 1152–1154) observes that a capitalism–democracy nexus underpins Schumpeter's famous claim about the peace-inducing qualities of capitalism. Schumpeter adduces empirical evidence in favor of this claim in a historical discussion about the nature of imperialism. His basic point is that modern capitalism discourages such imperialism; indeed that it creates pacifism, because the very premise of the market economy is that success is obtained via participation in the market, not conquest (Schumpeter 1991 [1919]: 192). But, Doyle argues, these pacific impulses can only come to the fullest within the context of democracy. As we shall see, this coupling is important for discussing some of the criticism directed against the economic dimension of the peace theory.

Regarding the pacific impact of free trade, the democratic peace theory seems to have a conspicuous Achilles' heel: the so-called first wave of globalization,[3] which rolled across the world in the mid-1800s and continued until the outbreak of World War I. A couple of figures demonstrate the explosion of trade during this period. The total French and British exports rose by a factor of 25 and 35, respectively, in the period from 1820 to 1913, and the French, German, and American export figures all increased by over 30 percent annually until the war broke out (McDonald & Sweeney 2007). In fact, the total world trade on the eve of World War I represented somewhere between one-fifth and one-quarter of the global GNP. By the late 1930s, this figure had fallen to less than one-tenth, and it was not until the 1970s that the pre-World War I level was again surpassed.

The first wave of globalization was generally something of a high point for European bourgeois civilization. In his memoirs from 1942, *The World of*

Yesterday, the Austrian writer Stefan Zweig described the years leading up to World War I as a 'Golden Age of Security'. Western Europe had enjoyed almost 100 years of relative peace and unprecedented economic growth. It was also an age where civil liberties enjoyed great respect. In *The Origins of Totalitarianism*, Hannah Arendt (1951: ch. 4) takes note of the outcry raised over any and every legal scandal during this period. She refers to the miscarriage of justice perpetrated on Captain Alfred Dreyfus, a Jew, which came to be known as the 'Dreyfus Affair' (mentioned in Chapter 1). Arendt points to the remarkable fact that this isolated act of power abuse attracted so much attention throughout Western Europe in the 1890s. The doctrine of equality before the law was so entrenched that the case involving the French captain alarmed the bourgeois civilization on the entire continent. Had the affair taken place a couple of generations later – in the dark decades between the World Wars – nobody would have batted an eye, Arendt concludes. For World War I ushered in a rebellion against Zweig's Golden Age. The faith in progress was replaced by pessimism.

The first wave of globalization simply did not realize Kant's perpetual peace. Instead, it ended with the Great War and its millions of dead and otherwise affected victims. Indeed, the outbreak of war in 1914 has been hailed as providing conclusive evidence against the pacifist impact of free trade. In *Imperialism, The Highest Stage of Capitalism* (1999 [1916]), Lenin went so far as to claim that free trade and capitalism promote war and domestic conflict instead of dampening them (for a counter-argument, see Schumpeter 1991 [1919]; cf. Doyle 1986: 1152–1154).

The democratic peace: a status

Generally speaking, what is there to say about these first two points of criticism? Beginning with the second point – the economic link in the chain – there is undoubtedly something in what the critics of the democratic peace thesis are objecting to. It is indeed striking that the first wave of globalization resulted in that which has since been labeled 'the second Thirty Years War' or 'the Great European Civil War'; that is, the pernicious period from 1914 until 1945. And it is all the more striking considering that many politicians and pundits – even on the very brink of the outbreak of World War I in 1914 – emphasized how the mutual economic dependence rendered a new major conflict unthinkable.

For example, the pacifist Norman Angell asserted in 1911 that a repeat of the past great wars in Europe, such as those during the period 1792 to 1815, was simply inconceivable. The ever-increasing trade between the great European powers meant that nobody was interested in provoking a war that would merely serve to impoverish the people (see Waltz 1959 [1954]: 74). This, too, was Zweig's message in *The World of Yesterday*, though he based it more on the liberal ethos of the age than on economic interdependence. Indeed, we meet this optimistic pacific outlook among many of the liberals of Zweig's generation. In his autobiography, the Whig[4] historian G.M. Trevelyan (1949) reports his visiting the Volturno battlefields north of Naples some time before World War I as part of his research to write a book on Garibaldi. Trevelyan (1949: 33–34) then remarks that:

> It would have been a rude shock to us to be told that, a generation later, British and Germans would be fighting each other over the same ground. The worst public catastrophe we then feared was that the Lords would succeed in throwing out the Parliament Bill. Italian freedom was a thing won and settled. Torture, wholesale executions and massacres in Europe, and wars that imperiled England's independence seemed far away, portions and parcels of the dreadful past.

While Angell, Zweig, and Trevelyan may in a sense be correct that an intra-European war was both madness economically and had – at least among the educated elite – become seen as barbarous culturally, the governments in Vienna, Moscow, Berlin, and Paris turned a deaf ear to the voice of reason in July and August 1914. The result was a war that nobody had really wanted, indeed which hardly anyone had any interest in (see Zagare 2009). In the famous words of A.J.P. Taylor (1972: 16):

> Men are reluctant to believe that great events have small causes. Therefore, once the Great War started, they were convinced that it must be the outcome of profound forces. It is hard to discover these when we examine the details. Nowhere was there conscious determination to provoke a war. Statesmen miscalculated. They used the instruments of bluff and threat which had proved effective on previous occasions. This time things went wrong. The deterrent on which they relied failed to deter; the statesmen became the prisoners of their own weapons. The great armies, accumulated to provide security and preserve the peace, carried the nations to war by their own weight.

Obviously, then, trade interdependence failed to prevent armed conflict in 1914. Nevertheless, there has been no shortage of attempts at saving Bastiat's proposition that trade prevents war. Recently, Patrick McDonald and Kevin Sweeney (2007) presented data supporting the pacifist impact of free trade. Boiled down to a single sentence, their point is that the first wave of globalization had little to do with free trade. The explosive growth in trade in the 19th century first and foremost led to a dramatic fall in freight rates, which was particularly owing to the widespread use of steam-engines on land and sea. In the decades leading up to World War I, duties were actually raised throughout much of Europe as a political reaction to the ever-increasing business transactions. Thus, increased economic exchange went hand in hand with protectionism. According to Paul Bairoch: "It can be concluded that the tariff barriers set up during the period of 1880 to 1914 merely replaced the previous natural barriers provided by high transport costs" (quoted in McDonald & Sweeney 2007: 387).

On this point, the first wave of globalization distinguishes itself from the contemporary second wave of globalization, which is very much driven by free trade agreements in the WTO (formerly GATT) as well as regional measures such as the European common market and NAFTA. With this observation in mind, McDonald and Sweeney (2007) argue that only *this* kind of free trade actually counteracts warfare. Here, the defense of the economic aspect of the peace theory becomes directly entangled in the political. As noted above, the general population – particularly in the role of consumers – has an economic interest in trade and will therefore press to avoid both protectionism and foolhardy foreign policy. For McDonald and Sweeney, however, the events of the first wave of globalization offer evidence that the parliamentary channel may also be used to press for protectionism and aggressive foreign policy, if specific domestic interests are not off-balanced by the right to vote for the general population. In this way, it is possible to argue that political democracy is a prerequisite for mutual economic dependence leading to peace.

This clarification leads us directly to the discussion about the empirical examples of warfare between democracies. Despite the numerous historical exceptions, this criticism does not really have much bite, since it is possible to account for almost all of the exceptions by tightening the definition of democracy. Take World War I, for instance. It has often been observed that the democratically elected officials throughout Europe supported the war appropriations and that the semi-democratic channels of the day thus fueled the fire. As already indicated, however, it is rather simple to refute this criticism by arguing that democratic government had yet to settle among the European great powers. Even in the United Kingdom, only 60 percent (of the men) had the right to vote, and the parliamentary principle had yet to be implemented in Germany. These were, at most, instances of minimalist democracy, not electoral democracy, polyarchy, or liberal democracy.[5] The democratic deficits were even greater in connection with the possible exceptions of the 19th century. The war between the USA and Great Britain in 1812 and the American Civil War can be rejected as contradicting the peace thesis, since both the parliamentary principle and equal and universal suffrage were still in their infancy in at least one of the two parties to the conflict. In the former case, it is probably erroneous even to talk about minimalist democracy – as is also the case for Germany in 1914.

So while the economic link in the chain may be a little rusty, it is not incorrect to use the word 'law' when it comes to the political link in the chain. It is virtually impossible to find examples of two modern, liberal democracies that have waged war against one another. Bruce Russett and Zeev Maoz (1993) have thus demonstrated that there is not a single such example in the period 1946 to 1986.[6] During the same period, there are 32 instances of wars between autocracies or between democracies and autocracies. What is more, democracies – with a few exceptions – have not even threatened each other during this period, while threats between autocracies or between autocracies and democracies have been legion. To summarize, whereas most researchers agree that the economic link in the causal chain is insufficient – possibly it is not even necessary – very few are ready to reject the political link, at least if the baseline is actual liberal democracy rather than minimalist democracy. This brings us to the final point in the assessment of the democratic peace thesis.

Belligerent democrats – a qualification to the peace thesis

We have concluded that peace holds between well-established democracies, which are particularly prevalent in the Western world. But we also know that there are a number of more unstable democracies in the developing countries, which we have referred to as minimalist or electoral democracies. The question then becomes whether they – or countries which are merely moving towards this destination for that matter – are also covered by the democratic peace.

This question not only holds a huge actuality, it also points back to some of the classics in the Western history of political thought. Niccolò Machiavelli argued that what he termed republics would be more war-prone – and more capable of waging war – than were non-democracies (Doyle 1986). These republics may be interpreted as what today we would call semi-democracies, and Machiavelli's classical contribution may therefore be said to write into the debate about belligerent democrats. One of the scholars who have addressed this issue is Georg Sørensen (2008: 153). On the one hand, he defends the validity of the peace thesis for liberal democracies. On the other hand, he adds that the connection does not necessarily hold outside of this group. In the thinner types of democracies, the causal mechanism underpinning this very relationship, that is, the democratic norms for conflict resolution, shared values, and mutual economic dependence, rarely exists.

Indeed, a growing body of literature – represented in particular by the work of Edward Mansfield and Jack Snyder (1995, 2005, 2009) – argues that the early stages of democratization are often conducive to both external and internal conflict. Harking back to Samuel P. Huntington (1968), Mansfield and Snyder argue that increasing mass political participation in the context of weak political institutions facilitates political leaders playing the nationalist card. More particularly, in cases of 'stalled transitions', weak political institutions often facilitate the waging of external wars. Mansfield and Snyder (2009: 384) distinguish between two paths. First, democratizing states may generally be characterized by weak political institutions which make them "prone to belligerent ethnic nationalism or sectarianism that induces neighboring states to attack." Contemporary Georgia, repeatedly threatened by Russia due to the existence of separatist regions such as Abkhazia and South Ossetia, is one such example. Second, states may have strong administrative institutions but weak democratic institutions which make them likely to develop 'counter-revolutionary nationalism' and initiate foreign wars. Germany under Otto von Bismarck in the late 19th century is an instance of this phenomenon.

Mansfield and Snyder (1995, 2005, 2009) use both quantitative analyses and historical case studies to corroborate their claims about democratization fueling the flames in cases with such weak institutions. However, others have criticized these analyses. As Lars-Erik Cederman et al. (2008: 518) note, all studies finding that semi-democracies or democratizing states are conflict-prone rest on an application of the POLITY index (more on this below). Indeed, Mansfield and Snyder simply identify a part of the POLITY spectrum, from –6 to 6 (on a scale ranging from -10 to 10), as that of democratizing states, and argue that within this terrain weak institutions make for conflicts. This is, to say the least, a very broad understanding of 'democratizing' countries, covering, for example, Burma (2008–2009), Egypt (1976–2009), Hungary (1867–1943), Iran (1982–2008), Kazakhstan (1991–2009), Mexico (1917–1999), Morocco (1800–1964), Singapore (1965–2009), Tanzania (1961–2009), Tunisia (1987–2009), Yemen (1993–2009), and Zimbabwe (1970–2009). Besides being very far from democracy – however defined – many of these countries did not as such 'democratize', i.e., move further towards democracy, in the enumerated periods.

What is more, in their attempt to get at the issue, Vipen Narang and Rebecca Nelson (2009) fail to find an empirical relationship between incomplete democratizers with weak central institutions and external conflict. Moreover, they question the theoretical basis of the argument, pointing out that "it is hard to conceive of a state with weak institutions that is simultaneously so strong that it can wage an interstate war, yet so weak at the center that it fails" (Narang & Nelson 2009: 359). This assertion is obviously plausible but also to some extent misses the mark, as the countries traveling along one of Mansfield and Snyder's two paths, the combination of strong administrative institutions and weak political institutions, would still be able to wage an external war, whereas those traversing the other path, as described above, might still attract belligerent neighbors – as the above-mentioned case of the Russian–Georgian conflicts testifies to.

The criticism does not end here, however. Michael McFaul (2007) puts the critical spotlight on Mansfield and Snyder's historical case studies. For instance, he argues that it is conceptual stretching "to analyze Prussia and then Germany as democratizing states in the various wars fought between 1864 and 1945" (McFaul 2007: 164). Notwithstanding this criticism, Mansfield and Snyder's perspective, which originally centered on external wars only, has recently migrated to the study of internal conflicts, including civil war, which we elaborate on below.

Peace between liberal democracies?

Even if we accept the validity of Mansfield and Snyder's findings, this does not undermine the democratic peace theory as it has been dealt with above. In fact, and as pointed out by Narang and Nelson (2009: 357), in their "qualification to the democratic peace theory" Mansfield and Snyder simply:

> contend that while mature democracies may be more pacific in their relations with each other, incompletely democratizing states with weak central institutions are more likely to initiate external wars than stable regimes or fully democratizing and autocratizing states.

As with the treatment of the historical exceptions above, this obviously implies that the peace thesis holds as long as we apply a relatively demanding definition of democracy (see also Cederman et al. 2008: 511). In this connection, it is once again worth mentioning that Kant (2003 [1795]: 490–491) – when framing the theory in the first place – defined the republican constitution in terms not only of securing the consent of the governed but also, and indeed more expressly, of the liberal elements we have added with our definition of liberal democracy.[7] This point serves to show that Mansfield and Snyder's qualification to the peace thesis is really a minor one.

Civil war – the dark side of democratization?

Mansfield and Snyder's qualification is nonetheless relevant as thinner types of democracy – or merely countries moving towards such democracy – obviously merit attention; not least due to the mushrooming of instances of such regimes since the end of the Cold War. The growing body of research that hones in on the internal dimension of the conflict-inducing effects of the early stages of democratization is the next stop on our journey.

A number of scholars have recently argued that the early stages of democratization are conducive to internal conflicts, including civil wars. Håvard Hegre et al. (2001) find an inverse U-shaped relationship between the level of democracy and civil war (see also Cederman et al. 2010). The theoretical premise of Hegre et al.'s (2001: 35–36) finding is that 'intermediate regimes' – what they also refer to as 'anocracies' – being partly open, partly repressive, are characterized by inherent contradictions that invite "protest, rebellion, and other forms of civil violence." This "political incoherence" facilitates the eruption of civil conflict. Narang and Nelson (2009), too, in spite of their rejection of any relationship between democratization and the waging of external wars, recognize this relationship. Notice, furthermore, that these arguments are to some extent indebted to the modernization revisionists discussed in Chapter 7, for instance, their assertion that rapid political and socio-economic modernization was conducive to post-colonial civil strife such as the war in Biafra of 1967 to 1970. The arguments of the modernization revisionists may arguably be extended to more contemporary cases, such as the internecine wars in the former Yugoslavia in the 1990s or the conflicts that regularly erupt in Sub-Saharan Africa.

There is an intuitive plausibility to these claims. As Cederman et al. (2008: 516) note, however, several scholars have rejected the empirical validity of this relationship. James Vreeland (2008), for instance, shows that the relationship fails to appear when measures of democracy other than the conventional POLITY index are used; indeed that the same happens if the problem that some of the POLITY codes of component indicators seem to measure civil war are accounted for. Once again, the link between democratization and conflict is thus not undisputed in the literature (see also Cheibub et al. 2010: 92–95). For this very reason, it seems fair to be somewhat hesitant in accepting the policy implications that have been made on the basis of the work on democratization and conflict. These policy implications have normally been taken to be that democracy promotion is a two-edged sword, and that the developed countries and international organizations should prioritize building strong institutions before advocating free elections. These recommendations are, obviously, heavily indebted to Samuel P. Huntington's (1968) famous call for prioritizing a high degree of government over the form of government – an emphasis later developed into the notion of an 'authoritarian transition to democracy' by Fareed Zakaria (1997, 2003; see Munck 2011: 6–7).

Notice that these policy implications can be criticized even without questioning the theoretical and empirical relationship between democratization and conflict. For instance, Thomas Carothers (2007) convincingly argues that the development of the rule of law is well-nigh impossible in the absence of some kind of electoral competition, meaning that the advocates of the authoritarian transition path commit what Carothers terms a 'sequencing fallacy' (see also Møller & Skaaning 2011). In support of this position, McFaul (2007: 166) argues that:

> Even without invoking the violence, repression, and disorder involved in producing strong state institutions in Europe in the eighteenth and nineteenth centuries or South Africa in the twentieth century, there is simply no just or practical way to ask citizens to accept disenfranchisement until their elites build strong institutions, especially when today's autocracies have such a poor record of actually building them.

Here, it is worth recalling that though Mansfield and Snyder (2007: 6–7) recommend that outside powers do not support what they term 'out-of-sequence' transitions they also recognize that external actors can do little to "re-engineer a country's political institutions." In that sense, the disagreement about sequencing might be smaller than first appears.

State repression

A related strand in the literature concerns the relationship between democracy and state repressive behavior vis-à-vis its own citizens. From a normative perspective this theme is relevant, as state coercive behavior has probably claimed more lives than other forms of political conflict in recent history (Davenport 2007: 11–12). As Christian Davenport (2007: 10–11) reports, most studies find that democracy reduces violations of personal integrity in the form of killings, disappearances, and torture. Here, too, a number of mechanisms can be identified. The first is that the democratic regime form increases the cost of state repressive behavior because such transgressions can be punished by the electorate. Other than that, democracy is believed to be conducive to tolerant values while the mechanisms of participation and contestation provide an outlet for protest, which removes the justification for repression.

As with international and civil wars, the general contours of this relationship are rather clear-cut. However, the findings also bear similarity to those mentioned above in another way. Some scholars have suggested that there is 'more murder in the middle', meaning that more state repression is seen in hybrid and transitional regimes than in clearly autocratic and democratic regimes (Fein 1995; Regan & Henderson 2002). The upshot of this is that transitions to democracy may increase repression but that successful democratizations sharply decrease such repression.

However, Davenport (2007: 10–11) argues that state repression is not influenced by regime type until high levels of democracy are achieved. If so, the relationship is more correctly characterized by a threshold effect.

Conclusions

The discussion about the relationship between democratization and conflict in general and the democratic peace theory in particular has once again demonstrated that it is useful to distinguish between thinner and thicker types of democracy. Liberal democracies seem to have the pacific consequences attributed to them by the peace theory, whereas the relationship between democratization and conflict is much more disputed. Indeed, much speaks in favor of accepting that some conflict-inducing consequences of the early stages of democratization are in existence.

The upshot of this is that the peace theory is still standing insofar as a thick definition is employed. However, the question is: which causal mechanisms have led to the association between liberal democracy and peace? The literature does not yet present any particularly convincing response to this question. The very fact that the relationship tends to break down using more minimalist versions of democracy, which obviously makes it easier to tease out the independent effects of democracy (cf. Carbone 2009: 126), certainly requires further scrutiny, since this basically means that it cannot be the isolated effect of consent, via elections, that provides the decisive mechanism.

This brings us to a related problem, namely the question of whether it is democracy or the structural background conditions that are decisive for the promotion of peace. As shown in previous chapters, we almost exclusively find liberal democracies among the countries characterized by a combination of affluence, strong civil societies, and linkage to the key Western areas. The circumstance that we do not really have full-fledged democracies without this package makes it difficult to assess the independent impact of (liberal) democracy. This has direct consequences for the democratic peace thesis. Perhaps this is actually a peace between states with the rule of law? Or perhaps it is a peace between modern, dynamic, and pluralist countries?

This completes the circle, since we are now back to the fundamental critique of democratic peace: that it does not hold true for all kinds of democracies. There is indeed good reason to not blindly accept its blessings. But one unwavering fact remains. If we apply a relatively thick definition of democracy, this is one of the absolute, strongest empirical relationships in the social sciences. In fact, it is in the same category as the finding that there has never been a democracy with a planned economy. In the final chapter of this book, we scrutinize whether democracy is also associated with such things as economic growth and equality – and whether these relationships hinge upon the distinction between thinner and thicker types of democracy.

13 Democracy, growth, equality, and famines

Twenty years ago, Samuel P. Huntington (1991: 263) argued that "Democracy becomes consolidated when people learn that democracy is a solution to the problem of tyranny, but not necessarily to anything else." This is, to say the least, a low-key attitude to the merits of democracy. It is also one that stands in stark contrast to the euphoric scenes that have often characterized the fall of many a dictator in many a place. Particularly memorable is the joy and hope of a new and better future which was expressed in the East-Central European capitals in 1989 to 1990 in connection with the collapse of communist one-party rule (Ash 1990). The vast majority of the people were beside themselves with glee, and everywhere there was hope for a new and better future – politically, economically, and socially. So who is right? The skeptic Huntington, or the optimistic masses in Europe, Africa, Asia, and Latin America that were liberated from autocratic rule in recent decades? In this chapter, our main emphasis lies on whether democracy has a competitive edge over other regime forms regarding equality, economic growth, and efficient reactions to large-scale human catastrophes. However, before delving into these issues, we address the normative and political import of focusing on these (potential) effects.

The debate about consequences

The debate about the consequences of democracy may be traced all the way back to Antiquity. Recall merely Aristotle's and Polybios' typologies of political regimes, which basically associated *demokratia* and *ochlokratia*, respectively, with the rule of the poor and their consequent proscription of the rich (see Chapter 1). This can in many ways be seen as a more radical and violent version of the contemporary 'medium voter theorem' which we return to below. But versions of Huntington's dictum may also be traced back to ancient Greece. Consider only Democritus' assertion that "Poverty in a democracy is as much to be preferred to what is called prosperity under despots as freedom is to slavery" (quoted in Russell 2004 [1946]: 78). Here, too, democracy is defended by its combating tyranny rather than its effects on economic development.[1] The debate is ancient, then, but as noted in the Introduction, it has come to the fore in recent decades. According to Giovanni Carbone (2009: 124), the very strength of the normative arguments for democracy, along with its vast spread over the last few decades, have produced a series of broader anticipations about the effects of democratic governance. Aside from what democracy may embody – be it political equality, individual freedom, or something else – a democratic political system is often expected to generate a number of side benefits such as better-consolidated state institutions; more firmly established rational-legal administrative structures; domestic and international peace; improved economic performance and development; and the adoption of redistributive and welfare policies. After all, the reasoning goes, if everyone is going to have a say on the way a country is governed, does it not follow that such self-evident public goods as peace or economic well-being should be among the obvious outcomes?

Carbone (2009: 136) goes so far as to state that the effects of democracy may paradoxically become a cause for its survival. Insofar as the people's expectations come to naught, they may turn their backs on democracy.

A democratic critique of democracy

Carbone's point finds quite a broad resonance in the recent literature. A good way of elucidating this is by returning to the fact that most democratic openings have been occasions of hope for a new future – expectations that were often built up under the impression of the dismal effects of the preceding autocracies. Take only Latin America in the 1960s, 1970s, and 1980s, where military rule was widespread. The longing for political freedom is naturally greatest while suffering from a lack of freedom, and it is probably no coincidence that social and economic hardships under autocratic rule are often attributed to the political oppression of the people. Once democracy has made its advent, high expectations therefore remain to be fulfilled. Robert A. Dahl (1989: 222) puts it in the following way:

Typical of democrats who live in countries governed by authoritarian regimes is a fervent hope that their country will one day reach the threshold of polyarchy. Typical of democrats who live in countries long governed by polyarchy is a belief that polyarchy is insufficiently democratic and should be made more so.

Researchers are people too, and a number of Latin American academics actively threw themselves into the fight against dictatorship. Worth naming here are Fernando Cardoso and Guillermo O'Donnell, both of whom remained in Brazil and Argentina, respectively, during spells with military juntas in order to create academic breathing spaces in the absence of political rights. Cardoso later became President of Brazil (1995–2002), while O'Donnell left Argentina to become a professor in the USA. O'Donnell in particular has invested much of his career pondering over the state of democracy and what democracy is about. This has led to a number of ground-breaking scientific articles which must at least be partly attributed to his own experiences with military rule in Argentina. As O'Donnell has since pointed out (see Munck & Snyder 2007: 294), his generation of democracy activists had rather high expectations concerning democracy. While they did not see democracy as the solution to all of life's problems, they were convinced that in addition to political rights, democracy would provide progress with respect to ensuring the civil rights of the people and decreasing economic disparities.

Argentina rid itself of military rule in 1983 and Brazil did so in 1988 as the third wave of democracy rolled over South America. But when O'Donnell (2007) looked back on the development in the 1990s, he was less than satisfied. His assessment was that democracy had yet to lead to an effective enforcement of civil rights and make an impact on the major social and economic ailments of the South American countries. O'Donnell therefore engaged in a research agenda focusing on the Latin American social and economic shortfalls. Simplifying somewhat, O'Donnell reports good news and bad news. The good news is that – to invoke the terminology of T.H. Marshall (1996 [1949]) – the third wave of democratization has led to the introduction of political citizenship in many developing countries. The bad news is that democracy has generally had very limited success with regard to civil citizenship,[2] not to mention social citizenship, which has not really gained ground in practice. O'Donnell observes that fundamental human rights are simply not respected in many of these countries. The legislation may well be full of flowery declarations regarding freedom of speech, equality before the law, and social benefits for those in need. However, aside from affluent parts of the larger cities, the liberal and social rights are not worth the paper on which they are written.

Democracy and equality

These disheartening observations on O'Donnell's behalf serve to frame the debate about democracy's consequences, which has gained momentum in the latest decades. A widespread consensus among economists and political theorists exists to the effect that we should expect that democracy leads to economic leveling (Gradstein & Milanovic 2004: 518; Przeworski 2007: 22). The mechanism providing the causal link is so intuitively convincing: the poor will use their political leverage, via the free vote, to secure economic redistribution. This mechanism has been formalized into the so-called 'median voter model' or 'median voter theorem' (cf. Meltzer & Richards 1981). Adam Przeworski (2007: 21–22) renders it in the following way:

> Each individual is characterized by an endowment of labor or capital and all individuals can be ranked from the poorest to the richest. Individuals vote on the rate of tax to be imposed on incomes generated by supplying these endowments to production. The revenues generated by this tax are either equally distributed to all individuals or spent to provide equally valued public goods, so that the tax rate uniquely determines the extent of redistribution. Once the tax rate is decided, individuals maximize utility by deciding in a

decentralized way how much of their endowments to supply. The median voter theorem asserts that there exists a unique majority rule equilibrium, this equilibrium is the choice of the voter with the median preference, and the voter with the median preference is the one with median income. And when the distribution of incomes is right-skewed, that is, if the median income is lower than the mean, as it is in all countries for which data exist, majority rule equilibrium is associated with a high degree of equality of post-fisc (tax and transfer) incomes, tempered only by the deadweight losses of redistribution.

This notion also infuses the 'economic' approaches to democratization of Daron Acemoglu and James Robinson (2006) and Carles Boix (2003), described in Chapter 7. Counter-arguments do exist of course. Most famous is 'Pareto's Law', the postulate of the Italian economist Vilfredo Pareto (1935 [1916]) to the effect that distribution of income takes the form of a stable pattern in which the richest 20 percent of the population retains around 80 percent of societal income, no matter the regime form. Formulating this law, Pareto drew both upon his statistical work on income distributions and upon his 'elite circulation theory'. The theory states that narrow elites continuously replace each other but always exercise power, meaning that democracy is merely a different façade of elite rule than autocracy (see Pareto 1991 [1901]). More particularly, democracy does not cater to the needs and wishes of the people, meaning that redistribution is not to be expected as an effect of democratization.

Another criticism of the postulate about the leveling consequences of democracy identifies empirical examples of countries that achieved relatively high levels of equality under autocracy – most famous here are the Asian tigers Singapore, South Korea, and Taiwan. Contrariwise, the post-communist countries have experienced rising, indeed sometimes skyrocketing, levels of inequality following their democratizations after the Cold War (Gradstein & Milanovic 2004: 516). Seen from the higher ground, there is thus room for doubt – but the assertion that democracy produces redistribution and decreases inequality nonetheless has the upper hand in terms of theoretical plausibility (cf. Carbone 2009: 131). What do the data show?

Based on general reviews of the extant empirical studies of this relationship, Larry Sirowy and Alex Inkeles (1990: 145; see also Carbone 2009: 132) find "no generalizable and robust confirmation of the thesis that democracy promotes greater equality," whereas Mark Gradstein and Branko Milanovic (2004) find some evidence of a positive impact of democracy upon equality. But the effects are not large, and Gradstein and Milanovic stress that the post-communist experience remains an important caveat.

Przeworski (2007: 21–22) takes on a more historical perspective and emphasizes that modern democracy, as conceived in the 18th and 19th centuries, originally represented an attempt to fight the privileges of aristocracy. This was obviously a revolutionary idea, but it concerned the leveling of political (and judicial) power, not economic power, meaning that it was blind to economic inequality. Democracy was simply not conceived as a weapon with which to secure redistribution – to use

Przeworski's formulation "the sin was original." On this basis, Przeworski (2007: 26) argues that the historical absence of a relationship between democracy and equality may not be so surprising. He does add that at least in the 20th century, democrats clearly did fight for economic redistribution. Nevertheless, he notes, we find little empirical support for the effectiveness of this push; the inequality levels are almost the same in democracies and autocracies when controlling for per capita income. More generally, in individual countries the income inequality has been remarkably stable over time, even where welfare states have been erected over the period (Przeworski 2007: 23). This does not mean that Przeworski accepts Pareto's Law. Indeed, he expressly denounces it, pointing to the difference between the low inequality levels in Western Europe and parts of East Asia on the one hand and the high inequality levels in Latin America on the other hand. However, he ponders whether the equality level achieved in countries such as Spain and South Korea, in which the ratio income of the top to the bottom quintile is about six, "is just the extent to which any political system can equalize assets or incomes" (Przeworski 2007: 26–27).

Democracy and growth

Democracy's effect on growth has received at least as much attention as its effects on inequality. As a number of scholars have pointed out, quite convincing theoretical contributions predict either that democracy is conducive to growth or that democracy hampers growth. Indeed, in an appraisal of the methods used to analyze this relationship, Jason Seawright (2010: 250) points out that the literature has identified at least five different such relationships:

> Variation across levels of democracy may (1) cause economic growth, (2) prevent economic growth, (3) be irrelevant to economic growth, (4) have a curvilinear relationship with growth, or (5) have other forms of mixed effects on growth.

The presence of such rampant disagreements obviously calls for more general attempts to take stock of the relationship. Two such general appraisals of this relationship, published with a decade's interval, take the inherent theoretical tension in the literature as the stepping stone for carrying out a general assessment.

Sirowy and Inkeles (1990) point to a general oscillation within the discipline, from theories asserting that democracy facilitates the creation of wealth to theories arguing that it stifles it. They term these positions the 'compatibility' and the 'conflict' perspective, respectively. The notion of compatibility, open to the point of view that all good things go together, is basically that of the classical versions of modernization theory (Sirowy & Inkeles 1990: 128) whereas the notion of conflict is indebted to many of the criticisms of modernization theory, which we also dealt with in Chapter 7, such as that of Huntington (1968). More particularly, the compatibility perspective emphasizes that political pluralism is necessary for economic pluralism and that free information is necessary for efficient government, both of which are conducive to growth. The conflict perspective, on the contrary, points to the disorder of premature democracy, the inability of democratic politicians to implement tough but needed policies, and the need for state involvement in development processes (Sirowy & Inkeles 1990: 128–132).

Carrying out an appraisal of the empirical results within the literature, Sirowy and Inkeles (1990: 128) end on a skeptical note. They fail to find any universal relationship between democracy and economic growth, and basically argue that economic progress can be achieved under different regime forms. This conclusion is widely echoed in Przeworski et al.'s (2000) subsequent attempt to get at the relationship. Przeworski et al. also begin by identifying convincing theoretical arguments to the effect that democracy can both be conducive and detrimental to growth. Regarding the latter view, they point to the classical work of Karl de Schweinitz (1959), who argued that in poor countries democracy leads to pressures for immediate consumption, thus decreasing the investments needed for growth.[3] Regarding the former view, they point to the work of scholars like Douglass North (1990), who basically says that the state always preys on society but that democratic institutions diminish this pernicious state of affairs. In outlining these positions, Przeworski et al. (2000: 144–145) conclude that both mechanisms are plausible and that it is therefore very difficult to predict whether rates of growth differ between democracies and autocracies. This must, in a nutshell, be left to empirical testing. Carrying out just such a test, Przeworski et al. (2000: ch. 3) find that, controlling for relevant factors, regimes have no general effect upon economic growth. This is most conspicuously the case in poor countries. Przeworski et al. accordingly observe that poverty constrains whatever the regime. Most importantly, poor countries cannot finance a capable state, meaning that neither democracies nor autocracies can squeeze out the investments needed for growth.

Where does this leave us? The lack of consistent findings may be taken to go some way to support the notion that democracy is not conducive to growth – but also that it does not cost growth (see Munck 2011: 6–7). Alternatively, it may follow from methodological problems. In this vein, Seawright (2010: 247, 261) argues that these "remarkably inconsistent findings" seem to reflect some fundamental problems of regression analysis, in particular the absence of consensus about which control variables to include.

Another important observation is that many of the studies which do assert that democracy breeds growth actually emphasize the liberal aspects of liberal democracy much more than the electoral ones. For instance, Mancur Olson (1993), with his theory of roving and stationary bandits, ultimately attributes democracy's superior record with respect to growth to "court systems, independent judiciaries and respect of law and individual rights," all of which make for secure property rights (Olson 1993: 572).[4] Now, these are obviously attributes linked to the rule of law rather than to free elections, and they present a reminder that the definition of democracy needs to be unpacked before theoretical relationships can be appraised.

To a lesser extent, the same is the case for John Gerring et al.'s (2005) more recent contribution. Gerring et al. argue that a relationship exists between the longevity (stock) of democracy and economic growth. Such is the case because democracy tends to build up physical, human, social, and political capital when it is stable and long-lasting, and all of these kinds of capital tend to facilitate economic growth. Physical capital refers to the level of equality, human capital to the education level and health of the population, social capital to the level of generalized trust, and political capital to the political system's learning capability and level of institutionalized (vs. personalized) rule. To have positive consequences for growth, democracy must survive 'its tumultuous youth' where 'democratic overload' is a persistent danger. But once democracy matures, the positive effects set in (Gerring et al. 2005: 335). However, it is obvious that this study, too, accentuates mechanisms, such as the institutionalization of a Weberian bureaucracy (among other things), that would be more pronounced under thicker than thinner versions of democracy.

Democracy and famines

Amartya Sen's (2003 [1996]) assertion that democracies are superior in averting immediate catastrophes such as famines has also been widely discussed in the literature. According to Sen, this relationship holds water empirically when controlling for factors such as affluence and it also holds across time in singular cases. India, for instance, suffered frequent famines until 1947 but these ended with the introduction of democracy. Indeed, Sen (2003 [1996]: 444–445) claims that no substantial famine has ever occurred in a democracy with a relatively free press. A number of mechanisms underpin this relationship. Democracy means that the ruling elite is punished for the occurrence of famine: via the ballot-box. Equally crucial is the issue of information. A free press and an active opposition make up a relatively effective system of early warning, meaning that the occurrence of famines cannot be withheld from public scrutiny.

An instructive comparison here is between democratic India and autocratic China. As Georg Sørensen (2008: 105–112) also notes, China has often failed when it comes to famines and other catastrophes – probably because nobody has dared (or been able) to hold the rulers accountable after they have committed catastrophic errors. Mao's Great Leap Forward (1958–1961), which cost the lives of between 16 and 30 million Chinese due to famine, offers a striking example (Sen 2003 [1996]: 445). The relatively recent famine in North Korea in 1996, known as the March of Tribulation, may likewise be adduced to support the argument.

Though the importance of Sen's theory is obvious, it has not been tested systematically in the subsequent literature. Recently, however, Oliver Rubin (2009) has sought to do just that. His first important observation is that the few prior attempts to appraise Sen's theory have upheld his claim but have done so via a focus on the relationship between famines and, for example, freedom or the size of the electorate rather than simply democracy (Rubin 2009: 701). Next, Rubin (2009: 702) argues that Sen's theory may be tested in two ways: either deterministically, meaning that no famines should ever have occurred in electoral democracies, or probabilistically, meaning that such democracies should be superior in averting famines compared to other regime forms.

The first claim Rubin tests via a 'critical case approach', where he is particularly interested in India due to the prominent role this case plays in Sen's formulation of his theory. Rubin (2009: 702) argues that it is possible to identify at least three potential famines in India following democratization, namely Bihar (1966), Maharashtra (1973), and Orissa in the 1990s. All three incidents occurred at the state level rather than at the national level. But Rubin further shows that the democratic process – especially the occurrence of a political blame game between the national and state-level governments – contributed to the crises. Further, he argues that similar blame games contributed to the food crises in Malawi (2002) and Niger (2005). On this basis, he rejects the deterministic version of Sen's theory.

Whether this rejection is warranted is questionable. Rubin's treatment of both of the key variables, that is, famine and democracy, is somewhat nonchalant. At most, he shows that – to use our conceptual distinctions – the identified cases are instances of minimalist or electoral democracy, and in the case of Niger (2005), even this could probably be contested. Whether a free press, a crucial link in Sen's theory, was in existence is thus only considered indirectly via the democracy criterion. Even more problematic is the absence of a clear definition of famine in the case studies. Recall here that Sen claims that no *substantial* famine ever occurred in a democracy with a relatively free press. It is not clear that the five incidents identified are instances of substantial famine. To make the case for this that concept obviously needs to be defined and operationalized. In doing so, these cases may easily fail to cross the threshold as the number of casualties was, by historical standards of famine, rather small.

That said, Rubin's points about the democratic process possibly exacerbating the crisis are clearly relevant – as is his observation that there have been no famines in China *after* the terrible one in 1958 to 1961. It is with such observations in mind that he sets out to test Sen's theory probabilistically, using a cross-national statistical analysis. Rubin (2009: 709–710) finds no robust evidence showing that democracies are better than autocracies at combating famines. His most important results are that poverty constrains, all else being equal, and that there is an independent effect of being situated in Africa, meaning that, controlling for other factors, African countries are more prone to experience famines. On this basis, Rubin (2009: 710–713) concludes that the relationship between democracy and famine is not clear empirically and that we need to appreciate the workings of different kinds of democracies to understand how democracy impacts upon the occurrence of famine.

Considering this conclusion it is somewhat paradoxical that Rubin only uses measures for electoral democracy as his explanatory variable. With thicker defini-tions and measures, the results may well have differed substantially. What is more, Sen's theory retains a certain intuitive plausibility, but it obviously needs to be tested more systematically. In addition, even if it holds up in such tests, this does not mean that democracies are generally superior in avoiding hardships. We have already seen that they seem to have little general effect upon inequality and growth. Sen (2003 [1996]: 446) frames this as follows: Whereas democracies have been good at avoiding disasters that are 'easy to understand', they have a much worse record with respect to solving more complex problems such as ordinary hunger or illiteracy. Returning to the country comparison, it is telling that autocratic China has outdistanced democratic India as regards the average standard of living and factors such as infant mortality, literacy, and life expectancy (Sørensen 2008: 105–112). In a nutshell, Indians die 'prematurely' for other reasons than famine in numbers equivalent to what would surely be instances of substantial famines, in spite of democracy and a free press.

Conclusions

In this chapter we have covered a number of recent debates, such as those concerning democracy's impact upon economic growth and redistribution, and whether democracy hinders famines. As in the previous chapter on democracy's effects upon conflict, our distinction between thinner and thicker types of democracy has been put to good use, as we have observed that different types of democracy seemingly have different consequences. Let us attempt to use this point to take stock with respect to Huntington's provocative claim about how democracy is not necessarily the solution to anything other than the problem with tyranny. Against the background of the preceding discussion, we can raise two objections against this statement, objections that somewhat paradoxically criticize Huntington for either claiming too much or not enough.

As far as the liberal democracies are concerned, there is hardly any doubt that we are dealing with the solution to more than merely the problem of tyranny. The liberal democracies are able to ensure the rule of law (in fact by definition) as well as growth and welfare. Whether these things are the results of democracy or whether they are merely the results of the same background factors that have contributed to democracy so far remains undecided. In any case, we can note that these things appear to go hand in hand. The situation is quite different with fledgling (mostly minimalist) democracies in the greater part of the developing countries. Strictly speaking, the question here is whether they are at all able to solve the problem of tyranny. Does Huntington claim too much here? As long as the citizens can vote the authorities in and out at the ballot-box, it is obviously not possible to talk about tyranny in the conventional, political sense. As far as this is concerned, Huntington (also here, by definition) is surely right; but if state power is not present, then private tyrants in the form of local strongmen (cf. Migdal 1988) can reign at will. And if democracy is not the solution to one of the other great problems facing humankind – the problem of lawlessness – it is not surprising that critics will emerge.

This brings us back to one of the major themes of this book: that free elections are not worth much in the absence of the rule of law. Research-wise, we are here faced with trade-off. The best way to scrutinize the effects of democracy is by using minimalist definitions which are capable of isolating the core of democracy (Carbone 2009: 126). With such definitions, the literature finds very little evidence of positive effects of democracy. With thicker definitions, on the other hand, the effects are much more visible. But here we do not really know what the 'root cause' is – particular attributes of liberal democracy, such as the rule of law, or deeper structural factors which promote the rule of law?

The lack of clear-cut findings about the consequences of democracy should not cloud the basic fact that democracy has an intrinsic normative value: it is an aim in itself rather than solely a means. This, of course, is also why so many people care about democracy – and why the laborious task of appraising democratic theory and the democratization literature is worthwhile. Bearing this in mind, it is time to conclude.

Concluding and looking ahead

Surprisingly similar notions of democracy have existed in two periods separated by almost 2000 years, namely Hellas in the classical period and the centuries after the French Revolution. To be sure, democrats in ancient Greece had no notion of two crucially important strands of the modern ideal of liberal democracy, namely representation and individual human rights. But the antique and modern conceptions share a general appreciation of three other values, namely self-government (popular sovereignty), liberty, and equality. It is all the more paradoxical that no direct relationship between ancient Greek democratic institutions and modern democratic institutions can be established. Instead, modern representative democracy owes a lot to medieval ecclesiastical and secular teaching about rulership and the practical use of institutions such as charters and estates of the realm. Furthermore, it draws on important elements of the republicanism which flourished during the Renaissance.

Even though the roots can be traced deep into medieval times, it was only in the 19th century that modern democracy came into existence. And until the turn of the century democracy was, at most, what we have termed minimalist democracy. Most evidently, equal and universal suffrage was still only beckoning dimly in the future. Nonetheless, the democracies of the 19th century capture staggering historical novelties. For the second time in history, the rule of the one or of the few was replaced by some version of the rule of the many (the people). Indeed, the construct of minimalist democracy captures the core of virtually any modern definition of democracy, namely popular sovereignty embodied by recurrent, competitive, and decisive elections which determine the appointment of government. The conceptual parts of our book document that this is the only defining property that finds virtually universal acceptance in democratic theory. Within the procedural approach to defining democracy, where democracy is viewed as a political method, some scholars have proposed augmenting the electoral core with political (civil) liberties, such as the freedoms of speech and association, and others have gone even further and added the rule of law in a more general sense. Meanwhile, those preferring more substantial definitions have emphasized attributes such as social equality, extensive participation, and thorough deliberation.

Based on the comparative perspective which underpins this book, we have argued that procedural definitions have more to offer when discussing empirical developments and relationships. What is more, we have demonstrated that the most influential procedural definitions can be situated in an overarching typology based on systematic distinctions between thinner (more minimalist) and thicker (more maximalist) definitions of democracy. This typology made for appreciating a pivotal message of this book, namely that we need to break down the concept of democracy into its constituent parts and to systematically distinguish between different definitions of democracy to understand the developments, causes, and consequences of democracy.

We first took advantage of this descriptively, mapping the spread of democracy since its second coming in the early 19th century. This made it possible to replicate Samuel P. Huntington's (1991) analysis of waves of democratization based on a minimalist definition of democracy. Our appraisal showed that 19th- and 20th-century democratizations have indeed been characterized by a 'two-steps-forward-one-step-back' pattern. But we also presented some important nuances to Huntington's framework. First, there has only been one genuine step backwards or reverse wave, namely the one engulfing particularly Europe during the interwar years. Second, we identified a number of conjunctures, most importantly in the aftermath of World War I, following World War II, and after the end of the Cold War, which seem at least as interesting as the more general wave movements. Finally, based on the fine-grained distinctions between liberal democracy, polyarchy, electoral democracy, and minimalist democracy we took a closer look at the regional developments since the early 1970s, concluding that great dissimilarities exist as regards regional patterns, and that a new reverse wave has not set in yet – but that the massive post-1989 democratization seems to have abated.

The very description of these political developments obviously cries out for explanation. Confronting the causes of democratization over the past 200 years, the combination of a comparative, historical perspective and an appreciation of different types of democracy, once again proved its worth. We identified four general explanatory currents: modernization theory, the social forces tradition, transitology, and international factors. In each case, we showed that some of the seeming disagreements within the traditions could be bridged by distinguishing between thinner and thicker types of democracy. Furthermore, we argued that a number of relationships are context-dependent, which underlines the need for comparisons across space and time. Finally, we emphasized that scholars increasingly attempt to combine insights from the perspectives, in particular by integrating structures and actors into general explanatory models. We endorsed these endeavors by pointing out that any convincing explanation of democratization needs to rest on solid micro-foundations. But we also raised a warning not to slight the structural factors which seem most crucial for explaining the large-scale regularities across space and time that were laid bare by our descriptive analyses.

When democracy means so much to so many, it is at least partly due to expectations about its consequences. The most important such consequence is tautological, namely the fact that democracy – whatever the conception – by definition rules out autocracy and, if thicker procedural definitions are employed, also safeguards certain individual liberties and the rule of law. More disputed is the issue of the causal consequences of democracy. We delved into this issue bereft of clear expectations. But what we found was a quite solid consensus about the pacific relationships between liberal democracies coupled with a massive disagreement regarding the effect of democracy on factors such as social equality and growth. Once again, it turned out that the distinction between thinner and thicker types of democracy was helpful in making sense of these controversies. Maintaining a thick definition – such as liberal democracy – a positive empirical relationship can be established between democracy on the one hand, and peace, equality, and prosperity on the other. Substituting this with a thin definition – such as minimalist democracy – these relationships are less evident. In fact, numerous scholars have identified adverse consequences of such regimes, stressing that political openings may facilitate violent conflict, hamper investments (and thus growth), and create political and social instability. This brings us to a more general problem. Only by isolating the electoral core of democracy can we test its effects convincingly. Using the definition of liberal democracy, we simply do not know which of the constituent attributes drives particular relationships. What is more, due to the fact that most liberal democracies are characterized by relatively similar structural conditions, it is difficult to tease out the effect of ulterior factors.

This last observation presents a platform for looking ahead. First, it is obvious that the concept of democracy needs to be further – and systematically – disaggregated into subcomponents in empirical studies. Scholars increasingly need to take a multifaceted view of democracy to investigate its causes and consequences. Our typology presents a very useful analytical device for doing this but much more is called for. By interchangeably isolating different attributes of democracy it should be possible to elucidate sequences and syndromes of democratization and de-democratization. That is to say, attributes which tend to go together, or follow one another, when a political regime slips away from, or moves towards, democracy. Furthermore, such a conceptual framework will pave the way for investigating whether causal relationships differ when different definitions of democracy are applied. Hopefully, such a disaggregated approach will make it possible to further bridge some of the seemingly irreconcilable findings about causes and consequences of democracy. Here, there is room for some optimism. Several datasets, such as *The Freedom in the World Survey* and *The Bertelsmann Transformation Index*, now make their subcomponent scores publicly available. And an ambitious new undertaking, the so-called *Varieties of Democracy* (V-dem) project, is expressly devoted to allowing scholars to investigate and combine even larger sets of subcomponents. When complete, the V-dem dataset will enable researchers to distinguish between no less than seven principles of democracy – electoral, liberal, consensus, majoritarian, participatory, deliberative, and egalitarian – based on several hundreds of indicators, covering all countries in the world from 1900 onwards (see Coppedge et al. 2011).

Second, our book has documented that a comparative, historical perspective on democracy and democratization is indispensable. Studies based on empirical snapshots fail to capture the contextual developments which created modern democracy and the possibility that relationships differ during different periods (cf.

Boix 2011). More generally, the past makes up a virtual laboratory for testing our theories about causes and consequences of democracy, often in the form of 'natural experiments'. Also in this regard, there is room for optimism as the historical dimension of democratization is attracting renewed attention. As mentioned in Chapter 11, Giovanni Capoccia and Daniel Ziblatt (2010) have recently proposed a new research agenda based on a 'historical turn'. The backdrop to these endeavors is the observation that the historical focus has been downplayed in recent decades as the massive democratization over the latest generation has tended to crowd out attention to developments in prior periods. As Capoccia and Ziblatt convincingly argue, the consequent 'ahistorical' analyses suffer from an implausible assumption of causal homogeneity, a lack of micro foundations for causal relationships, and problems of circular causality (Capoccia & Ziblatt 2010: 935–938). This, then, is why a historical turn is needed. It still remains to be seen if this historical turn becomes a reality, but the omens are promising.

It follows from our prior endorsement of integrated causal models that the disaggregated and historical approaches which we recommend are to be nested in explanatory frameworks that combine different factors, including both structures and actors. If anything there currently seems to be a danger of over-emphasizing actors, something that is in fact reflected in Capoccia and Ziblatt's research agenda. Our book serves as a reminder about the importance of structural conditions, a reminder that is especially timely when distinguishing between thicker and thinner democracies. One of the more particular factors that has been under-appreciated is the state as both a more general entity and as a bureaucratic structure. To quote Gerardo Munck's (2011: 10) recent appraisal:

> the paucity of empirical analysis of the state compared to analyses of modernization theory is striking. While the role of state is thus increasingly addressed in research on democracy, more theoretical and empirical research is needed to develop this relatively new line of inquiry.

One such new line of research is to be found in the interface between state formation and democratization. An established current in historical sociology has emphasized the way state formation and democratization were interwoven – and often mutually reinforcing – in Europe and the European settler colonies, but outside of this area, the situation has been quite different (see Vu 2010). Jacob Hariri (forthcoming) can thus explain much of the democratic variation outside Europe using the diversity in pre-colonial state development that can be accounted for by the timing of the Neolithic revolution. Given a premise about the unique European development and subsequent export of constitutionalism (relatively similar to that described in Chapter 4 of this book), Hariri's point is that non-democracy is more likely, the stronger the non-European states were. For this allowed non-European states to keep European pro-democratizing influence (including outright colonization) at bay. This interesting finding is a good example of some of the gains which can be made by focusing attention on the relationship between the state and democracy.

These gains are desirable exactly because "the organisation and establishment of democracy" is arguably the major problem of our time – as it was for Alexis de Tocqueville (1988 [1835]: 311). In this book we have attempted to shed light on this problem from a variety of angles. We have demonstrated some of the important strides made by the democratization literature, especially after World War II. Nonetheless, it is surely no exaggeration to say that much work still needs to be done.

Notes

Introduction

1 Invoking Aristotle, Marsilius of Padua (1956 [1324]: 46–47) could on this basis argue in favor of something which comes pretty close to democracy (see also Held 2006: 38–39).
2 Acquinas' treatment is especially symptomatic because he simultaneously proclaimed the mixed constitution, with its democratic elements, the preferable form of government (see Chapter 1).
3 Or at least as the worst form of government except all the others that have been tried, as Sir Winston Churchill once phrased it.
4 This statement is, at least, valid until the economic crisis which has engulfed a number of long-established democracies in Western Europe.

1 Conceptions of democracy in ancient Greece

1 There are exceptions, however. Some German and Scandinavian scholars have emphasized the existence of a Germanic *Urdemokratie*, whereas some French scholars, following Rousseau, have found the cradle of democracy in the political communities of Switzerland. We are indebted to Mogens Herman Hansen for pointing this out. That some disagreement exists is also reflected in Tocqueville's (1988 [1840]: 439) dismissive remark that the only thing which ancient and modern democracy had in common was the word itself. Against such objections, Dahl (1998: 102) argues that to deny Athens the status of democracy would be like asserting that the brothers Wright did not invent the airplane because it looks so different from the airplanes of today.
2 To quote Giovanni Sartori (1987: 279): "Modern men want another democracy, in the sense that their ideal of democracy is not at all the same as that of the Greeks. It would be strange, indeed, if this were not so. In more than two thousand intervening years Western civilization has enriched, modified, and articulated its value goals. It has experienced Christianity, humanism, the Reformation, a 'natural rights' conception of natural law, and liberalism. How can we possibly think that when we advocate democracy today, we are pursuing the same aims and ideals as the Greeks? How can it escape us that democracy, for us, embodies values of which the Greeks were not and could not be aware?"
3 Hansen (2010b: 1-9) identifies no less than nine different meanings of *eleutheria/ eleutheros*. At least one of these corresponds to Berlin's positive conception of liberty – namely that found in Plato's writings – several to his negative conception of liberty, and several to each of Constant's two different conceptions of liberty, i.e., ancient and modern.
4 We owe this argument to Hansen (2010d: 338–339).

5   Even this point should not be stated too categorically, however. Hansen (1999: 3) draws attention to the fact that Aristotle in *Politics* "refers to a type of democracy where the only function of the Assembly of the People is to choose the magistrates and call them to account for their conduct in office, while all political decisions are taken by the magistrates without the People having any say." This seemingly comes pretty close to our notion of indirect (though not representative) democracy. The problem is, though, that we only have sufficient knowledge about the direct democracy of Athens, meaning that we are, willy-nilly, forced to rely on "a comparison of Athenian and modern democracy, rather than a comparison of ancient and modern democracy."

6   Except for the case of compulsory voting in a few countries such as Australia and Belgium.

7   In classical Greece, *Idiōtēs* was normally used to denote the citizen who uses his political rights but does not take on offices, rather than the purely private person (Hansen 1999: 144, 308).

8   Lord Acton (1972 [1877]: 63) conveys this charge in a symptomatic way when noting that "the possession of unlimited power, which corrodes the conscience, hardens the heart, and confounds the understanding of monarchs, exercised its demoralising influence on the illustrious democracy of Athens. It is bad to be oppressed by a minority, but it is worse to be oppressed by a majority."

9   Interestingly, Aristotle judged that among the good constitutions, *basileia* (i.e., monarchy) was the best form and *politea* the worst, whereas under the perverse constitution, the order was reversed so that *demokratia* was the best form and *tyrannis* the worst (Hansen 1993: 101). Russell (2004 [1946]: 183) points out that Aristotle thereby "arrives at a qualified defense of democracy; for most actual governments are bad, and therefore, among the actual governments, democracies tend to be best."

10 We here arguably find a reminiscence of the way in which the *poleis* first democratized as a response to the advent of infantry warfare (Weber 2003 [1927]: 324–325; Hintze 1975 [1906]: 183–184; McNeill 1982: 5–20; Bobbit 2002: xxii).

2 Conceptions of democracy from ancient Rome to our time

1   Modern republicanism is normally subdivided into a neo-Athenian and neo-Roman branch (see Hansen (2007: 53), who points out that neo-Athenian is in fact a misnomer and that neo-Aristotelian would be a much better term). This presents quite a tight overlap with David Held's distinction, as the neo-Athenian strand is obviously closer to development republicanism whereas the neo-Roman strand is closer to protective republicanism (and thus to liberalism) (see Held 2006: 35–37). However, the distinction between a neo-Athenian and neo-Roman branch applies to the modern current of republicanism, whereas Held's is, at least to a larger extent, an attempt to capture the historical republicanism. For that reason, we prefer Held's terminology here.

2   There are exceptions, such as Bentham and John Stuart Mill.

3   See also the uncannily similar contemporary definition of Alf Ross (1952) [1946]).

4   Notice, however, that the process criteria are equally befitting for the ideal version of direct and the ideal version of representative democracy. It is only with his seven criteria for polyarchy that Dahl delimits his thought to representative democracy.

5   We have excluded Held's references in the quote.

6   For more comprehensive accounts of the different meanings of democracy, including some not discussed in this chapter, see Held (2006), Cunningham (2001), and Coppedge et al. (2011).

3 Typologies of democratic and autocratic regimes

1 It should be noted that this scheme is based on a standard, Aristotelian – or classical – logic and does not apply if other logic systems, such as those of radial concepts and family resemblance, are employed (Collier & Mahon 1993). Elsewhere, we have argued that these other logical systems are inappropriate to capture the conceptual and empirical distinctions between regime forms (Møller & Skaaning 2010, 2011).

2 Naess et al. (1956: 130–131) tellingly quote Bryce to the effect that democracy is "merely a form of government, not a consideration of the purposes to which government may be turned."

3 It should be noticed that O'Donnell (2001: 7) argues for creating a "realistic and restricted, but not necessarily minimalist" definition, which seemingly incorporates some kind of social rights (see Møller & Skaaning 2011: ch. 3). This does not neatly fit our analytical separation between procedural and substantive definitions.

4 A typology is a combination of multiple classifications. Classifications are uni-dimensional, as they divide the empirical cases with respect to a single characteristic, while typologies are multi-dimensional and refer to two or more characteristics (see Bailey 1994).

5 In reality, a few examples existed until recently, namely a number of small European principalities such as Liechtenstein and Monaco. But they have also recently left this category.

6 That is, in a society characterized by the rule of law, the public rules are general, prospective, clear, certain, and equally applied (cf. Hayek 1960; Fuller 1969; Raz 1979) – and followed by the public administration.

7 This does not necessarily mean that there will be more minimalist democracies than liberal democracies in our actual tallies. Rather, the point is that the liberal democracies are *also* minimalist, since the total number of countries living up to the definition of a given rung on the ladder are taking the sum total of that rung together with those above it. As mentioned above, we score the countries according to the most demanding definition they live up to.

8 The focus on modern autocracies means that Linz does not include regime types that rest on the Weberian notion of traditional legitimacy, first and foremost monarchies.

9 In his first comprehensive attempt to develop a typology of autocratic regimes, Linz (2000 [1975]) distinguishes between no less than seven sub-types of authoritarian regimes, namely bureaucratic-military, organic statist, mobilizational post-democratic, post-independence mobilizational, racial and ethnic, defective and pre-totalitarian, and post-totalitarian. Regarding totalitarian regimes, he mentions three kinds: fascist, communist, and nationalist.

10 More particularly, electoral regimes are divided into three sub-types: the no-party regime, the one-party regime, and the limited multi-party regime. Elections are held in no-party regimes but political parties (or at least candidates representing a party) are prohibited, whereas in one-party regimes all parties but the ruling one are forbidden from competing in elections. Finally, in limited multi-party regimes, at least some independent or opposition candidates are able to participate in the elections. These elections, however, are not free and fair as the process is biased in ways that favor the incumbents (Hadenius & Teorell 2007: 147; cf. Levitsky & Way 2002; Schedler 2002; Howard & Roessler 2006).

11 And no other suited measures have similar cross-spatial and temporal coverage.

12 For detailed criticisms of the Freedom House data, see Kenneth Bollen and Pamela Paxton (2000), Gerardo Munck and Jay Verkuilen (2002), Hans-Joachim Lauth (2004), and Diego Giannone (2010).

4 Medieval foundations of the second coming of democracy

1 This chapter heading is borrowed from Dunn's (2005) notion of democracy's second coming, which is broadly equivalent to Dahl's (1989) second democratic transformation, which we referred to in Chapters 1 and 2.

2 Strictly speaking, the formalization of *habeas corpus* occurred later than the signing of the Magna Carta. But the judicial institution has been attributed to the tradition established by the Magna Carta.

3 Western/Latin Christendom covers the areas historically Christianized from Rome and therefore answering to the Roman Church up until the Reformation. Eastern/Orthodox Christendom – in Eastern Europe – was Christianized from Constantinople by the Orthodox Church.

4 As opposed to the ancient conception of popular sovereignty described in Chapter 1.

5 Of course, based on our distinctions democracy only saw the light of day in the 19th century. Viewed through these spectacles, Downing is first and foremost trying to explain the survival of constitutionalism.

6 Alexis de Tocqueville (1983 [1856]: 47–48), in *The Old Regime and the French Revolution*, touches upon this point in the following way. Noting that "parochial self-government was common to all races in which formerly the feudal system had prevailed," he goes on to observe that "Transported overseas from feudal Europe and free to develop in total independence, the rural parish of the Middle Ages became the township of New England."

7 According to Holmes (1982: 25), Constant was not opposed to democracy as such. But he was surely skeptical about widening suffrage too much.

8 Though de Tocqueville saw the aristocracy as the true defenders of liberty, with the masses instead desiring equality.

9 According to Dunn (2005: 168), this balance is skewed in favor of egoism.

5 Waves of democratization

1 This suggestion makes it all the more interesting that Huntington himself cannot quite figure out which leg to stand on. In the overall tallies, he counts the USA as being democratic in 1828, but elsewhere in the book he writes that the USA first became democratic after having granted genuine political rights to African Americans in the 1960s. He displays the same lack of consistency in relation to Switzerland, which is referred to as being democratic in the 19th century in one place, whereas elsewhere it is first registered as being a democracy after finally granting suffrage to women in 1975 (Huntington 1991: 7, 15).

2 O'Donnell (2010: 23) conveys this nicely via his notion of democracy's 'open-ended character', meaning that "the 'proper' drawing of the external and internal boundaries . . . is a matter of perpetual political deliberation and contention."

3 In the case of new countries, we count them as democratic transitions if they are democratic in their first year of existence. Consequently, if a new country is autocratic from its independence, we do not count it as a democratic breakdown.

4 For critical assessments of the dataset, see Gleditsch and Ward (1997); Munck and Verkuilen (2002); Lauth (2004); and Shawn Treier and Simon Jackman (2008).

5 As such, we consider all of the countries that achieve the respective scores of 2 or 3 on the 'competitiveness of executive recruitment', 3 or 4 on 'openness of executive recruitment', 0, 3, 4, or 5 on 'competitiveness of participation', and 4, 5, 6, or 7 on 'constraints on the power of the chief executive' as democratic; Doorenspleet terms these 'competitive regimes'.

6 The third wave of democratization in different regions

1 Similar observations have been made on the regional level for Latin America (Smith & Ziegler 2008), Sub-Saharan Africa (van de Walle 2002), and Asia (Croissant 2004).

2 Note, once more, that we refer to countries according to the 'most demanding' political regime type they qualify for, even though liberal democracies also fulfill the criteria for polyarchy, and so on and so forth.

3 On August 26, 2003, in his remarks to the 85th American Legion Convention, George W. Bush argued that "Iraq's progress towards self-determination and democracy brings hope to other oppressed people in the region and throughout the world. . . . The people who yearn for liberty and opportunity in countries like Iran and throughout the Middle East are watching and they are praying for our success in Iraq."

4 More generally, Diamond has warned about a reverse wave at least since the end of the 1990s. Diamond (1996) thus wrote an article in the mid-1990s entitled "Is the Third Wave Over? ", and at the turn of the millennium Diamond (2000) wrote another article in the same vein, "Is Pakistan the (Reverse) Wave of the Future?", in which he pointed out how General Musharraf's coup in Pakistan might indicate a forthcoming reverse wave. The inclination to blow the whistle can actually be traced all the way back to Huntington's *The Third Wave* from 1991 in which he refers to the reintroduction of autocracy in Haiti, Sudan, and Suriname, more than hinting that the third wave of democratization was already being displaced by a reverse wave.

7 Modernization theory

1 The following sections, including the way they are structured, primarily build upon Robin Randall and Vicky Theobald (1998).

2 Lipset (1994) himself has – with reference to Weber – noted the significance of Protestantism.

3 The exception here is Libya, where a civil war and an outside intervention led to the overthrow of the Gaddafi regime in 2011.

4 However, it obviously does not fit with Lipset's causal mechanisms, which are specifically based on the modernization process facilitating democratization.

5 This is not to say that we would be better off without a state; the alternative to the public mafia organization is private Mafiosi or anarchy (cf. Holmes 1995).

6 Recent studies have questioned the existence of a general, negative relationship between oil and democracy (Dunning 2008; Haber & Menaldo 2011).

7 The final word has obviously not been said here, however. Acemoglu et al. (2008) argue that neither the endogenous nor the exogenous relationship can be corroborated empirically. Acemoglu et al. observe that the modernization relationship is spurious. Regarding the co-variation between affluence and democracy, they argue that the critical juncture occurred about 500 years ago, providing Western European countries and some of their colonies with a set of institutions (centered on constraining executive power) which facilitated both the development of affluence and that of democracy.

8 In addition, Boix (2003: 41) argues that economic development decreases the specificity of assets, which in turn increases capital mobility. This shift from relying on the exploitation of immobile assets (land, mines, oil, etc. – recall the resource curse discussed above) to relying on manufacturing industries and human capital-intensive businesses makes the capital of the elites more tax-elastic. This development in turn eases the demands of the working class, rendering democracy more likely.

9 Przeworski has recently construed this as an attempt "to see what the facts were that needed to be explained, then explain them. . . . I did not want to write models until I knew what I wanted to explain" (see Munck & Snyder 2007: 473).

8 The social forces tradition

1   We have borrowed the phrase 'the social forces tradition' from Eva Bellin (2000).
2   As Paul Pierson (2000: 264) has argued, the point about timing only genuinely makes sense given the path-dependency notion of *increasing returns*. Because these returns are increasing, the effects of a certain factor (critical juncture) will be a function of when it occurred. Cross-spatial analysis at one point in time is unable to appreciate this; instead 'historical causes' are needed.
3   The terms bourgeoisie and middle class are used interchangeably in this chapter.
4   In addition, Therborn (1977: 8) emphasizes that non-sovereign states and constitutional monarchies in which the cabinet is not responsible to the parliament do not count as democracies.
5   Requiring that the government enjoys a continuous confidence from the legislature (if the head of government is not directly elected such as in presidential systems, where the confidence of the president thus serves as a functional equivalent).
6   To quote: "The author sees the development of a democracy as a long and certainly incomplete struggle to do three closely related things: 1) to check arbitrary rulers, 2) to replace arbitrary rules with just and rational ones, and 3) to *obtain a share* for the underlying population in the making of the rules" (Moore 1991 [1966]: 413; emphasis added).
7   In this chapter, we pay no attention to the South American side of the story.
8   Differing from the way the term is otherwise used in this book, liberal must here be understood in purely economic terms, meaning that the state is not intervening in the (market) economy.
9   Herbert Kitschelt (1992: 1029) provides an interesting defense of Moore worth mentioning in this connection: "In the spirit of Luebbert's structuralism, however, it must be noted that countries where peasants coalesced with fascism had a different legacy of agricultural property rights than countries where they did not. Conversely, if historical patterns of landholding and their political consequences did not matter, political choice on part of socialist party leaders is clearly critical in accounting for interwar regime outcomes."
10 Note that Moore's view of the enclosures has been heavily criticized (Rothman 1970: 67–70; Femia 1972: 25).

9 Transitology

1   Parts of this chapter build on a dissertation written by Mads Viskum (2009).
2   For example, a promise to the authorities that they will not be prosecuted for violations of human rights that have taken place under their autocratic regime – as occurred in South Africa (see above).
3   Here it should be noted that O'Donnell and Schmitter (1986) were largely preoccupied by the 'rightist' autocracies of Latin America; hence their famous warning not to touch the property rights of the bourgeoisie. When taking this into account, it is not that surprising that their formula fails when applied to 'leftist' autocracies (communist regimes) where the bourgeoisie was not in existence and property rights were tenuous.
4   Schmitter (2010: 21) hastens to point out that these problems are not exclusive to new democracies. The established democracies are also marked by disillusionment, meaning that this is a more general democratic crisis. O'Donnell (2010a: 31) cannot subscribe to this claim, as the entire premise for his 'democratic critique of democracy' is that the low-quality democracies in many developing countries distinguish themselves considerably from the consolidated liberal democracies. In his opinion, there is a world of difference between the problems with ensuring basic rights and keeping the rulers on the straight and narrow in, for example, South America as opposed to the dwindling political participation in the Northwestern democracies. The same is the case with the extent of the political corruption in the two areas.

10 International factors

1 Or, as they put it earlier in the book, "transitions from authoritarian rule and immediate prospects for political democracy were largely to be explained in terms of national forces and calculations. External actors tended to play an indirect and usually marginal role" (O'Donnell & Schmitter 1986: 5).

2 There is one very prominent exception to this assertion. In comparative historical analyses of state formation and regime change, the external dimension – in the guise of geopolitical competition – has always figured prominently (see, e.g., Weber 2003 [1927]; Hintze 1975 [1906]; Schumpeter 1991 [1917/1918]); Tilly 1975, 1984, 1990; Skocpol 1979; Downing 1992; Ertman 1997).

3 A disciplinary divide seems to have been at least partially responsible for this disjunction. A telling illustration is that Dankwart Rustow (1970: 348) acknowledges the potential impact of international influences upon transitions to democracy but argues that this should be left to IR scholars, whereas scholars versed in comparative politics handle the internal dimension of transitions.

4 It is worth mentioning, however, that seven of their 35 cases do not fit their expectations (Levitsky & Way 2010: 341).

5 In our empirical appraisals, we have employed Marshall's own conceptual distinctions rather than those of our typology of democracy and non-democracy, meaning, for instance, that civil rights include the rule of law (see Møller & Skaaning 2011: ch. 5).

6 In 1960, American President John F. Kennedy stated that "Governments of the civil-military type of El Salvador are the most effective in containing communist penetration in Latin America." However, this logic is not unique to the Cold War. Already in 1939, American President Franklin D. Roosevelt remarked about the dictator in Nicaragua that "Somoza may be a son of a bitch, but he's our son of a bitch."

7 The economic criterion is that the countries had to have competitive market economies in order to assume actual membership.

8 Vachudova (2005) does not actually include the three Baltic countries and Slovenia in her analysis, but they may be situated with Poland, the Czech Republic, and Hungary in the category she terms 'liberal'.

11 Combining agency and structure

1 To be sure, Guillermo O'Donnell and Philippe Schmitter (1986) paid lip-service to the constraining effect of deeper structures, and Seymour M. Lipset (1959) and others in the structuralist camp have based their argument on some kind of analytical micro foundation. However, they did not as such integrate these aspects into their respective analyses.

2 Kitschelt (1992: 1028) thus observes that "I know of no single process-oriented study that supplies a systematic comparative analysis of regime transitions for a large number of instances."

3 With stateness, Linz and Stepan (1996: 7) understand the extent to which (1) the state can claim the legitimate use of force within the territory; and (2) there is congruence between polity and demos (i.e., the extent to which significant parts of the population want to create an independent state or join a different state).

4 As philosophers of science have noted, a causal relationship can actually be in existence even though there is no co-variation (see Smelser 1976: 210), but we do not pursue this point here.

5 This is, as Kitschelt (2003) points out, basically an ontological argument. However, there is also a methodological aspect to it, as it undermines the validity of what Kitschelt terms a 'tournament of variables'; that is, standard, multiple regression techniques. The more proximate variables will simply wash out the deeper structural

variables because they are more closely linked to the outcome on the temporal dimension, something that tells us precious little about the general causal chain.

6 Crucially, the countries obtain different values on these variables based on pre-1989 scores.

7 There are exceptions, of course. Most prominently, Mongolia has developed into a minimalist democracy, even though it is situated to the very east of the setting.

8 The remaining post-communist countries were excluded owing to the absence of valid data on one or more variables.

9 As Mahoney and Snyder (1999: 18) pertinently argue, and as alluded to above, the structuralist basis is of course less pronounced here than in the 'destined pathways' approach of scholars such as Moore (1991 [1966]) and Luebbert (1991).

12 Democracy and conflict

1 This mechanism is especially important between developed countries which also tend to be democracies, as wars with relatively distant autocracies (e.g., in Iraq or Afghanistan) are much less costly than, say, war between France and Germany would be.

2 For a more general discussion of the conflict-proneness of the direct democracies of ancient Greece, see David Pritchard (2010).

3 The 'second' wave of globalization has flooded the world since World War II and particularly since the 1970s.

4 On Trevelyan's status as a Whig historian, see E.H. Carr (1961: 22–23).

5 Notice, though, that a country such as the United Kingdom obviously offered a liberal version of minimalist democracy (i.e., one also characterized by civil liberties and the rule of law). An important point here is therefore that the 19th-century Western European instances of minimalist democracy differ from the minimalist democracies of the contemporary era, where the liberal attributes are not present.

6 We can safely extend these empirical conclusions up until the present, and probably also back to the beginning of modern democracy.

7 In addition, Russett (2003 [2000]: 493) defines democracy in terms of polyarchy, rather than using a truly minimalist definition.

13 Democracy, growth, equality, and famines

1 Up to a point, at least. One may thus argue that Democritus' dictum is not so different from the thoughts conveyed by Aristotle and Polybios as appears at first sight. Recall from Chapter 1 that the Greek notion of liberty, *eleutheros*, carried many different meanings. In the context of Democritus' quote, it basically refers to the poorer citizens. Arguably, Democritus is thus equalizing democracy with the rule of the poor, thereby rendering the liberty infusing democracy as the liberty of the poor against the rich. We are indebted to Mogens Herman Hansen for pointing this out.

2 For example, the Latin American countries are peppered by that which O'Donnell refers to as 'brown zones'; that is, areas in which the fundamental civil rights of the people are not maintained by the authorities.

3 We have met a related – albeit more radical – argument in this vein in both Chapters 2 and 4, namely the 19th-century warning by liberals that democracy would pave the way for an attack on the property rights of the elite: and thereby capitalism as a system (see also Boix & Stokes 2003: 538).

4 The historical validity of this theory – which states that roving bandits pillage society, stationary bandits provide some public goods but extract the maximum possible amount of resources from society whereas democratic rulers tax less – is very questionable. Comparative historical analyses have shown that the development or intensification of constitutionalism allowed states to tax more, not less, because the citizens became stakeholders, as demonstrated by, for example, Thomas Ertman (1997) in his comparison of constitutionalist Great Britain and absolutist Prussia and France.

Bibliography

Acemoglu, Daron & James A. Robinson (2006). *Economic Origins of Dictatorship and Democracy*. Cambridge: Cambridge University Press.

Acemoglu, Daron, Simon Johnson, James A. Robinson & Pierre Yared (2008). "Income and Democracy." *American Economic Review* 98(3): 808–842.

Acemoglu, Daron, Simon Johnson, James A. Robinson & Pierre Yared (2009). "Reevaluating the Modernization Hypothesis." *Journal of Monetary Economics* 56(8): 1043–1058.

Acton, Lord John (1972 [1877]). *Essays on Freedom and Power*. Gloucester: Peter Smith.

Adcock, Robert & David Collier (2001). "Measurement Validity: A Shared Standard for Qualitative and Quantitative Research." *American Political Science Review* 95(3): 529–546.

Alexander, Amy C., Ronald Inglehart & Christian Welzel (2012). "Measuring Effective Democracy: A Defense." *International Political Science Review* 33(1): 41–62.

Almond, Gabriel & James Coleman (eds) (1960). *The Politics of Developing Areas*. Princeton, NJ: Princeton University Press.

Almond, Gabriel & G. Bingham Powell (1966). *Comparative Politics: A Developmental Approach*. Boston, MA: Little, Brown & Company.

Alvarez, Michael, José A. Cheibub, Fernando Limongi & Adam Przeworski (1996). "Classifying Political Regimes." *Studies in Comparative International Development* 31(2): 529–546.

Anckar, Carsten (2008). "Size, Islandness, and Democracy: A Global Comparison." *International Political Science Review* 29(4): 433–459.

Anderson, Perry (1974). *Lineages of the Absolutist State*. London: Verso.

Arendt, Hannah (1958 [1951]). *The Origins of Totalitarianism*. New York: Harcourt Brace.

Arias-King, Fredo (2005). "From Brezhnev Doctrine to Sinatra Doctrine." *Demokratizatsiya* 13(2): 289–297.

Aristotle (2008 [350 BC]). *Politics*. New York: Cosimo.

Ash, Timothy Garton (1990). *We the People: The Revolution of '89*. Cambridge: Granta Books.

Bailey, Kenneth (1994). *Typologies and Taxonomies: An Introduction to Classification Techniques*. Thousand Oaks, CA: Sage.

Barkan, Joel D. (2000). "Protracted Transitions in Africa's New Democracies." *Democratization* 7(3): 227–243.

Bartolini, Stefano (1993). "On Time and Comparative Research." *Journal of Theoretical Politics* 5(2): 131–167.

Bellin, Eva (2000). "Contingent Democrat: Industrialist, Labor and Democratization in Late-Developing Countries." *World Politics* 52(2): 175–205.

Bellin, Eva (2004). "The Robustness of Authoritarianism in the Middle East." *Comparative Politics* 36(2): 139–157.

Bendix, Reinhard (1964). *Nation-Building and Citizenship*. New York: John Wiley.

Berger, Peter (1992). "The Uncertain Triumph of Democratic Capitalism." *Journal of Democracy* 3(3): 7–16.

Berg-Schlosser, Dirk (2009). "Long Waves and Conjunctures of Democratization," pp. 41–54 in Christian W. Haerpfer, Patrick Bernhagen, Ronald F. Inglehart & Christian Welzel (eds), *Democratization*. Oxford: Oxford University Press.

Berg-Schlosser, Dirk & Jeremy Mitchell (2003). *Authoritarianism and Democracy in Europe, 1919-1939: Comparative Analyses*. London: Macmillan.

Berlin, Isaiah (2002 [1958]). "Two Concepts of Liberty," pp. 166–217 in Isaiah Berlin, *Liberty*. Oxford: Oxford University Press.

Berlin, Isaiah (2002 [1995]). "Liberty," pp. 283–286 in Isaiah Berlin, *Liberty*. Oxford: Oxford University Press.

Berman, Sheri (1997). "Civil Society and the Collapse of the Weimar Republic." *World Politics* 49(2): 401–429.

Bermeo, Nancy (1997a). *Getting Mad or Going Mad? Citizens, Scarcity and the Breakdown of Democracy in Interwar Europe*. Center for the Study of Democracy Working Paper 97–06.

Bermeo, Nancy (1997b). "Myths of Moderation: Confrontation and Conflict During Democratic Transitions," pp. 120–140 in Lisa Anderson (ed.), *Transitions to Democracy*. New York: Columbia University Press.

Bideleux, Robert & Ian Jeffries (1998). *A History of Eastern Europe: Crisis and Change*. London: Routledge.

Bloch, Marc (1971a [1939]). *Feudal Society (I): The Growth of Ties of Dependence*. London: Routledge.

Bloch, Marc (1971b [1939]). *Feudal Society (II): Social Classes and Political Organization*. London: Routledge.

Bobbit, Philip (2002). *The Shield of Achilles: War, Peace, and the Course of History*. New York: Alfred A. Knopf.

Boix, Carles (2003). *Democracy and Redistribution*. Cambridge: Cambridge University Press.

Boix, Carles (2011). "Democracy, Development, and the International System." *International Political Science Review* 105(4): 809–828.

Boix, Carles & Susan Stokes (2003). "Endogenous Democratization." *World Politics* 55(4): 517–549.

Bollen, Kenneth & Pamela Paxton (2000). "Subjective Measures of Liberal Democracy." *Comparative Political Studies* 33(1): 58–86.

Bonald, Louis Gabriel Ambroise de (1796). *Théorie du pouvoir politique et religieux, dans la société civile*. http://classiques.uqac.ca/classiques/de_bonald_louis/theorie_pouvoir_pol/theorie_pouvoir.html (last visited April 18, 2012).

Bradford, Alfred S. (2001). *With Arrow, Sword, and Spear: A History of Warfare in the Ancient World*. Westport, CT: Praeger.

Bratton, Michael & Nicolas van de Walle (1997). *Democratic Experiments in Africa: Regime Transitions in Comparative Perspective*. Cambridge: Cambridge University Press.

Brinks, Daniel & Michael Coppedge (2006). "Diffusion is No Illusion: Neighbor Emulation in the Third Wave of Democracy." *Comparative Political Studies* 39(4): 463–489.

Brownlee, Jason (2007). *Authoritarianism in an Age of Democratization*. New York: Cambridge University Press.

Brownlee, Jason (2009). "Portents of Pluralism: How Hybrid Regimes Affect Democratic Transitions." *American Journal of Political Science* 53(3): 515–532.

Brucker, Gene A. (1984). *Florence: The Golden Age, 1138–1737*. New York: Abbeville Press.

Bryce, James (1921) *Modern Democracies*. New York: Macmillan.

Bunce, Valerie (1995). "Should Transitologists be Grounded?" *Slavic Review* 54(1): 111–127.

Bunce, Valerie (1999). "The Political Economy of Postsocialism." *Slavic Review* 58(4): 756–793.

Bunce, Valerie (2000). "Comparative Democratization: Big and Bounded Generalizations." *Comparative Political Studies* 33(6/7): 703–734.

Bunce, Valerie (2003). "Rethinking Recent Democratization: Lessons from the Postcommunist Experience." *World Politics* 55(2): 167–192.

Burkhart, Ross E. & Michael S. Lewis-Beck (1994). "Comparative Democracy: The Economic Development Thesis." *American Political Science Review* 88(4): 903–910.

Burnell, Peter (ed.) (2000). *Democracy Assistance: International Co-operation for Democratization*. London: Frank Cass.

Burton, Michael, Richard Gunther & John Higley (1992). "Introduction: Elite Transformations and Democratic Regimes," pp. 1–37 in John Higley & Richard Gunther (eds), *Elites and Democratic Consolidation in Latin America and Southern Europe*. Cambridge: Cambridge University Press.

Callaway, Rhonda & Elizabeth Matthews (2008). *Strategic US Foreign Assistance: The Battle Between Human Rights and National Security*. Aldershot: Ashgate.

Capoccia, Giovanni (2005). *Defending Democracy: Reactions to Extremism in Interwar Europe*. Baltimore, MD: Johns Hopkins University Press.

Capoccia, Giovanni & R. Daniel Kelemen (2007). "The Study of Critical Junctures: Theory, Narratives, and Counterfactuals in Historical Institutionalism." *World Politics* 59(3): 341–369.

Capoccia, Giovanni & Daniel Ziblatt (2010). "The Historical Turn in Democratization Studies: A New Research Agenda." *Comparative Political Studies* 43(8): 931–968.

Carbone, Giovanni (2009). "The Consequences of Democratization." *Journal of Democracy* 20(2): 123–137.

Cardoso, Fernando H. & Enzo Faletto (1979). *Democracy and Development in Latin America*. Berkeley: University of California Press.

Carothers, Thomas (1991). *In the Name of Democracy: US Policy toward Latin America in the Reagan Years*. Berkeley: University of California Press.

Carothers, Thomas (1999). *Aiding Democracy Abroad: The Learning Curve*. Washington, D.C.: Carnegie Endowment for International Peace.

Carothers, Thomas (2002). "The End of the Transition Paradigm." *Journal of Democracy* 13(1): 5–21.

Carothers, Thomas (2004). *Critical Mission: Essays on Democracy Promotion*. Washington, D.C.: Carnegie Endowment for International Peace.

Carothers, Thomas (2007). "The 'Sequencing' Fallacy." *Journal of Democracy* 18(1): 12–27.

Carr, E.H. (1961). *What is History?* New York: Vintage.

Cederman, Lars-Erik, Simon Hug & Andreas Wenger (2008). "Democratization and War in Political Science." *Democratization* 15(3): 509–524.

Cederman, Lars-Erik, Simon Hug & Lutz Krebs (2010). "Democratization and Civil War: Empirical Evidence." *Journal of Peace Research* 47(4): 377–394.

Cheibub, Jose A., Jennifer Gandhi & James Vreeland (2010). "Democracy and Dictatorship Revisisted." *Public Choice* 143(1/2): 67–101.

Chu, Yun.-han, Michael Bratton, Marta Lagos, Sandeep Shastri & Mark Tessler (2008). "Public Opinion and Democratic Legitimacy." *Journal of Democracy* 19(2): 74–87.

Clague, Christopher, Susanne Gleason & Stephen Knack (2001). "Determinants of Lasting Democracy in Poor Countries: Culture, Development, and Institutions." *Annals of the American Academy of Political and Social Science* 573(1): 16–41.

Coleman, James (1990). *Foundations of Social Theory*. Cambridge, MA: Harvard University Press.

Collier, David & Robert Adcock (1999). "Democracy and Dichotomies: A Pragmatic Approach to Choices about Concepts." *Annual Review of Political Science* 2: 537–565.

Collier, David & Steven Levitsky (1996). *Democracy 'with Adjectives': Conceptual Innovation in Comparative Research*. The Helen Kellogg Institute for International Studies, University of Notre Dame, Working Paper 230.

Collier, David & Steven Levitsky (1997). "Democracy with Adjectives. Conceptual Innovation in Comparative Research." *World Politics* 49(3): 430–451.

Collier, David & James E. Mahon (1993). "Conceptual 'Stretching' Revisited: Adapting Categories in Comparative Analysis." *American Political Science Review* 87(3): 845–855.

Collier, Ruth B. (1999). *Paths toward Democracy: The Working Class and Elites in Western Europe and South America*. Cambridge: Cambridge University Press.

Collier, Ruth & David Collier (1991). *Shaping the Political Arena: Critical Junctures, the Labor Movement, and Regime Dynamics in Latin America*. Princeton, NJ: Princeton University Press.

Collins, Randall (1986). *Max Weber: A Skeleton Key*. Beverly Hills, CA: Sage.

Constant, Benjamin (1988 [1819]). "The Liberty of the Ancients Compared with that of the Moderns," pp. 309–328 in Benjamin Constant, *Political Writings*. Cambridge: Cambridge University Press.

Coppedge, Michael & John Gerring, with David Altman, Michael Bernhard, Steven Fish, Allen Hicken, Matthew Kroenig, Staffan I. Lindberg, Kelly McMann, Pamela Paxton, Holly A. Semetko, Svend-Erik Skaaning, Jeffrey Staton & Jan Teorell (2011). "Defining and Measuring Democracy: A New Approach." *Perspectives on Politics* 9(2): 247–267.

Corzier, Michel, Samuel P. Huntington & Joji Watanuki (1975). *The Crisis of Democracy Report on the Governability of Democracies to the Trilateral Commission*. New York: New York University Press.

Coulborn, Rushton (1956). *Feudalism in History*. Princeton, NJ: Princeton University Press.

Creel, Herrlee (1970). *The Origins of Statecraft in China*. Chicago, IL: University of Chicago Press.

Croissant, Aurel (2004). "From Transition to Defective Democracy: Mapping Asian Democratization." *Democratization* 11(5): 156–178.

Crouch, Colin (2004). *Post-Democracy*. Cambridge: Polity Press.

Cunningham, Frank (2001). *Theories of Democracy: A Critical Discussion*. London: Routledge.

Dahl, Robert A. (1956). *A Preface to Democratic Theory*. Chicago, IL: University of Chicago Press.

Dahl, Robert A. (1971). *Polyarchy: Participation and Opposition*. New Haven, CT: Yale University Press.

Dahl, Robert A. (1982). *Dilemmas of Pluralist Democracy: Autonomy vs. Control*. New Haven, CT: Yale University Press.

Dahl, Robert A. (1985). *A Preface to Economic Democracy*. Cambridge: Polity Press.

Dahl, Robert A. (1989). *Democracy and Its Critics*. New Haven, CT: Yale University Press.

Dahl, Robert A. (1998). *On Democracy*. New Haven, CT: Yale University Press.

Dahl, Robert A. & Edward R. Tufte (1974). *Size and Democracy*. Stanford, CA: Stanford University Press.

Darden, Keith & Anna Grzymala-Busse (2006). "The Great Divide: Literacy, Nationalism, and the Communist Collapse." *World Politics* 59(1): 83–118.

Davenport, Christian (2007). "State Repression and Political Order." *Annual Review of Political Science* 10: 1–23.

Diamond, Larry (1992). "Economic Development and Democracy Reconsidered," pp. 93–139 in Gary Marks & Larry Diamond (eds), *Reexamining Democracy: Essays in Honor of Seymour Martin Lipset*. Newbury Park, CA: Sage.

Diamond, Larry (1996). "Is the Third Wave Over?" *Journal of Democracy* 7(3): 20–37.

Diamond, Larry (1999). *Developing Democracy: Toward Consolidation*. Baltimore, MD: Johns Hopkins University Press.

Diamond, Larry (2000). "Is Pakistan the (Reverse) Wave of the Future?" *Journal of Democracy* 11(3): 91–106.

Diamond, Larry (2002). "Thinking about Hybrid Regimes." *Journal of Democracy* 13(2): 21–35.

Diamond, Larry (2008). "The Democratic Rollback: The Resurgence of the Predatory State." *Foreign Affairs* 87(2): 36–48.

Diamond, Larry (2010). "Why Are There No Arab Democracies?" *Journal of Democracy* 21(1): 93–104.

Diamond, Larry (2011). "The Impact of the Economic Crisis: Why Democracies Survive?" *Journal of Democracy* 22(1): 17–30.

Diamond, Larry & Leonardo Morlino (2004). "Quality of Democracy: An Overview." *Journal of Democracy* 15(4): 20–31.

Diamond, Larry, Juan J. Linz & Seymour M. Lipset (1990). *Democracy in Developing Countries*. Boulder, CO: Lynne Rienner.

Doorenspleet, Renske (2000). "Reassessing the Three Waves of Democratization." *World Politics* 52(3): 384–406.

Doorenspleet, Renske (2005). *Democratic Transitions: Exploring the Structural Sources of the Fourth Wave*. Boulder, CO: Lynne Rienner.

Downing, Brian M. (1992). *The Military Revolution and Political Change: Origins of Democracy and Autocracy in Early Modern Europe*. Princeton, NJ: Princeton University Press.

Doyle, Michael (1986). "Liberalism and World Politics." *American Political Science Review* 80(4): 1151–1169.

Dunn, John (2005). *Democracy: A History*. New York: Atlantic Monthly Press.

Dunning, Thad (2008). *Crude Democracy: Natural Resource Wealth and Political Regimes*. New York: Cambridge University Press.

Easter, Gerald (1997). "Preference for Presidentialism: Postcommunist Regime Change in Russia and the NIS." *World Politics* 49(2): 184–211.

Epstein, David L., Robert Bates, Jack Goldstone, Ida Kristensen & Sharyn O'Halloran (2006). "Democratic Transitions." *American Journal of Political Science* 50(3): 551–569.

Ertman, Thomas (1997). *Birth of the Leviathan*. New York: Cambridge University Press.

Ertman, Thomas (1998). "Democracy and Dictatorship in the Interwar Western Europe Revisited." *World Politics* 50(3): 475–505.

Fein, Helen (1995). "More Murder in the Middle: Life-Integrity Violations and Democracy in the World." *Human Rights Quarterly* 17(1): 170–192.

Femia, Joseph V. (1972). "Barrington Moore and the Preconditions for Democracy." *British Journal of Political Science* 2(1): 21–46.

Finer, Samuel E. (1962). *The Man on Horseback: The Role of the Military in Politics*. New York: Praeger.

Finer, Samuel E. (1997a). *The History of Government (II): The Intermediate Ages*. Oxford: Oxford University Press.

Finer, Samuel E. (1997b). *The History of Government (III): Empires, Monarchies, and the Modern State*. Oxford: Oxford University Press.

Fish, M. Steven (1998a). "Democratization's Requisites: The Postcommunist Experience." *Post-Soviet Affairs* 14(3): 212–247.

Fish, M. Steven (1998b). "The Determinants of Economic Reform in the Postcommunist World." *East European Politics and Societies* 12(1): 31–78.

Fish, M. Steven (2006). "Stronger Legislatures, Stronger Democracies." *Journal of Democracy* 17(1): 5–20.

Fish, M. Steven & Omar Choudhry (2008). "Democratization and Economic Liberalization in the Postcommunist World." *Comparative Political Studies* 40(3): 254–282.

Føllesdal, Andreas & Simon Hix (2006). "Why there is a Democratic Deficit in the EU." *Journal of Common Market Studies* 44(3): 533–562.

Frank, Andre Gunder (1966). *Capitalism and Underdevelopment in Latin America*. New York: Monthly Review Press.

Freedom House (2012). *Freedom in the World Survey*. http://www.freedomhouse.org (last visited April 17, 2012).

Fried, Charles (2007). *Modern Liberty and the Limits of Government*. New York: W.W. Norton & Company.

Friedman, Milton (1962). *Capitalism and Freedom*. Chicago, IL: University of Chicago Press.

Friedrich, Carl J. & Zbigniew K. Brzezinski (1968). *Totalitarian Dictatorship and Autocracy*. Cambridge, MA: Harvard University Press.

Fukuyama, Francis (1992). *The End of History and the Last Man*. New York: Free Press.

Fukuyama, Francis (2010). "Foreword," pp. xi–xvii in Samuel P. Huntington, *Political Order in Changing Societies*. New Haven, CT: Yale University Press.

Fukuyama, Francis (2011). *The Origins of Political Order: From Prehuman Times to the French Revolution*. London: Profile Books.

Fuller, Lon (1969). *The Morality of Law*. New Haven, CT: Yale University Press.

Gallie, Walter B. (1956). "Essentially Contested Concepts." *Proceedings of the Aristotelian Society* 56: 167–198.

Gandhi, Jennifer (2008). *Political Institutions under Dictatorship*. New York: Cambridge University Press.

Ganshof, F.L. (1952 [1944]). *Feudalism*. London: Longmans.

Geddes, Barbara (1999). "What Do We Know about Democratization after Twenty Years." *Annual Review of Political Science* 2: 115–144.

Gerhard, Dietrich (1970). "Otto Hintze: His Work and Significance in Historiography." *Central European History* 3(1/2): 17–48.

Gerring, John (1999). "What Makes a Concept Good? An Integrated Framework for Understanding Concept Formation in the Social Sciences." *Polity* 31(3): 357–393.

Gerring, John (2001). *Social Science Methodology: A Criterial Framework*. Cambridge: Cambridge University Press.

Gerring, John (2011). "The Social Science of Democracy?" *Perspectives on Politics* 9(2): 377–381.

Gerring, John, Phillip Bond, William Barndt & Carola Moreno (2005). "Democracy and Economic Growth: A Historical Perspective." *World Politics* 57(3): 323–364.

Gerschenkron, Alexander (1962). *Economic Backwardness in Historical Perspective.* Cambridge, MA: Harvard University Press.

Giannone, Diego (2010). "Political and Ideological Aspects in the Measurement of Democracy: The Freedom House Case." *Democratization* 17(1): 68–97.

Giddens, Anthony (1984). *The Constitution of Society.* Berkeley: University of California Press.

Gledtisch, Kristian & Michael Ward (1997). "Double Take: Reexamining Democracy and Autocracy in Modern Polities." *Journal of Conflict Resolution* 41(3): 361–383.

Gleditsch, Kristian & Michael Ward (2006). "Diffusion and the International Context of Democratization." *International Organization* 60(4): 911–933.

Goldscheid, Rudolf (1958 [1925]). "A Sociological Approach to Problems of Public Finance," pp. 202–213 in Richard Musgrave & Alan Peacock (eds), *Classics in the Theory of Public Finance.* London: Macmillan.

Gradstein. Mark & Branko Milanovic (2004). "Does Liberte = Egalite ? A Survey of the Empirical Links between Democracy and Inequality with Some Evidence on the Transition Economies." *Journal of Economic Surveys* 18(4): 515–537.

Grandin, Greg (2004). *The Last Colonial Massacre: Latin America in the Cold War.* Chicago, IL: University of Chicago Press.

Gress, David (1998). *From Plato to NATO: The Idea of the West and Its Opponents.* London: The Free Press.

Grugel, Jean (2002). *Democratization: A Critical Introduction.* Basingstoke: Palgrave.

Grzymala-Busse, Anna & Pauline J. Luong (2002). "Reconceptualizing the State: Lessons from Post-Communism." *Politics & Society* 30(4): 529–554.

Haber, Stephen & Victor Menaldo (2011). "Do Natural Resources Fuel Authoritarianism? A Reappraisal of the Resource Curse." *American Political Science Review* 105(1): 1–26.

Habermas, Jürgen (1989 [1962]). *The Structural Transformation of the Public Sphere.* Cambridge: Polity Press.

Habermas, Jürgen (1996). *Between Facts and Norms.* Cambridge, MA: MIT Press.

Hadenius, Axel & Jan Teorell (2007). "Pathways from Authoritarisnism." *Journal of Democracy* 18(1): 143–156.

Haerpfer, Christian W. , Patrick Bernhagen, Ronald F. Inglehart & Christian Welzel (eds) (2009). *Democratization.* Oxford: Oxford University Press.

Haggard, Stephan & Robert Kaufman (1997). *The Political Economy of Democratic Transitions.* Princeton, NJ: Princeton University Press.

Hall, John A. (1985). *Powers & Liberties: The Causes and Consequences of the Rise of the West.* Oxford: Basil Blackwell.

Hall, John A. (1989). "They Do Things Differently There, or, the Contribution of British Historical Sociology." *British Journal of Sociology* 40(4): 544–564.

Hall, John W. (1962). Feudalism in Japan – A Reasessment." *Comparative Studies in Society and History* 5(1): 15–51.

Hall, Peter A. (2003). "Aligning Ontology and Methodology in Comparative Research," pp. 373–406 in James Mahoney & Dietrich Rueschemeyer (eds), *Comparative Historical Analysis in the Social Sciences.* Cambridge: Cambridge University Press.

Hansen, Mogens Herman (1989). *What Athens a Democracy?* Historisk-Filosofiske Meddelelser 59. København: Det Kongelige Danske Videnskabernes Selskab.

Hansen, Mogens Herman (1993). "Aristotle's Alternative to the Sixfold Model of Constitutions," pp. 91–101 in P. Piérart (ed.), *Aristote et Athènes*. Paris.

Hansen, Mogens Herman (1999). *The Athenian Democracy in the Age of Demosthenes* (2nd edn). London: Oxford University Press.

Hansen, Mogens Herman (2007). *Den moderne republikanisme og dens kritik af det liberale demokrati*. Historisk-Filosofiske Meddelelser 100. København: Det Kongelige Danske Videnskabernes Selskab.

Hansen, Mogens Herman (2010a). "The Mixed Constitution Versus the Separation of Powers: Monarchical and Aristocratic Aspects of Modern Democracy." *History of Political Thought* 31(3): 509–531.

Hansen, Mogens Herman (2010b). "Democratic Freedom and the Concept of Freedom in Plato and Aristotle." *Greek Roman and Byzantine Studies* 50: 1–27.

Hansen, Mogens Herman (2010c). "Introduction," pp. vii–xxxviii in *Démocratie Athénienne – Démocratie Moderne: Tradition et Influences*. Geneve: Entretiens sur L'Antiquité Classique 56.

Hansen, Mogens Herman (2010d). "Ancient Democratic *Eleutheria* and Modern Liberal Democrats' Conception of Freedom," pp. 307–353 in *Démocratie Athénienne – Démocratie Moderne: Tradition et Influences*. Geneve: Entretiens sur L'Antiquité Classique 56.

Hariri, Jacob (forthcoming). "The Autocratic Legacy of Early Statehood." *American Political Science Review*.

Hayek, Friedrich August von (1944). *The Road to Serfdom*. Chicago, IL: University of Chicago Press.

Hayek, Friedrich August von (2006 [1960]). *The Constitution of Liberty*. Chicago, IL: University of Chicago Press.

Hedström, Peter & Richard Swedberg (1996). "Social Mechanisms." *Acta Sociologica* 39(3): 281–308.

Hegre, Håvard, Tanja Ellingsen, Scott Gates & Nils Petter Gleditsch (2001). "Toward a Democratic Civil Peace? Democracy, Political Change, and Civil War, 1816-1992." *American Political Science Review* 95(1): 33–48.

Held, David (2006). *Models of Democracy*. Cambridge: Polity Press.

Hintze, Otto (1962 [1929]). "Wesen und Verbreitung des Feudalismus," pp. 84–119 in Otto Hintze, *Staat und Verfassung*. Göttingen: Vandenhoeck & Ruprecht.

Hintze, Otto (1962 [1930]). "Typologie der ständischen Verfassungen des Abendlandes," pp. 120–139 in Otto Hintze, *Staat und Verfassung*. Göttingen: Vandenhoeck & Ruprecht.

Hintze, Otto (1975 [1906]). *The Historical Essays of Otto Hintze*. Oxford: Oxford University Press.

Hintze, O. (1975 [1931]). *The Historical Essays of Otto Hintze*. Oxford: Oxford University Press.

Hippel, Karin von (2000). *Democracy by Force: US Military Intervention in the Post-Cold War World*. New York: New York University Press.

Hobbes, Thomas (1985 [1651]). *Leviathan*. Harmondsworth: Penguin.

Holmes, Stephen (1979). "Aristippus in and out of Athens." *American Political Science Review* 73(1): 113–128.

Holmes, Stephen (1982). *Benjamin Constant and the Making of Modern Liberalism*. New Haven, CT: Yale University Press.

Holmes, Stephen (1995). *Passion and Constraint: On the Theory of Liberal Democracy*. Chicago, IL: University of Chicago Press.

Howard, Marc & Philip Roessler (2006). "Liberalizing Electoral Outcomes in Competitive Authoritarian Regimes." *American Journal of Political Science* 50(2): 365–381.

Huber, Evelyn & John Stephens (1995). "Conclusion: Agrarian Structures and Political Power in Comparative Perspective," pp. 183–232 in Evelyn Huber & Frank Safford (eds), *Agrarian Structure and Political Power in Latin America*. Pittsburgh: University of Pittsburgh Press.

Hui, Victoria T. (2004). "Towards a Dynamic Theory of International Politics: Insights from Comparing the Ancient Chinese and Early Modern European Systems." *International Organization* 58(1): 175–205.

Hui, Victoria T. (2005). *War and State Formation in Ancient China and Early Modern Europe*. Cambridge: Cambridge University Press.

Hume, David (1993 [1748]). *An Enquiry Concerning Human Understanding*. Indianapolis: Hackett.

Huntington, Samuel P. (1968). *Political Order in Changing Societies*. New Haven, CT: Yale University Press.

Huntington, Samuel P. (1971). "The Change to Change: Modernization, Development, and Politics." *Comparative Politics* 3(3): 283–322.

Huntington, Samuel P. (1991). *The Third Wave: Democratization in the Late Twentieth Century*. Norman: University of Oklahoma Press.

Huntington, Samuel P. (1996). *The Clash of Civilizations and the Remaking of World Order*. New York: Simon & Schuster.

Inglehart, Ronald (1977). *The Silent Revolution: Changing Values and Political Styles Among Western Publics*. Princeton, NJ: Princeton University Press.

Inglehart, Ronald (1997). *Modernization and Postmodernization: Cultural, Economic, and Political Change in 43 Societies*. Princeton, NJ: Princeton University Press.

Inglehart, Ronald & Christian Welzel (2005). *Modernization, Cultural Change, and Democracy*. Cambridge: Cambridge University Press.

Inglehart, Ronald & Christian Welzel (2009). "How Development Leads to Democracy: What We Know about Modernization." *Foreign Affairs* 88(2): 33–48.

Janos, Andrew (2000). *East Central Europe in the Modern World: The Politics of the Borderlands from Pre- to Postcommunism*. Stanford, CA: Stanford University Press.

Jones, Eric (2008 [1981]). *The European Miracle: Environments, Economies and Geopolitics in the History of Europe and Asia*. Cambridge: Cambridge University Press.

Kant, Immanuel (2003 [1795]). *Perpetual Peace*. Indianapolis: Hackett.

Karatnycky, Adrian & Peter Ackerman (2005). *How Freedom is Won: From Civic Resistance to Durable Democracy*. New York: Freedom House.

Karl, Terry L. (1990). "Dilemmas of Democratization in Latin America." *Comparative Politics* 23(1): 1–21.

Karl, Terry L. (1998). *The Paradox of Plenty: Oil Booms and Petro-States*. Berkeley: University of California Press.

Karl, Terry L. (2005). *From Democracy to Democratization and Back: Before Transitions from Authoritarian Rule*. Center on Democracy, Development, and the Rule of Law Working Paper No. 45.

Karl, Terry L. & Philippe C. Schmitter (1991). "Modes of Transition in Latin America, Southern and Eastern Europe." *International Social Science Journal* 128: 269–284.

Karl, Terry L. & Philippe Schmitter (1995). "From an Iron Curtain to a Paper Curtain: Grounding Transitologists or Student of Postcommunism?" *Slavic Review* 54(4): 965–978.

Kelley, Judith (2009). "The More the Merrier? The Effects of Having Multiple International Election Monitors." *Perspectives on Politics* 7(1): 59–64.

Kelsen, Hans (1920). *Vom Wesen und Wert der Demokratie*. Tübingen: J.C.B. Mohr.

Kelsen, Hans (1955). "Foundations of Democracy." *Ethics* 66(1): 1–101.

Kitschelt, Herbert (1992). "Political Regime Change: Structure and Process-Driven Explanations." *American Political Science Review* 86(4): 1028–1034.

Kitschelt, Herbert (1993). "Comparative Historical Research and Rational Choice Theory: The Case of Transitions to Democracy." *Theory and Society* 22(3): 413–427.

Kitschelt, Herbert (1999). *Accounting for Outcomes of Post-Communist Regime Change: Causal Depth or Shallowness in Rival Explanations?* Paper presented at the APSA Annual Meeting, Atlanta, September 2–5, 1999.

Kitschelt, Herbert (2003). "Accounting for Postcommunist Regime Diversity: What Counts as a Good Cause?" pp. 125–152 in Grzegorz Ekiert & Stephen E. Hanson (eds), *Capitalism and Democracy in Central and Eastern Europe: Assessing the Legacy of Communist Rule*. Cambridge: Cambridge University Press.

Kitschelt, Herbert, Zdenka Mansfeldova, Radoslaw Markowski & Gábor Tóka (1999). *Post-Communist Party Systems: Competition, Representation, and Inter-Party Cooperation*. Cambridge: Cambridge University Press.

Klingemann, Hans-Dieter (1999). "Mapping Political Support in the 1990s: A Global Analysis," pp. 31–56 in Pippa Norris (ed.), *Critical Citizens: Global Support for Democratic Governance*. Oxford: Oxford University Press.

Krasner, Stephen (2005). "The Case for Shared Sovereignty." *Journal of Democracy* 16(1): 69–83.

Lauth, Hans-Joachim (2004). *Demokratie und Demokratiemessung: Eine konzeptionelle Grundlegung für den interkulturellen Vergleich*. Wiesbaden: VS Verlag für Sozialwissenschaften.

Lazarsfeld, Paul F. & Allen H. Barton (1951). "Qualitative Measurement in the Social Sciences: Classification, Typologies, and Indices," pp. 155–192 in David Lerner & Harold D. Lasswell (eds), *The Policy Sciences*. Stanford, CA: Stanford University Press.

Lenin, Vladimir (1999 [1916]). *Imperialism, The Highest Stage of Capitalism*. Broadway: Resistance Books.

Lenin, Vladimir (2004 [1917]). *The State and the Revolution*. Whitefish: Kessinger.

Levi, Margaret (1988). *Of Rule and Revenue*. Berkeley: University of California Press.

Levitsky, Steven & Lucan A. Way (2002). "The Rise of Competitive Authoritarianism." *Journal of Democracy* 13(2): 51–65.

Levitsky, Steven & Lucan A. Way (2005). "International Linkage and Democratization." *Journal of Democracy* 16(3): 20–34.

Levitsky, Steven & Lucan A. Way (2006). "Linkage versus Leverage: Rethinking the International Dimension of Regime Change." *Comparative Politics* 38(4): 379–400.

Levitsky, Steven & Lucan Way (2010). *Competitive Authoritarianism*. New York: Cambridge University Press.

Lieberman, Evan S. (2005). "Nested Analysis as a Mixed-Method Strategy for Comparative Research." *American Political Science Review* 99(3): 435–452.

Lijphart, Arend (1971). "Comparative Politics and the Comparative Method." *American Political Science Review* 65(3): 682–693.

Lijphart, Arend (1996). "The Puzzle of Indian Democracy: A Consociational Interpretation." *American Political Science Review* 90(2): 258–268.

Lindberg, Staffan (2006). *Democracy and Elections in Africa*. Baltimore, MD: Johns Hopkins University Press.

Lindberg, Staffan (ed.) (2009). *Democratization by Elections: A New Mode of Transition*. Baltimore, MD: Johns Hopkins University Press.

Lindblom, Charles (1977). *Politics and Markets: The World's Political Economic Systems.* New York: Basic Books.

Linz, Juan J. (1975). "Totalitarian and Authoritarian Regimes," pp. 175–411 in Fred Greenstein & Nelson Polsby (eds), *Handbook of Political Science: Macropolitical Theory.* Reading, MA: Addison-Wesley.

Linz, Juan J. (1978). *The Breakdown of Democratic Regimes: Crisis, Breakdown, & Reequilibrium,* Baltimore, MD: Johns Hopkins University Press.

Linz, Juan (2000 [1975]). *Totalitarian and Authoritarian Regimes.* Boulder, CO: Lynne Rienner.

Linz, Juan J. & Alfred Stepan (1978). *The Breakdown of Democratic Regimes.* Baltimore, MD: Johns Hopkins University Press.

Linz, Juan J. & Alfred Stepan (1996). *Problems of Democratic Transition and Consolidation: Southern Europe, South America, and Post-Communist Societies.* Baltimore, MD: Johns Hopkins University Press.

Lipset, Seymour M. (1959). "Some Social Requisites of Democracy: Economic Development and Political Legitimacy." *American Political Science Review* 53(1): 69–105.

Lipset, Seymour M. (1994). "The Social Requisites of Democracy Revisited." *American Sociological Review* 94(4): 1–22.

Livingstone, Grace (2009). *America's Backyard: The United States and Latin America from the Monroe Doctrine to the War on Terror.* London: Zed Books.

Locke, John (1993 [1690]). "Second Treatise of Government," pp. 261–386 in John Locke, *Political Writings of John Locke.* New York: Mentor.

Loftager, Jørn (2004). *Politisk offentlighed og demokrati i Danmark.* Århus: Aarhus Universitetsforlag.

Luebbert, Gregory M. (1991). *Liberalism, Fascism, or Social Democracy: Social Classes and the Political Origins of Regimes in Interwar Europe.* Oxford: Oxford University Press.

Machiavelli, Niccolò (1970 [1517]). *The Discourses.* Harmondsworth: Penguin.

Madison, James, Alexander Hamilton & James Jay (1987 [1787/1788]). *The Federalist Papers.* Harmondsworth: Penguin.

Mahoney, James (2000). "Path Dependence in Historical Sociology." *Theory and Society* 29(4): 507–548.

Mahoney, James (2003a). "Knowledge Accumulation in Comparative Historical Research: The Case of Democracy and Authoritarianism," pp. 131–174 in James Mahoney & Dietrich Rueschemeyer (eds), *Comparative Historical Analysis in the Social Sciences.* Cambridge: Cambridge University Press.

Mahoney, James (2003b). "Strategies of Causal Assessment in Comparative Historical Analysis," pp. 337–382 in James Mahoney & Dietrich Rueschemeyer (eds), *Comparative Historical Analysis in the Social Sciences.* Cambridge: Cambridge University Press.

Mahoney, James & Gary Goertz (2006). "A Tale of Two Cultures: Contrasting Quantitative and Qualitative Research." *Political Analysis* 14(3): 227–249.

Mahoney, James & Dietrich Rueschemeyer (eds) (2003). *Comparative Historical Analysis in the Social Sciences.* Cambridge: Cambridge University Press.

Mahoney, James & Richard Snyder (1999). "Rethinking Agency and Structure in the Study of Regime Change." *Studies in Comparative International Development* 34(2): 3–32.

Mainwaring, Scott (1992). "Transitions to Democracy and Democratic Consolidation: Theoretical and Comparative Issues," pp. 294–341 in Scott Mainwaring, Guillermo O'Donnell & J. Samuel Valenzuela (eds), *Issues in Democratic Consolidation: The New*

South American Democracies in Comparative Perspective. Notre Dame: University of Notre Dame Press.

Mair, Peter (2008). "Democracies," pp. 108–132 in Daniele Caramani (ed.), *Comparative Politics.* Oxford: Oxford University Press.

Maistre, Joseph de (1847 [1809]). *Essay on the Generative Principle of Political Constitutions.* Boston, MA: Little, Brown.

Manin, Bernard (1997). *The Principles of Representative Government.* Cambridge: Cambridge University Press.

Mansfield, Edward & Jack Snyder (1995). "Democratization and the Danger of War." *International Security* 20(1): 5–38.

Mansfield, Edward & Jack Snyder (2005). *Electing to Fight: Why Emerging Democracies go to War.* Cambridge, MA: MIT Press.

Mansfield, Edward & Jack Snyder (2009). "Pathways to War in Democratic Transitions." *International Organization* 63(2): 381–390.

Marshall, T.H. (1996 [1949]). *Citizenship and Social Class.* London: Pluto.

Marsilius of Padua (1956 [1324]). *The Defender of Peace.* New York: Columbia University Press.

Marx, Karl (1988 [1871]). *The Civil War in France.* New York: International Publishers.

Marx, Karl (2007 [1867]). *Capital: A Critique of Political Economy.* New York: Cosimo Classics.

Marx, Karl & Friedrich Engels (1998 [1848]). *The Communist Manifesto.* London: Verso.

Mason, David (1996). *Revolution and Transition in East-Central Europe.* Boulder, CO: Westview Press.

McDonald, Patrick J. & Kevin Sweeney (2007). "The Achilles' Heel of Liberal IR Theory? Globalization and Conflict in the Pre-World War I Era." *World Politics* 59(3): 370–403.

McFaul, Michael (2002). "The Fourth Wave of Democracy and Dictatorship: Noncooperative Transitions in the Postcommunist World." *World Politics* 54(2): 212–244.

McFaul, Michael (2007). "Are New Democracies War-Prone?" *Journal of Democracy* 18(2): 160–167.

McFaul, Michael (2010). "The Missing Variable: The International System as the Link between Third and Fourth Wave Models of Democratization," pp. 3–29 in Valerie Bunce, Michael McFaul & Kathryn Stoner-Weiss (eds), *Democracy and Authoritarianism in the Postcommunist World.* Cambridge: Cambridge University Press.

McNeill, William H. (1982). *The Pursuit of Power: Technology, Armed Forces, and Society since 1000 A.D.* Oxford: Blackwell.

Mearsheimer, John (2005). "Hans Morgenthau and the Iraq War: Realism versus Neo-Conservatism." http://www.openDemocracy.com (last visited April 17, 2012).

Meltzer, Allan & Scott Richards (1981). "A Rational Theory of the Size of Government." *Journal of Political Economy* 89(5): 914–927.

Merkel, Wolfgang (2004). "Embedded and Defective Democracies." *Democratization* 11(1): 33–58.

Merkel, Wolfgang (2008). "Democracy through War?" *Democratization* 15(3): 487–508.

Merkel, Wolfgang (2010). "Are Dictatorships Returning? Revisiting the 'Democratic Rollback' Hypothesis." *Contemporary Politics* 16(1): 17–31.

Migdal, Joel (1988). *Strong Societies and Weak States.* Princeton, NJ: Princeton University Press.

Mill, John Stuart (1984 [1869]).*The Subjection of Women.* Cambridge, MA: MIT Press.

Mill, John Stuart (1993 [1861]). "Considerations on Representative Government," pp. 188–428 in John Stuart Mill, *Utilitarianism, On Liberty, Considerations on Representative Government, Remarks on Bentham's Philosophy.* London: Dent.

Mills, C. Wright (1959). *The Sociological Imagination*. Oxford: Oxford University Press.

Milton, John (1927 [1644]). *Areopagitica*. London: Noel Douglas.

Møller, Jørgen (2007). "The Gap between Electoral and Liberal Democracy Revisited: Some Conceptual and Empirical Clarifications." *Acta Politica* 42(4): 380–400.

Møller, Jørgen (2008). "A Critical Note on 'The Rise of Illiberal Democracy'." *Australian Journal of Political Science* 43(3): 555–561.

Møller, Jørgen (2009). *Post-communist Regime Change: A Comparative Study*. London: Routledge.

Møller, Jørgen (forthcoming). "When One Might Not See the Wood for Trees: The 'Historical Turn in Democratization Studies, Critical Junctures, and Cross-case Comparisons'." *Democratization*.

Møller, Jørgen & Svend-Erik Skaaning (2009). "The Three Worlds of Post-Communism: Revisiting Deep and Proximate Explanations." *Democratization* 16(2): 298–322.

Møller, Jørgen & Svend-Erik Skaaning (2010). "Beyond the Radial Delusion: Conceptualizing and Measuring Democracy and Non-Democracy." *International Political Science Review* 31(3): 261–283.

Møller, Jørgen & Svend-Erik Skaaning (2011). *Requisites of Democracy: Conceptualization, Measurement, and Explanation*. London: Routledge.

Montesquieu, Charles de (1989 [1757]). *Spirit of the Laws*. Cambridge: Cambridge University Press.

Moore, Barrington (1991 [1966]). *Social Origins of Dictatorship and Democracy: Lord and Peasant in the Making of the Modern World*. London: Penguin.

Moravcsik, Andrew (2002). "In Defense of the Democratic Deficit: Reassessing Legitimacy in the European Union." *Journal of Common Market Studies* 40(4): 603–624.

Moravscik, Andrew & Milada Vachudova (2003). "National Interests, State Power, and EU Enlargement." *East European Politics and Societies* 17(1): 42–57.

Mouritsen, Hans (2001). *Plebs and Politics in the Late Roman Republic*. Cambridge: Cambridge University Press.

Munck, Gerardo (2001). "The Regime Question: Theory Building in Democracy Studies." *World Politics* 54(1): 119–144.

Munck, Gerardo (2011). "Democratic Theory after Transition from Authoritarian Rule." *Perspectives on Politics* 9(2): 333–343.

Munck, Gerardo L. & Carol S. Leff (1997). "Modes of Transition and Democratization: South America and Eastern Europe in Comparative Perspective." *Comparative Politics* 29(3): 343–362.

Munck, Gerardo & Richard Snyder (2007). *Passion, Craft and Method in Comparative Politics*. Baltimore, MD: Johns Hopkins University Press.

Munck, Gerardo & Jay Verkuilen (2002). "Conceptualizing and Measuring Democracy: Evaluating Alternative Indices." *Comparative Political Studies* 35(1): 5–34.

Munck, Gerardo & Jay Verkuilen (2005). "Research Designs," pp. 385–395 in Kimberly Kempf-Leonard (ed.), *Encyclopedia of Social Measurement, Vol. 3*. San Diego, CA: Academic Press.

Myers, A.R. (1975). *Parliaments and Estates in Europe to 1789*. London: Thames & Hudson.

Naess, Arne, Jens Christophersen & Kjell Kvalo (1956). *Democracy, Ideology and Objectivity: Studies in the Semantics and Cognitive Analysis of an Ideological Controversy*. Oslo: Universitetsforlaget.

Narang, Vipin & Rebecca Nelson (2009). "Who Are These Belligerent Democratizers? Reassessing the Impact of Democratization on War." *International Organization* 63(2): 357–379.

Nodia, Ghia (1996). "How Different Are Postcommunist Transitions?" *Journal of Democracy* 7(4): 15–29.

Norris, Pippa (2011). *Democratic Deficit: Critical Citizens Revisited.* New York: Cambridge University Press.

North, Douglass C. (1981). *Structure and Change in Economic History.* New York: W.W. Norton.

North, Douglass C. (1990). *Institutions, Institutional Change, and Economic Performance.* Cambridge: Cambridge University Press.

North, Douglass C. & Robert P. Thomas (1973). *The Rise of the Western World: A New Economic History.* Cambridge: Cambridge University Press.

O'Donnell, Guillermo (1973). *Modernization and Bureaucratic-Authoritarianism: Studies in South American Politics.* Berkeley, CA: Institute of International Studies.

O'Donnell, Guillermo (1992). "Transitions, Continuities, and Paradoxes," pp. 17–56 in Scott Mainwaring, Guillermo O'Donnell & J. Samuel Valenzuela (eds), *Issues in Democratic Consolidation: The New South American Democracies in Comparative Perspective.* Notre Dame: University of Notre Dame Press.

O'Donnell, Guillermo (1993). "On the State, Democratization and Some Conceptual Problems: A Latin American View with Glances at Some Postcommunist Countries." *World Development* 21(8): 1355–1369.

O'Donnell, G. (1998). *Polyarchies and the (Un)Rule of Law in Latin America.* Paper Presented at the Meeting of the Latin American Studies Association, Chicago, September.

O'Donnell, Guillermo (2001). "Democracy, Law, and Comparative Politics." *Studies in Comparative International Development* 36(1): 7–36.

O'Donnell, Guillermo (2002). "In Partial Defence of an Evanescent 'Paradigm'." *Journal of Democracy* 13(3): 6–12.

O'Donnell, Guillermo (2004). "Human Development, Human Rights, and Democracy," pp. 9–92 in Guillermo O'Donnell, Jorge V. Cullell & Osvaldo M. Iazzetta (eds), *The Quality of Democracy: Theory and Applications.* Notre Dame: Notre Dame University Press.

O'Donnell, Guillermo (2007). *Dissonances: Democratic Critiques of Democracy.* Notre Dame: University of Notre Dame Press.

O'Donnell, Guillermo (2010a). *Democracy, Agency, and the State: Theory with Comparative Intent.* Oxford: Oxford University Press.

O'Donnell, Guillermo (2010b). "Schmitter's Retrospective: A Few Dissenting Notes." *Journal of Democracy* 21(1): 29–32.

O'Donnell, Guillermo, Philippe Schmitter & Laurence Whitehead (eds) (1986). *Transitions from Authoritarian Rule: Tentative Conclusions about Uncertain Democracies.* Baltimore, MD: Johns Hopkins University Press.

Olson, Mancur (1993). "Dictatorship, Democracy, and Development." *American Political Science Review* 87(3): 567–576.

Orwell, George (1962 [1946]). "Politics and the English Language," pp. 143–157 in George Orwell, *Inside the Whale and Other Essays.* Harmondsworth: Penguin.

Oxhorn, Philip (2003). "Social Inequality, Civil Society, and the Limits of Citizenship in Latin America," pp. 35–63 in Susan Eckstein & Timothy Wickham-Crowley (eds), *What Justice? Whose Justice? Fighting for Fairness in Latin America.* Berkeley: University of California Press.

Paine, Thomas (1996 [1791]). *Rights of Man.* Ware: Wordsworth.

Palma, Giuseppe di (1990). *To Craft Democracies: An Essay on Democratic Transitions.* Berkeley: University of California Press.

Pareto, Vilfredo (1935 [1916]). *Mind and Society*. New York: Harcourt.

Pareto, Vilfredo (1991 [1901]). *The Rise and Fall of Elites: An Application of Theoretical Sociology*. New Jersey: Transaction Publishers.

Peeler, John (1985). *Latin American Democracies: Colombia, Costa Rica, Venezuela*. Chapel Hill: University of North Carolina Press.

Peeler, John (2004). *Building Democracy in Latin America*. Boulder, CO: Lynne Rienner.

Pevehouse, Jon (2005). *Democracy from Above: International Organizations and Democratization*. New York: Cambridge University Press.

Pierson, Paul (2000). "Path Dependence, Increasing Returns, and the Study of Politics." *American Political Science Review* 94(2): 251–267.

Pocock, J.G.A. (1957). *The Ancient Constitution and the Feudal Law*. Cambridge: Cambridge University Press.

Pocock, J.G.A. (1975). *The Machiavellian Moment: Florentine Political Thought and the Atlantic Republican Tradition*. Princeton, NJ: Princeton University Press.

Poggi, Gianfranco (1978). *The Development of the Modern State: A Sociological Introduction*. Stanford, CA: Stanford University Press.

Poggi, Gianfranco (1991). *The State: Its Nature, Development, and Prospects*. Stanford, CA: Stanford University Press.

Pop-Eleches, Gregore (2007). "Historical Legacies and Post-Communist Regime Change." *Journal of Politics* 69(4): 908–926.

Posner, Richard A. (2003). *Law, Pragmatism, and Democracy*. Cambridge: Cambridge University Press.

Pridham, Geoffrey (1997). "The International Dimension of Democratization: Theory, Practice, and Inter-Regional Comparisons," pp. 7–29 in Geoffrey Pridham, Eric Herring & George Sanford (eds), *Building Democracy? The International Dimension of Democratization in Eastern Europe*. London: Leicester University Press.

Pridham, Geoffrey (2000). *The Dynamics of Democratization: A Comparative Approach*. London: Continuum.

Pritchard, David M. (2010). "The Symbiosis between Democracy and War: The Case of Athens," pp. 1–62 in David Pritchard (ed.), *War, Democracy and Culture in Classical Athens*. Cambridge: Cambridge University Press.

Przeworski, Adam (1991). *Democracy and the Market: Political and Economic Reforms in Eastern Europe and Latin America*. Cambridge: Cambridge University Press.

Przeworski, Adam (2005). "Democracy as an Equilibrium." *Public Choice* 123(3/4): 253–273.

Przeworski, Adam (2007). "Democracy, Equality, and Redistribution," pp. 281–312 in Richard Bourke & Raymond Gauss (eds), *Political Judgment: Essays for John Dunn*. Cambridge: Cambridge University Press.

Przeworski, Adam (2009). "Conquered or Granted: A History of Suffrage Extensions." *British Journal of Political Science* 39(2): 291–321.

Przeworski, Adam & Fernando Limongi (1997). "Modernization: Theories and Facts." *World Politics* 49(2): 155–183.

Przeworski, Adam, Michael E. Alvarez, José A. Cheibub & Fernando Limongi (2000). *Democracy and Development: Political Institutions and Well-Being in the World, 1950–1990*. Cambridge: Cambridge University Press.

Puddington, Arch (2008). "Is the Tide Turning?" *Journal of Democracy* 19(2): 61–73.

Puddington, Arch (2010). "The Erosion Accelerates." *Journal of Democracy* 21(2): 36–50.

Putnam, Robert (1988). "Diplomacy and Domestic Politics: The Logic of Two-Level Games." *International Organization* 42(3): 427–460.

Putnam, Robert (1993). *Making Democracy Work: Civic Traditions in Modern Italy.* Princeton, NJ: Princeton University Press.

Randall, Vicky & Robin Theobald (1998). *Political Change and Underdevelopment: A Critical Introduction to Third World Politics.* Basingstoke: Macmillan.

Rawls, John (1971). *A Theory of Justice.* Oxford: Oxford University Press.

Raz, Joseph (1979). *The Authority of Law: Essays on Law and Morality.* Oxford: Clarendon Press.

Regan, Patrick M. & Errol A. Henderson (2002). "Democracy, Threats and Political Repression in Developing Countries: Are Democracies Internally Less Violent?" *Third World Quarterly* 23(1): 119–136.

Reiter, Dan & Allan Stam (2002). *Democracies at War.* Princeton, NJ: Princeton University Press.

Rigger, Shelley (2000). "Machine Politics and Protracted Transition in Taiwan." *Democratization* 7(3): 135–152.

Robinson, James (2006). "Economic Development and Democracy." *Annual Review of Political Science* 9: 503–527.

Rohlfing, Ingo (2009). "What You See and What You Get: Pitfalls and Principles of Nested Analysis in Comparative Research." *Comparative Political Studies* 41(11): 1492–1514.

Ross, Alf (1952 [1946]). *Why Democracy?* Cambridge, MA: Harvard University Press.

Ross, Michael (2001). "Does Oil Hinder Democracy?" *World Politics* 53(3): 325–361.

Ross, Michael (2012). *The Oil Curse: How Petroleum Wealth Shapes the Development of Nations.* Princeton, NJ: Princeton University Press.

Rostow, Walt (1960). *The Stages of Economic Growth: A Non-Communist Manifesto.* Cambridge: Cambridge University Press.

Rothman, Stanley (1970). "Barrington Moore and the Dialectics of Revolution: A Review Essay." *American Political Science Review* 64(1): 61–82.

Rousseau, Jean-Jacques (1993 [1762]). "The Social Contract," pp. 180–309 in Jean-Jacques Rousseau, *The Social Contract and Discourses.* London: Dent.

Rubin, Oliver (2009). "The Merits of Democracy in Famine Protection – Fact or Fallacy?" *European Journal of Development Research* 21(5): 699–717.

Rudolph, Lloyd & Susanne Rudolph (1967). *The Modernity of Tradition: Political Development in India.* Chicago, IL: University of Chicago Press.

Rueschemeyer, Dietrich, Evelyne H. Stephens & John Stephens (1992). *Capitalist Development and Democracy.* Chicago, IL: University of Chicago Press.

Ruggiero, Guido de (1927). *The History of European Liberalism.* Oxford: Oxford University Press.

Ruggiero, Guido de (1928). *The History of European Liberalism.* Boston, MA: Beacon Press.

Russell, Bertrand (2004 [1946]). *A History of Western Philosophy.* London: Routledge.

Russett, Bruce (2003 [2000]). "How Democracy, Interdependence, and International Organizations Create a System of Peace," pp. 492–496 in Robert A. Dahl, Ian Shapiro & Jose A. Cheibub (eds), *The Democracy Sourcebook.* Cambridge, MA: MIT Press.

Russett, Bruce & Zeev Maoz (1993). "Normative and Structural Causes of Democratic Peace." *American Political Science Review* 87(3): 640–654.

Rustow, Dankwart (1970). "Transitions to Democracy: Toward a Dynamic Model." *Comparative Politics* 2(3): 337–363.

Sandbrook, Richard (1996). "Transitions without Consolidation: Democratization in Six African States." *Third World Quarterly* 17(1): 69–87.

Sartori, Giovanni (1970). "Concept Misformation in Comparative Politics." *American Political Science Review* 64(4): 1033–1053.

Sartori, Giovanni (1984). "Guidelines for Concept Analysis," pp. 15–85 in Giovanni Sartori (ed.), *Social Science Concepts: A Systematic Analysis*. Beverly Hills, CA: Sage.

Sartori, Giovanni (1987). *The Theory of Democracy Revisited.* Chatham, NJ: Chatham House.

Schedler, Andreas (2001). "Measuring Democratic Consolidation." *Studies in Comparative International Development* 36(1): 66–92.

Schedler, Andreas (2002). "The Menu of Manipulation." *Journal of Democracy* 13(2): 36–50.

Schedler, Andreas (ed.) (2006). *Electoral Authoritarianism: The Dynamics of Unfree Competition*. Boulder, CO: Lynne Rienner.

Schedler, Andreas (2010). "Authoritarianism's Last Line of Defense." *Journal of Democracy* 21(1): 69–80.

Schimmelfennig, Frank & Ulrich Sedelmeier (2005). *The Europanization of Central and Eastern Europe*. Ithaca, NY: Cornell University Press.

Schmitter, Philippe (2010). "Twenty-Five Years, Fifteen Findings." *Journal of Democracy* 21(1): 17–28.

Schumpeter, Joseph A. (1974 [1942]). *Capitalism, Socialism and Democracy*. London: Unwin University Books.

Schumpeter, Joseph A. (1991 [1917/1918]). "The Crisis of the Tax State," pp. 99–140 in Joseph A. Schumpeter, *The Economics and Sociology of Capitalism*. Princeton, NJ: Princeton University Press.

Schumpeter, Joseph A. (1991 [1919]). "The Crisis of the Tax State," pp. 99–140 in Joseph A. Schumpeter, *The Economics and Sociology of Capitalism*. Princeton, NJ: Princeton University Press.

Schweinitz, Karl de (1959). "Industrialization, Labor Control, and Democracy." *Economic Development and Cultural Change* 7(4): 385–404.

Seawright, Jason (2010). "Regression-Based Inference: A Case-Study in Failed Causal Inference," pp. 247–272 in David Collier & David Brady (eds), *Rethinking Social Inquiry: Diverse Tools, Shared Standards*. Plymouth: Rowman & Littlefield.

Sen, Amartya (2003 [1996]). "Democracy Favors Development," pp. 444–446 in Robert A. Dahl, Ian Shapiro & Jose A. Cheibub (eds), *The Democracy Sourcebook*. Cambridge, MA: MIT Press.

Share, Donald (1987). "Transitions to Democracy and Transition through Transaction." *Comparative Political Studies* 19(4): 525–548.

Shin, Doh C. (2008). "The Third Wave in East Asia: Comparative and Dynamic Perspectives." *Taiwan Journal of Democracy* 4(4): 91–131.

Shin, Doh C. & Junhan Lee (2003). "Comparing Democratization in the East and the West." *Asian Pacific: Perspectives* 3(1): 40–49.

Sirowy, L. and Inkeles, Alex (1990). "The Effects of Democracy on Economic Growth and Inequality: A Review." *Studies in Comparative International Development* 25(1): 126–157.

Skaaning, Svend-Erik (2011). "Democratic Survival or Autocratic Revival." *Zeitschrift für vergleichende Politikwissenschaft*, Special Issue 1: 247–265.

Skocpol, Theda (1973). "A Critical Review of Barrington Moore's Social Origins of Dictatorship and Democracy." *Politics and Society* 4(1): 1–34.

Skocpol, Theda (1979). *States and Social Revolutions: A Comparative Analysis of France, Russia and China*. Cambridge: Cambridge University Press.

Skocpol, Theda (1984). "Sociology's Historical Imagination," pp. 1–21 in Theda Skocpol (ed.), *Vision and Method in Historical Sociology*. Cambridge: Cambridge University Press.

Smelser, Niel (1976). *Comparative Methods in the Social Sciences*. Englewood Cliffs, NJ: Prentice-Hall.

Smith, Peter H. & Melissa R. Ziegler (2008). "Liberal and Illiberal Democracy in Latin America." *Latin American Politics and Society* 50(1): 31–57.

Snyder, Richard (2003). "Imperial Temptations." *The National Interest* 71(Spring): 29–40.

Sørensen, Curt (1979). "Marx' og Engels' demokratiteori." *Politica* 11(2): 40–91.

Sørensen, Georg (ed.) (1993). *Political Conditionality*. London: Frank Cass.

Sørensen, Georg (2008). *Democracy and Democratization: Processes and Prospects in a Changing World*. Boulder, CO: Westview Press.

Stepan, Alfred & Graeme Robertson (2003). "An 'Arab' More Than a 'Muslim' Gap." *Journal of Democracy* 14(3): 30–44.

Stephens, John D. (1989). "Democratic Transition and Breakdown in Western Europe, 1870–1939: A Test of the Moore Thesis." *American Journal of Sociology* 94(5): 1019–1077.

Stephens, John & Gerhard Kümmel (2003). "Class Structure and Democratization," pp. 39–63 in Dirk Berg-Schlosser & Jeremy Mitchell (eds), *Authoritarianism and Democracy in Europe, 1919–1939: Comparative Analyses*. London: Macmillan.

Stephenson, Carl (1942). *Medieval Feudalism*. Ithaca, NY: Cornell University Press.

Stokke, Olav (ed.) (1995). *Aid and Political Conditionality*. London: Frank Cass.

Strayer, Joseph R. (1987 [1965]). *Feudalism*. Malabar: Krieger Publishing.

Svensson, Palle (1979). "Den klassiske demokratiske teori." *Politica* 11(2): 5–39.

Svensson, Palle (1995). *The Brno Lectures*. Århus: Institut for Statskundskab.

Svolik, Milan (2008). "Authoritarian Reversals and Democratic Consolidation." *American Political Science Review* 102(2): 153–168.

Talmon, Jacob (1952). *The Origins of Totalitarian Democracy*. London: Secker & Warburg.

Taylor, A.J.P. (1972). *The First World War*. New York: Perigee.

Therborn, Göran (1977). "The Rule of Capital and the Rise of Democracy." *New Left Review* 103: 3–41.

Tierney, Brian (1982). *Religion, Law, and the Growth of Constitutional Thought, 1150–1650*. Cambridge: Cambridge University Press.

Tilly, Charles (ed.) (1975). *The Formation of National States in Western Europe*. Princeton, NJ: Princeton University Press.

Tilly, Charles (1984). *Big Structures, Large Processes, Huge Comparisons*. New York: Russell Sage Foundation.

Tilly, Charles (1990). *Coercion, Capital and European States, AD 990–1992*. Oxford: Blackwell.

Tilly, Charles (1995). "Democracy is a Lake," pp. 365–387 in George R. Andrews & Herrick Chapman (eds), *The Social Construction of Democracy, 1870–1990*. New York: New York University Press.

Tilly, Charles (2002). *Stories, Identities, and Political Change*. Oxford: Rowman & Littlefield.

Tocqueville, Alexis de (1983 [1856]). *The Old Regime and the French Revolution*. New York: Anchor Books.

Tocqueville, Alexis de (1988 [1835/1840]). *Democracy in America*. New York: Harper & Row.

Tolstrup, Jakob (2009). "Studying a Negative External Actor: Russia's Management of Stability and Instability in the 'Near Abroad'." *Democratization* 16(5): 922–944.

Tolstrup, Jakob (forthcoming). "When Can External Actors Influence Democratization? Leverage, Linkages, and Gate Keeper Elites." *Democratization*.

Treier, Shawn & Simon Jackman (2008). "Democracy as a Latent Variable." *American Journal of Political Science* 52(1): 201–217.

Trevelyan, G.M. (1949). *An Autobiography and Other Essays.* London: Longmans.

Vachudova, Milada (2005). *Europe Undivided: Democracy, Leverage, & Integration.* Oxford: Oxford University Press.

Valenzuela, J. Samuel (1992). "Democratic Consolidation in Post-Transitional Settings: Notion, Process, and Facilitating Conditions," pp. 57–104 in Scott Mainwaring, Guillermo O'Donnell & J. Samuel Valenzuela (eds), *Issues in Democratic Consolidation: The New South American Democracies in Comparative Perspective.* Notre Dame: University of Notre Dame Press.

Viskum, Mads (2009). *Kan demokrati konstrueres uden forudsætninger: En teoretisk og empirisk evaluering af transitologien.* Master's dissertation, Department of Political Science, Aarhus University. http://www.mit.ps.au.dk/mema/2009/Mads_Maarup_Viskum.pdf

Vreeland, James (2008). "The Effects of Political Regime on Civil War: Unpacking Anocracy." *Journal of Conflict Resolution* 52(3): 401–425.

Vu, Tuong (2010). "Studying the State through State Formation." *World Politics* 62(1): 148–175.

Walle, Nicolas van de (1995). "Crisis and Opportunity." *Journal of Democracy* 6(2): 128–141.

Walle, Nicolas van de (2002). "Africa's Range of Regimes." *Journal of Democracy* 13(2): 66–80.

Wallerstein, Immanuel (1974). *The Modern World-System: Capitalist Agriculture and the Origins of the European World-Economy in the Sixteenth Century.* New York: Academic Press.

Wallerstein, Immanuel (1980). *The Modern World-System: Mercantilism and the Consolidation of the European World-Economy, 1600–1750.* New York: Academic Press.

Wallerstein, Immanuel (1989). *The Modern World-System: The Second Great Expansion of the Capitalist World-Economy, 1730–1840s.* San Diego, CA: Academic Press.

Waltz, Kenneth (1959 [1954]). *Man, the State and War.* New York: Columbia University Press.

Warren, Mark (2000). *Democracy and Association.* Princeton, NJ: Princeton University Press.

Weber, Max (1981 [1927]). *General Economic History.* New Brunswick, NJ: Transaction Books.

Weber, Max (2003 [1927]). *General Economic Theory.* Mineola: Dover Press.

Weber, M. (2005 [1904/1905]) *The Protestant Ethic and the Spirit of Capitalism.* London: Routledge.

Weiner, Myron (1987). "Empirical Democratic Theory and the Transition from Authoritarianism to Democracy." *PS: Political Science & Politics* 20(4): 861–866.

Welzel, Christian (2009). "Theories of Democratization," pp. 74–91 in Christian W. Haerpfer, Patrick Bernhagen, Ronald F. Inglehart & Christian Welzel (eds), *Democratization.* Oxford: Oxford University Press.

Weyland, Kurt (2009). "The Diffusion of Revolution: '1848' in Europe and Latin America." *International Organization* 63(3): 391–423.

Weyland, Kurt (2010). "The Diffusion of Regime Contention in European Democratization, 1830–1940." *Comparative Political Studies* 43(8): 1148–1176.

Whitehead, Laurence (1996). "Three International Dimensions of Democratization," pp.

3–25 in Laurence Whitehead (ed.), *The International Dimensions of Democratization*. Oxford: Oxford University Press.

World Bank (2011). Corruption and Economic Development. http://www1.worldbank.org/ publicsector/anticorrupt/corruptn/cor02.htm (last visited December 12, 2011).

Wright, Joseph & Matthew Winters (2010). "The Politics of Effective Foreign Aid." *Annual Review of Political Science* 13: 61–80.

Wucherpfennig, Julian & Franziska Deutsch (2009). "Modernization and Democracy: Theories and Evidence Revisited." *Living Reviews in Democracy* 1: 1–9.

Zagare, Frank C. (2009). "Explaining the 1914 War in Europe." *Journal of Theoretical Politics* 21(1): 63–95.

Zakaria, Fareed (1997). "The Rise of Illiberal Democracies." *Foreign Affairs* 76(6): 22–43.

Zakaria, Fareed (2003). *The Future of Freedom: Illiberal Democracy at Home and Abroad*. New York: Norton.

Ziblatt, Daniel (2006). "How Did Europe Democratize?" *World Politics* 58(2): 311–338.

Index

New eBook Library Collection

An environmentally friendly book printed and bound in England by www.printondemand-worldwide.com

PEFC Certified

This product is
from sustainably
managed forests
and controlled
sources

www.pefc.org

PEFC/16-33-415

This book is made entirely of sustainable materials; FSC paper for the cover and PEFC paper for the text pages.

#0152 - 100714 - C0 - 234/156/14 - PB